c/o Cunard House

88 Leadenhall Street London EC3

c/o Cunard House

88 Leadenhall Street London EC3

Bill Ferguson

Whittles Publishing

Published by
Whittles Publishing Ltd,
Dunbeath,
Caithness, KW6 6EG,
Scotland, UK

www.whittlespublishing.com

© 2025 Bill Ferguson

ISBN 978-184995-582-9

Printed and bound by CPI Group (UK) Ltd, Croydon, CR0 4YY

Contents

Aknowledgements vii
Publisher's note viii
Background ix
The British Merchant Navy in the mid-20th century xii

1 Genesis: Country boy to Seaman 1

2 TSMV *Port Brisbane* 3

Foreign parts at last 14
South of the Line 19
Homeward bound 32

3 MV Port Lincoln 41

First Voyage 41
Second Voyage 62

3 TSMV Port Auckland 72

First Voyage 72

5 TSMV Port Pirie 85

6 MV Port Townsville 91

7 TSMV Port Auckland revisited 110

Second Voyage 110
Third Voyage 118

8   TSMV Port Hobart   126

    First Voyage   126
    Second Voyage   133

9   The Interregnum   141

    TSMV Port Sydney   141
    TSMV Port Napier   143
    TSMV Port New Plymouth   147
    TSMV Port Vindex   149

10   TSMV Port Nicholson   152

    Alpha: from the builders' yard   152
    The maiden voyage   157
    Second voyage   167
    Third voyage   171
    Omega: fourth voyage   177

11   Epilogue   193

Acknowledgements

I most gratefully acknowledge the generous help from my wife Jane, from Helen and Sion Morgan, T. Alan Nickell, the late and distinguished marine artist Robert Blackwell and Mrs Lyn Blackwell, the maritime author Henry Spong, Stuart J. Kirkby, Gordon Kirkby, and the late John Corin, publicity officer of the Port of Bristol, who 50 years ago suggested the creation of an account of Jack's maritime life and supplied many of the photographs. The late and distinguished maritime historian C.J. (Jim) Crissup, and the late Richard Cornish, an expert on the British Merchant Navy and a former chief engineer in the Blue Funnel line of Alfred Holt. Thanks also go to Andy King, curator of the former Bristol Industrial Museum (now the M Shed), and to John Chapman of Digital Problem Solving Ltd, a steady hand on the helm, the corrector of many errors and my computer expert: 'When things go wrong call for John!'

Many of the photographs used in this account were donated over 50 years ago, and almost inevitably the questions of who, where and when – all those years ago – arise. While the history of many of them is lost in the mists of time, photographs were given by Geoffrey Bates, John Corin, C.J. Crissup, Richard Cornish, Don Western and Stuart Kirkby. In the case of John Corin many of the photographs were created by photographers such as Colin Momber, Fred Sharp, Bromheads and John himself. Several of the photographs were part of the archive of the former Port of Bristol Authority and are now in the custody of the Bristol City Museums and Art Galleries (BCM&AG), and their kindness in allowing their reproduction is most gratefully acknowledged, along with that of Colin Momber, Don Western and Stuart Kirkby. In any case of a photograph being misattributed, please accept my sincere apologies and please contact the publisher, to correct any further edition of this book.

Publisher's note

This book has been written from the perspective of a Merchant Navy sailor of the 1950s–60s, so you will find that some of the opinions and viewpoints differ from ours of the 2020s; please see this account as the literary equivalent of a series of photographs taken back then.

Background

Amongst the many British shipping companies of the 19th century were four that became involved in each other's commercial interests, mainly through the New Zealand refrigerated trade.

The major company, the Tyser Line, had originally acted for the New Zealand Shipping Company. Tyser then chartered, and later owned, a number of vessels, and after much effort entered into the New Zealand and Australian trade; he also became involved in the trade from North America to New Zealand and Australia.

Through his trade with India he became involved with J.P. Corry's Star Line. This company had been involved in the North American timber trade before sending its vessels to India. Tyser chartered some of its refrigerated vessels for his New Zealand frozen meat trade.

T.B. Royden & Co. Ltd was originally a shipbuilder on the River Mersey. It branched out into shipping in the India–Japan–America trade. Tyser chartered two of its vessels to carry wool from New Zealand; these vessels were succeeded by the refrigerated steamer *Indramayo*, which Tyser used on a commission basis for his New Zealand trade.

William Milburn, a ship owner from Northumberland, had become involved in the New Zealand trade through Shaw Savill & Albion Line, which chartered his vessels. Milburn used his steam-powered vessel *Port Jackson* in his new Anglo-Australasian Steam Navigation Company. Towards the end of the 19th century he was using eight vessels to trade with Australia and New Zealand.

In 1914 those companies combined, to create the Commonwealth and Dominion Line; it carried refrigerated cargo to Britain and Europe. Its new vessels had 'Port' added to their names, and they flew the Tyser house flag.

An honour for Port Line: *Port Brisbane* features on a commemorative stamp.

In 1916 the Commonwealth and Dominion Line was purchased by Cunard, whose funnel colours were adopted for the vessels of the newly titled Cunard Line Australasian Service, Commonwealth and Dominion Line Ltd. In November 1937 the name was changed to

Port Line Ltd, and so it remained until the demise of this once premier British shipping company 67 years after its foundation.

The title of this account relates to Cunard House, the headquarters of Port Line Ltd, at 88 Leadenhall Street, London EC3, where mail for its seagoing staff was sent, to be forwarded to the appropriate vessel. In addition, the building was a regular haunt for some staff going to, or returning from, a Port boat.

Port Auckland and *Port Nicholson*, from a painting by Robert Blackwell

The Company

GENERAL PLAN OF A MID-20th CENTURY CONVENTIONAL REFRIGERATED/CARGO LINER
THE IDENTIFIED DETAILS ARE THOSE MENTIONED IN THE TEXT

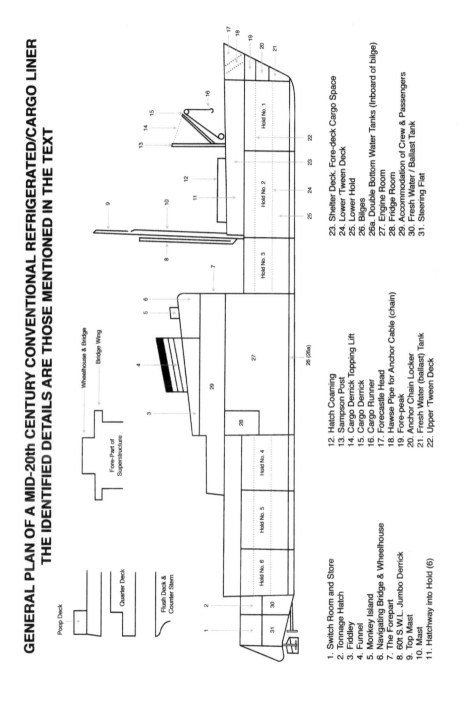

1. Switch Room and Store
2. Tonnage Hatch
3. Fiddley
4. Funnel
5. Monkey Island
6. Navigating Bridge & Wheelhouse
7. The Forepart
8. 60t S.W.L. Jumbo Derrick
9. Top Mast
10. Mast
11. Hatchway into Hold (6)

12. Hatch Coaming
13. Sampson Post
14. Cargo Derrick Topping Lift
15. Cargo Derrick
16. Cargo Runner
17. Forecastle Head
18. Hawse Pipe for Anchor Cable (chain)
19. Fore-peak
20. Anchor Chain Locker
21. Fresh Water (ballast) Tank
22. Upper 'Tween Deck

23. Shelter Deck. Fore-deck Cargo Space
24. Lower 'Tween Deck
25. Lower Hold
26. Bilges
26a. Double Bottom Water Tanks (Inboard of bilge)
27. Engine Room
28. Fridge Room
29. Accommodation of Crew & Passengers
30. Fresh Water / Ballast Tank
31. Steering Flat

Ship plan diagram (courtesy Gordon Kirkby)

The British Merchant Navy in the mid-20th century

The British Merchant Navy is a trade – an ancient and honourable occupation, but nonetheless still a trade, much the same as that of a silversmith, metal worker, plumber, carpenter or whatever. Trade is a conduit encompassing goods and services being exchanged between individuals, organisations and nations. The ships of the Merchant Navy carry items of trade wherever such goods are required, and vessels have been doing this since the days of the prehistoric canoe.

The occupational titles of the Merchant Navy, as listed below, directly relate to any certificated merchant trade insofar as the title 'master' defines the master of a trade, in this case a seafaring trade. In the Merchant Navy the master is the commander of a vessel, and upon them is bestowed the title of captain. In other trades the master will have a principal assistant known as a mate, and in the Merchant Navy the master's deputy, who is fully qualified to do the job as a master, is also known as the mate. The mate in turn has qualified assistants, also known as mates, and defined in rank and qualification as second, third and fourth mate etc. Yet again, as in other trades, in order to become a mate it is necessary (with the exception of some qualified ratings) to have served time as an apprentice and to have attended a suitable training establishment. The mates and the master are known as officers, denoting the responsibility they hold by virtue of their rank.

In the case of the other ranks of the Merchant Navy, the titles reflect the skilled work that their holders are required to undertake. For example, the boatswain equates to the manager in a similar trade ashore, and the boatswain's underlings are, according to their various qualifications, skilled in the arts of the seafarer, and enter their working lives ranked as boys[1] recruited from approved sea training schools. They relate to semi-skilled workers ashore until, achieving the necessary sea time, they obtain their qualification through examination.

---

1 This account extends to the mid-1960s, and the first girls were accepted into the Merchant Navy in the 1970s in specific roles.

With the exception of one ship, all the post-war Port Line vessels were powered by engines. MV (Motor Vessel) denotes a unit with a single engine and screw, whilst TSMV (Twin-Screw Motor Vessel) denotes a vessel with two engines driving two screws.

Throughout the period in question the Ministry of Transport (MOT) and its predecessor, the Board of Trade (BOT), controlled all legal aspects concerning crew members, machinery, certificates of competency, discipline, food, cargo and training establishments – and above all, the safety of ships and personnel of the British Merchant Navy, mainly encompassed by the Articles of Agreement under which all mariners serve in British ships.

Deck department rank structure of Port Line Ltd, 1956–1966

MOT / BOT Certificate Held	RANK / RATING	TITLE	ALTERNATIVE TITLE
Master Mariner/ Extra Master	Master	Captain	Old Man, Father
Master Mariner	First Mate	First Officer, Chief Officer	Mate, Mr Mate
Master Mariner/ First Mate	Second Mate	Second Officer	Second
Second Mate / First Mate	Third Mate	Third Officer	Third
Second Mate	Fourth Mate	Fourth Officer	Fourth
Approved Training School	Apprentice	Apprentice	Midi, Cadet, Snotty
Time-served Apprenticeship	Artificer/Shipwright	Carpenter	Chippy
Able Seaman	Chief Petty Officer	Boatswain	Bosun (Bose)
Able Seaman	Petty Officer	Boatswain's Mate	Lamp-trimmer (Lampy)
Able Seaman	Quartermaster	Quartermaster	Helmsman
Able Seaman	Able Seaman	Able Seaman	AB
Efficient Deck Hand	Efficient Deck Hand	Efficient Deck Hand	EDH
Approved Training School	Ordinary Seamen	Senior & Junior Seamen	SOS, JOS
Approved Training School	Deck Boys	Deck Boys	Peggy

Vessel sizes are shown in this book as grt (gross registered tons); a ship's total internal volume is expressed in registered tons, each of which is equal to 100 cubic feet.

1

Genesis: country boy to seaman

'It's a simple choice, son – if you want to go to sea for a career, join the Merchant Navy. If you want to join the Royal Navy you must be prepared for a career – whether seaman or admiral – consisting of simply swinging around the buoys in some Godforsaken harbour. Roughly 80 per cent of your service will be in harbour. Think about it and decide. Oh, by the way, throw that *Midshipman Easy* book on the fire; it bears no relationship to the rather sorry post-war naval service.' So Jack had been told by his mother's cousin, a former Royal Naval commander, and he had made up his mind there and then that it was to be a career in the Merchant Navy for him.

Those words went through his mind again as with considerable trepidation he approached his destination, a private (as opposed to state-run) sea training school.

As he settled into his new home the staff attempted to instil in him the rudiments of the art of seamanship, from ropework to basic navigation with the chief officer. This officer, who held the qualifications of a master mariner, repeatedly reminded the boys that he had been in their position 20 years ago, and that with diligence and hard work – emphasising his point with a flourish of his uniform sleeve and its three gold bands – they too could have that insignia of rank on their sleeve. With all due modesty he nonchalantly brushed imaginary specks of chalk from the gold bands, as the autumn sunlight gave an added lustre to the gold wire. Many of those boys did eventually wear the four gold bands of command, whilst others, despite much effort and anguish over the next five years, would not achieve it.

The mess room, no doubt as an inspiration to young minds, displayed many illustrations of the great ships of the day: P&O Line's *Himalaya*, Orient Line's *Orion*, New Zealand Line's *Rangitane* and the then revolutionary shape of the *Port Brisbane*, representing the Port Line.

Life in this training establishment, or 'stone frigate' as shore-based nautical premises were known, went on in its usual pattern; the bullying of the juniors by the seniors, much as in public schools of the time. Thrashing took place with an instrument known as a stonikey, a 12-inch length of rope concealed in a coat sleeve, convenient for slipping into the hand, for painful use on the buttocks – and even more painful when used on the bonier parts of the anatomy.

Not all was, however, doom and gloom and studying; if the trainee was a confirmed member of the Anglican faith, then – much to the anguish of his fellows – he would be given two fried eggs on a Sunday. Envy of such luxury was, with little doubt, the reason for a large number of trainees ending up in Canterbury Cathedral to be confirmed as Anglicans, and all for the guarantee of a second fried egg on a Sunday – providing they had been to communion that morning!

Fun was had by listening to Bill Haley and the Comets' records in the hall and, in the senior dormitory, by watching Slack Agnes in an adjoining dwelling with a well-illuminated bedroom window slowly undressing and playing to the gallery in few, if any, clothes, mesmerising the adolescents in that dormitory. It was essential to have a lookout on duty; when an inspection occurred and the officer looked in the dorm, a very gentle snore would pervade the air, with everyone tucked up in their bunks.

The establishment was commanded by a naval commander with a Merchant Navy chief officer and what appeared to be former Whale Island officers / instructors. They were as hard as nails, but even in their dotage could outrun the boys up Army Hill. These disciplinarians were not to be disobeyed; any bad behaviour would swiftly become a very painful experience for the miscreant.

In time Jack was promoted, so each Wednesday he could enjoy the privilege of an evening on the town, from 6 to 8:30 p.m. This sometimes involved dodging Slack Agnes and her sometimes less than chaste chums. On those occasions the five shillings per week spending money was quickly spent on cinema tickets or in the milk bars, and perhaps on the local girls – excluding Agnes. Whilst her bare, but somewhat solid, figure was a nocturnal vision of interest, her draped frame was not so interesting to most of the boys.

With final examinations over, it was time for the trainees to be appointed by the captain to their various merchant passenger liners; quality ships by any standards. Goodbye to runs up the hill. Farewell to sailing the drop-keeled whalers in the icy winter winds of the English Channel dressed only in a very porous jumper and almost non-existent shorts, and with blue bare feet. Jack was pleased to leave behind his poor reputation for sailing competence, which had been gained when he had run a whaler aground with the drop-keel down. It was with little difficulty that the young graduates of the establishment left behind them all the constant parading, and seemingly saluting of every passing seagull – along with the very doubtful charms of Slack Agnes and her chums.

However, it was with no less trepidation than they had experienced on their arrival that they left the security and certainty of what they had come to know for the uncertain world of work, and the challenges presented by a career with the deck department of the Merchant Navy.

2

TSMV *Port Brisbane*

'Port *what*?' Jack's mother queried in a tone which only went to emphasise the fact that both she and her opinions were not to be taken lightly by anyone, least of all the most junior member of her family.

'Port Line,' Jack almost whispered into the telephone, with no small amount of trepidation.

'Who on *earth* would call a shipping company *Port* Line?' asked Mother. From her tone of voice it was clear that she was not happy about Jack's appointment. It appeared that she doubted whether he had passed his exams. Jack attempted to explain that Port Line was part of the Cunard group of shipping companies trading with refrigerated cargo from New Zealand and Australia. If he expected that the revelation of the Port Line antecedence would alleviate her ire, he was mistaken. It would appear that the word 'cargo' only served to increase it. She had first-hand knowledge of the shipping world, in that as a young woman before the Great War she had travelled on her uncle's tugs as he brought sailing vessels and Greek tramp ships into the Bristol dock systems. To her, the word 'cargo' meant scruffy vessels, sailing or steam, with indifferent masters and crew; add to that her image of the word 'port' – a filthy place – and all in all it was perhaps understandable that Mother's mind was set. The boy tried to interject, but without success; she asserted that she would immediately phone her cousin who, she believed, had influence with P&O, and in the morning she would ring the captain, to give him a piece of her mind – and she promptly rang off.

Jack was in one sense relieved that the phone call had ended, but was understandably concerned about the call to his captain in the morning. She always communicated with the head of whatever organisation she was dealing with, from headmasters to the chairmen of companies to dukes. As the lights were turned off in the dormitories, the boy, lying in his bunk, wondered just how the captain would deal with her. If she wasn't happy with his replies she would be knocking on his door before he could bat an eyelid.

'Halt! Left turn! Off cap!' bellowed Mr Smith as he marched Jack into the captain's day cabin the next morning. The captain, a kindly man – in contrast to many of his officers – had his head down, studying whatever was on his desk.

3

The Port Line house flag

'Stand at ease,' the captain told Jack, and without raising his eyes he continued, 'I've had a conversation with your mother. She most certainly is a formidable lady. I understand from her that your uncle, who apparently has paid your fees here, has some influence with the P&O Line, but I've told her that this establishment does not send its young men to that company.' The captain looked directly at Jack, and leaning back, continued, 'I do hope that I have laid to rest any misconceptions about the quality of Port Line in your mother's mind. This was no doubt aided by your uncle telling her much the same last evening, and that the Port Line's original name was the Commonwealth and Dominion Line. I do believe that although she still seems to believe that the word 'port' is associated with filthy docks and even filthier workers, she now accepts, very reluctantly, that you may be appointed to one of its vessels.' In a very authoritative tone of voice he continued, 'However, it is not a case of 'may': you will join one of their vessels next week. You are dismissed.'

As Jack stood to attention, put his cap on, and turned to his right, the captain added, 'By the way, I did assure your mother that your appointment to Port Line had nothing to do with examination results, and whilst you were not at the top of the class, you were far above the bottom. I'm sending you to Port Line, as both your instructors and I believe that company will be suitable for the advancement of your career.'

It was on a fine January day in the 1950s that Jack, along with his friend from training, stood at the wicket gate of King George V Dock in London, and looked in amazement at the life inside it. In every direction was the hustle and bustle of a busy dock, with wagons full of cargo being pulled along the rails at the dock wall and under the veranda of No 8 berth, lorries totally ignoring the 20 mph signs, cyclists dodging vehicles, and hundreds of dockworkers handling carcasses of lamb, boxes of butter, bags of milk powder and bales of wool. It was a never to be forgotten first sight of a world that both boys would become very familiar with over the years.

Soon they were joined by a man from the Mission – the Mission to Seamen, which looked after the welfare of boys such as Jack and his chum. The man pointed beyond the end of the transit shed to the bow of a vessel; it was grey with a white apron at deck level, and set off in black was the name *Port Brisbane*. 'That's a ship of the company you two'll work for,' explained the man. 'We'll go to the Port Line dock office and find out what your first ship will be.'

They made their way along the dock road until a very modern, clean building came into view, with a freestone carving of the Port Line coat of arms. The Mission man took the boys into the crew manager's office; it was he who would decide which ship they joined.

The crew manager was usually present whenever crew signed Articles.[2] Unfortunately, the crew manager had problems spelling Jack's mother's name, Inez, to the clerk, so Jack intervened in the belief that he was being helpful. The manager's humiliation and anger would dog Jack for the rest of his career with Port Line.

The spat with the crew manager had taken place in the crew's recreation room on *Port Brisbane*, the most distinctive ship in the fleet, and a unique vessel of royal patronage. It had been the first merchant ship to host Queen Elizabeth, King George VI's wife, and Princess Margaret; the occasion was the inspection of the interior of No 3 hold. And it was *Port Brisbane* that was to become Jack's first seaborne home; life would never be the same again!

But Jack found it very humbling – *not* something to tell his mother about – when he was appointed to the petty officers' mess as a peggy – the mess steward and general servant for the occupiers of that mess room. (The term 'peggy' came from the time when seamen with a peg leg were employed as mess-men.) This was not what Jack had gone to sea for, and he was bitterly disappointed, first about the lowly position, and secondly because on the training ship no one had mentioned that on a cargo vessel this was usually the fate of a boy entrant. The pattern was to work as a peggy all morning, then work on deck during the afternoon and as a peggy again for dinner.

From a working perspective, the ship's boatswain – abbreviated to bosun or more commonly bose – was the manager of Jack and the deck crew. The bosun was under the overall charge of the first mate, the second in command of a vessel, and the bosun was responsible for all the work on deck, in the hatches and above. His assistant was

---

2 The Board of Trade/Ministry of Transport documents which agree the responsibility of the shipping company towards the crew, and the conduct and responsibility of the crew toward the master of the vessel and the company.

Port Brisbane (courtesy PBA-BM&AG ; Port of Bristol Authority - British Museum and Art Gallery)

the bosun's mate, normally known as the lamp-trimmer or Lampy – a very responsible job in the days before ships had electricity for its navigation lights. These days, Lampy was the deck department's storekeeper. Jack soon learned the eternal truth about the storekeepers of any trade: the less they could issue from their stock the happier they were – and lampies in particular!

This particular bosun was a fair but sometimes indecisive individual, so to Jack and his fellow boys he was easy meat for minor deception. In fact, the bosun probably knew what they were up to, but chose to ignore boyhood excesses when they fiddled their duties.

The magnificent 11,942-ton *Port Brisbane* had been built in 1949 by Swan, Hunter & Wigham Richardson Ltd, and was believed to be the most expensive cargo ship built until 1949. Now she was to sail from London to Avonmouth, Jack's home port, then to Liverpool. Coastal voyages around Britain and the near continent were known as home trade voyages, and for them a relief crew, from master to boy seamen, would temporarily relieve the deep-sea crew for their leave or replacements.

On leaving or entering port, the crew would go to their harbour stations at one of the four positions to be manned. The fo'c'sle gang looked after the mooring lines, tug lines and if required the anchors; the stern or after end gang had the same duties, excluding anchors. The quartermasters looked after the gangway and the pilot's arrival and departure. Finally, and most importantly, the bridge staff under the master controlled everyone – and, where possible, everything. Jack was posted on the foc'sle head as the stopper boy; his duty was to hitch a secured small rope onto the larger mooring line to take the weight of that line until it could be secured on the mooring bitts, two metal bollards, on deck.

In the darkness the ship slowly moved astern, towed through the locks into Gallions Reach of the Thames. She would then head for the English Channel before rounding Cornwall and going up to Avonmouth. With the ship heading downriver Jack's duties were finished for the night, and the throb of the ship's engines soon sent him off to sleep.

On the second morning aboard Jack looked out of the porthole to see the green fields of Somerset as they headed up the Bristol Channel. The bells in the accommodation rang to summon the sailors to their harbour stations and to secure the tugs off Portishead. The tugs then took *Port Brisbane* past the entrance locks of the dock in a wide sweep to stem the tide as she slowly approached the lock from around the North Pier. In those days the end of the pier was a wooden extension, and on this particular Friday – as if as moved by a powerful hand, and despite the tugs' endeavours – the vessel laid her 11,942 tons onto this wooden structure and simply pushed it over. No damage was done to the vessel, but someone would have a bit of explaining to do.

When the vessel was berthed at O Shed in the Royal Edward dock, Jack approached the bosun to explain that he lived nearby, and ask if he could have the Saturday afternoon off to go home for a few hours. The bosun had no objection and sent him off to see the mate, who agreed on condition that Jack's chum would cover his peggy duties.

On Saturday the vessel needed a supply of fresh water. Water was part of the carpenter's remit, and this man had just joined the vessel. Unlike most chippies in the Port Line he was not a company man; he had got the job by being in the Avonmouth seamen's pool at the right moment, replacing the company carpenter who had fallen ill. But he was fond of his drink, and instead of waiting aboard for the watermen he took himself off to the nearby Royal Hotel, telling an apprentice which pipe on the foc'sle the hose should be connected to.

Jack, meanwhile, had finished his Saturday morning duties and was changing into his shore clothes. On the foc'sle the watermen had arrived and connected their hose, as instructed by the apprentice, and promptly began to deliver 50 tons of water. The mate had noted the apprentice lounging on the foredeck and on returning noted that he was still there. Going over to the boy, the officer discovered why this was so …

As Jack was packing his weekend bag his cabin door opened: the first mate was standing there, and told him and his chum to be on the foc'sle in less than five minutes. The boys were surprised not only by the presence of this officer at their door, but also by him even knowing where they were accommodated. How much they had yet to learn! Mr Mate knew everything about everybody, even boy seamen. Jack, still in his going-ashore livery, went to the foc'sle and found three apprentices and the bosun there, with the hatch lid to the forepeak open. Jack was sent back to his cabin to change into his working gear and on his return found his chum and the apprentices hauling up dustbins of water from the forepeak and emptying them onto the deck.

The chippy had identified the wrong hole for the hose, so the forepeak was flooded. It would have been simple to have opened the scupper leading to the chain locker below, let the water drain into the locker and then use the chain locker pump to empty the water into the dock. However, even in those pre-anti-pollution days the Bristol Port Authority would have taken a very dim view of anyone polluting their muddy dock water with even muddier water from the *Port Brisbane*'s chain locker.

By 3 p.m. and with many blisters, the job was done, and the mate thanked the boys for 'volunteering' to work on their Saturday afternoon in port. Jack, taking into account his travelling time on the not-too-regular bus service to Bristol and out to Wraxall in north Somerset, was rather dejected, as his afternoon at home was ruined, and it must have shown.

'Didn't I give you permission to go home this afternoon?' asked the mate.

'Yes, Sir,' said Jack.

'As you've worked so willingly and well you may have the rest of today and until 16:00 hrs tomorrow off duty. That'll be okay, won't it, Bosun?' The bosun, not daring to quibble with his boss, promptly agreed to these new terms for Jack's leave.

By the Sunday afternoon Jack was back, to hear that first mate had found the errant carpenter in the Royal Hotel, and sacked him there and then.

Jack resumed his duties in the PO's mess, all the time learning things which would be of use to him in life – such as in order to make tea he needed to put tea leaves into the 7-pint pot of boiling water. He also learned, when he delivered those 7 pints to the mess and a quartermaster threw the offending liquid in him, that he needed to be fleet of foot at times; and that drying the deck was not a quick task with nine men waiting for their tea – in a now slightly dented tea pot with the enamel coating pinging off. The quartermaster, reprimanded by the bosun, had to apologise to the boy. This went along the lines of 'We all make mistakes, boy; make sure you don't make the same mistake when I'm around!'

Soon the *Port Brisbane* sailed from Avonmouth, without causing any more damage to the North Pier, heading for Liverpool. There, the most memorable task that the boys, apprentices and junior deck officers had to undertake was a series of visits to the five refrigerated holds in an effort to prevent the stevedores (dockers working on ships, as opposed to those working on shore) urinating on the chilled lamb carcasses destined for human consumption. It was no easy task, as those men were very threatening, indeed in some cases carrying out the threat to the point of aggression. It was not at all a nice first memory of Liverpool. The image of the city did improve on subsequent visits, but Jack's opinion concerning the Liverpool docker never changed.

From the less-than-inspiring Liverpool the vessel returned to London, and there the crew signed Foreign Going Articles. As before, the crew manager and Jack had words over the pronunciation of the name 'Inez', and it was there that Jack met Captain Francis William Bailey, his master for the next five and a half months. Bailey had a long and distinguished career with Port Line even though his first command, the *Port Bowen*, had run aground in New Zealand and eventually became a total loss. He had also been a prisoner of war during the Second World War. Eventually he became the commodore master of the company and was awarded the OBE.

The discharge of the New Zealand cargo completed, *Port Brisbane* was loaded with steel, motor vehicles (either in parts or complete), machinery, ladies' stockings – welded inside galvanised water butts to prevent theft – Dinky and many other toys, clothes, bags of carbon black, Kilner jars and various household items. She was loaded down to her 'marks', the safe loading scale for vessels introduced by Samuel Plimsoll, the MP for Bristol in the 19th century.

After a fortnight alongside, the vessel was secured for sea, and down the Thames she sailed en route for a destination not often visited by Port boats: Port of Spain in Trinidad. This was to be a real eye-opener for the country boy turned mariner, very green as he was in the matter of what might be called worldliness. Within days the sun shone constantly, and the vessel settled down to the deep-sea routine. The 12 passengers soon acquainted themselves with their areas of the vessel and made valiant efforts to understand the complexities of deck golf, the leading recreation for the exclusive Port Line passengers. There were two 'younger' female passengers, one the doctor's wife and the other a single woman, and as the days at sea increased so did the attractiveness of these two. Soon the single woman teamed up with a younger man travelling with his father. The budding romance was watched with a mixture of envy and amusement by the 80 men of the crew; while the pair tried every hidey-hole on the vessel for a private kiss and cuddle, some sailor or another, with profuse apologies of course, would interrupt their passion.

When this 'childish' and 'quite deplorable' conduct was brought to the attention of Authority, one wag asserted: 'She should thank us, not complain about us. At least she won't get up the duff with us around, will she?' A month later, though, the young woman must have been relieved that her romance had, thanks to the sailors, not taken a more serious turn, as on arrival at Auckland her beau and his father were escorted off the vessel by police detectives, allegedly for financial misdemeanours in the United Kingdom.

As the majority of Port Line's passengers were elderly, it was not surprising that younger single people, isolated in the oceans, would turn to each other for some light relief from conversations about money, arthritis, and how quickly one's offspring had risen up the greasy pole to become an admiral or a general or an air marshal, a director or a prelate of the church.

In those days the elderly female passengers did not consider trousers, or indeed shorts, suitable attire for women – particularly younger women. This fact was emphasised by the truly menacing stares of some ladies of advanced age when they saw any female under 50 wearing a blouse with the top button undone – or indeed anything but a substantial dress or heavy skirt. On this voyage the doctor's wife did conform to the standards considered appropriate by the matriarchs, but she annoyed them considerably when at deck golf she tucked her skirt hem into her knickers to allow freedom of movement for her legs and to prevent the skirt blowing over her head. However, she did allow the breeze to lift up her blouse every so often whilst carefully keeping it buttoned up; it was almost possible to hear the elderly females tut-tutting two decks below the golf course.

As the temperature increased the bosun and his men built the vessel's swimming pool from a wooden frame covered in canvas, with a constant supply of seawater. The passengers had the use of the pool in daytime, the crew using it in the late afternoon and evenings. While the sight of the younger ladies wearing quite revealing – for the 1950s – costumes caused near-apoplexy in the passenger circles, it elicited no small amount of delight within the crew quarters.

At 17 knots the vessel ploughed on through a 20-foot swell from the South Atlantic. As there was no storm, though, sunshine glistened in the very small wavelets riding the swell. The *Port Brisbane* was a good seakeeping ship, and with the cargo well stowed and the wind on her forepart she could be steered with just one finger on the wheel. As the passengers either lounged about or played deck golf for the umpteenth time in the truly perfect weather, the bosun and his men were washing down the foredeck. This foredeck was unique in ships of this nature, in that on this deck were two hatches which gave access to the No 1 and No 2 cargo holds. As the bosun directed the water from his hose onto the deck, his sailors, armed with (top quality) Bass brooms, swept any detritus into the scuppers and over the ship's side.

The third mate, as officer of the watch, was looking out through the wheelhouse windows when he saw movement under a winch bed on the foredeck. Instantly he was transformed into a man of action and, grabbing the loudhailer, bawled to the bosun, 'There's a rat behind you!'

The bosun, what with the noise of the water from his hose plus the breeze of the ship's passage through the ocean, could not understand what the third mate was saying. Cupping his hand to his ear, he shouted, 'What?'

'There's a *rat* behind you!'

Jack, standing on No 3 hatch below the bridge, was witnessing the start of a maritime pantomime never repeated during the rest of his maritime career. It was almost unheard of for a rat to be found on, of all vessels, a Port boat. Even though the *Port Brisbane* was not carrying any food on this outward leg, rats were not tolerated under any circumstances.

Within seconds, Captain Bailey was on the bridge and, wresting the loudhailer from his third mate, took command of this most serious matter: 'Bosun, kill the damned thing *now!*' – the first of many commandments issued from his lips, as it became apparent that he needed no loudhailer to make himself heard on the foredeck. After all, it was claimed that he had first gone to sea in a sailing vessel when, it was alleged, ships were made of wood and the men were made of iron. 'It's gone to port – no, it's behind the hatch, heading to starboard – *kill* it, man!' he shouted. 'Don't just stand there. I said kill it, not wave your broom at it, you damned fool.'

Able Seaman Smith took umbrage at being called a damned fool, but as it came from the Old Man he thought it best, for the sake of a 'Very Good' entry in the Ability column of his discharge book, to ignore this – in his carefully considered opinion – most unjust and unwarranted title.

News travelled very fast and the forward-facing saloon windows were soon filled with passengers watching a hunt which instead of a fox, a horse, hounds and hunting pink had a hose, denims, Bass brooms and the master of hounds ensconced on the starboard bridge wing. The seamen, chasing the rodent around the hatchways, under the winches and across the foredeck, made every effort to assault the beast with their brooms.

Meanwhile, the lamp-trimmer, keeper and – in his opinion – owner of all the deck stores, watched the rise and fall of his brooms with some trepidation in case they were damaged or, horror upon horror, the heads fell off.

Ratty had now made his way under the fairlead mounting on the starboard side of the foredeck and was determined to stay in this steel shelter to protect himself from the brooms wielded by seamen totally unconcerned about both their value and the delicate mental health of Scrooge Lampy where his stores were concerned.

Under the influence of broom handles being pushed through the water holes in the mounting base of the fairlead, Ratty decided it would be in his best interests to make a run for the sanctuary of the scupper pipe leading from the after end of the foredeck down to the scupper on the well deck, where Jack was standing on the canvas-covered No 3 hatch. Not trusted with a broom, Jack had simply let his fertile mind wander to the saying relating to speed, 'like a rat up a drain pipe' – only in this case it was a rat down a scupper drainpipe, and this particular rat had a very good turn of speed, probably a gold standard in the rat Olympics.

As the rat disappeared down the pipe the bosun promptly put the hose down it, fully expecting the rat to appear at the bottom. Ten seamen expected the same, and in a concerted rush slid down the ladder to the well deck.

No rat appeared. Minutes went past, and still no rat.

'Put another hose up the pipe,' roared Captain Bailey, 'and *drown* the bugger.'

Whether someone on the bridge brought the attention of the master to the fact that time was on the march or whether he was considering the well-being of his men, he issued an unexpected commanded. This was announced through the formerly discarded loudhailer, and in a more conciliatory tone: 'Bosun, take the men to smoke-ho for 15 minutes, then back here.'

The charitable break may, however, have been because the Captain's tiger – his personal steward – had just told his master that his tea and tabnab (a small cake, sweet pastry or other delicacy) was getting cold in his day cabin. But the captain's most generous concession swiftly deleted the pleasure that Jack had in watching the Rat Pantomime amid the gentle sun-dappled sea swell in mid-Atlantic; as he swiftly came back to reality from his rat-up-a-drainpipe reverie, it dawned on him, as the men filed past him on their way to the mess room for their own tea and tabnab, that he should already have had their tea brewed. Instead, here was he, the peggy, at the back of the column heading for the mess – and no tea, never mind tabnab, was prepared for their 15-minute break.

On Jack's late arrival at the mess he had to face the music, with irate men demanding where the bloody peggy was and voicing what they would do to him when he arrived. He shot into the mess and out again, clutching the large and dented teapot, and ran towards the water urn in the hope that it was boiling. Thankfully, it was, and he put more tea leaves than usual into the pot in the belief that the men wouldn't notice the strength, but presume that it had been brewed. Luckily, despite the fact that he was late, no one seemed to notice that the unbrewed tea was hotter than usual. The catering boy – a second tripper and plainly used to handling irate sailors – arrived with their tabnabs, and before anyone could shout a complaint about his late arrival, he loudly observed, 'If you buggers come in early you're lucky to get tabnabs at all – the baker ain't 'appy.' He slammed them down on the table, turned on his heel and left, to a stunned silence. That a catering boy could say such a thing to hardened seamen took them all by surprise – and it became a very useful tool in the Jack's war chest when dealing with his seniors.

Soon, but not soon enough for Jack, the sailors filed out of the mess ready to witness the rat – by now, drowned – emerging from the scupper pipe. Jack filed after them and took his position on the No 3 hatch cover. The bosun returned to his position befitting his unchallenged authority, and ordered that his hose be turned off at the hydrant. His deliberations were interrupted by His Master's Voice, on this occasion not appealing to the dog Nipper but to him. In a slightly exasperated tone, Captain Bailey, now refreshed by his afternoon tea, explained carefully and loudly, 'Would it not make more sense, Bosun, if you kept your hose going and turned off the hose going up the pipe so that the animal's body will come down it?'

Heard quite clearly by Jack, and possibly also heard on the foredeck, Captain Bailey addressed someone on the bridge with his still resounding Force-9-gale voice: 'That man's a fool. God help us if we ever have to rely on his intelligence.' Perhaps rather unfairly, Jack took some satisfaction from the master's comments on the ability of his bosun.

As there appeared to be little activity except between Bailey and the bosun, the sailors were either leaning on the starboard rail of the well deck or standing by the scupper awaiting the arrival of the corpse from the foredeck scupper pipe. Soon it

Playing card

appeared, and the distinctive voice from the bridge commanded, 'Get it over the side.'

The lamp-trimmer, standing outside his storeroom door on the port side of the for'ard bulkhead, heaved a sigh of relief. Soon his beloved brooms would be returned to him as he looked over the hatch towards the starboard rail where the men were preparing to give Ratty a less than ceremonial burial at sea.

Ratty, at that very moment, stood up, shook himself and took off along the starboard scupper with a commendable turn of speed as the voice from on high declared what might be acknowledged as stating the bloody obvious: 'It's alive! Kill it now, *kill it!*' The command was given in a tone of voice demanding some degree of urgency in its execution. The line of sailors armed with the brooms – the claimed personal possessions of the by now aghast lamp-trimmer – rose and fell in a line that closely resembled the hammers of a grand piano striking the wires. Unfortunately for both Ratty and poor Lampy, the symmetry of the wonderfully executed Overture to a Rodent ended with the death of Ratty in his last dash towards the stevedores' lavatory door; said lavatory a unique invention on a vessel, and a sanctuary for the stevedores to dally whilst reading the *Daily Mirror*, *Daily Herald* or, if a foreman, *The Guardian*. In the same crisis as the brooms rose and fell, with agile Ratty avoiding all but the deadly broom of AB McLeod, who was last in the executioners' line, the heads of eight brooms out of the ten issued that day entered – without any ceremony or concern on the part of their handlers – the mid-Atlantic Ocean.

As the sailors returned the broken handles of their instruments of death, the lamp-trimmer was truly distraught, his day, and probably his voyage itself, now totally ruined by a rat and a beautifully orchestrated but over-enthusiastic team of sailors under the baton of the brilliant and most distinguished conductor, Maestro Bailey.

The body of Ratty was consigned to the four winds of Heaven and the deep. Amen.

Foreign parts at last

After Jack had tripped over the wooden grating in front of the binnacle, the reflection of the green light from the gyro compass illuminated his face as he took the helm in the darkened wheelhouse for the very first time. Eleven thousand tons of ship worth millions of pounds was in his hands, although the duty quartermaster who had relinquished the helm to the lad was instructing him in the art of keeping the vessel on course – subject to the engineers maintaining the same revolutions on both screws. In the hectic turning of the wheel to limit the clicks of the gyro compass as each wayward degree was crossed, it was remarkably easy to forget when the wheel was amidships. So the most important lesson for Jack was to feel for the brass cap on the central spoke of the wheel indicating when it was amidships, rather than trying in the gloom to look for it. Every once in a while the duty officer would come over and check the course and walk quietly away, but this initiation into the art of steering a large vessel was certainly daunting for the boy.

The period of tuition was one hour every evening. After two hours Jack was on his own with no quartermaster to hold his hand – just him in the wheelhouse, with the officer of the watch and quite often an apprentice practising Morse code with the Aldis lamp. The apprentice would use the reflection of the light off the jumbo derrick, enabling the duty officer, Jack and the apprentice himself to read whatever he was signalling. Sometimes a message would be very amusing, and a major problem for young Jack was keeping his eyes on the gyro compass instead of reading the witty remarks emanating from the lamp.

The purpose of Jack, first-trip boys and first-trip apprentices learning to steer was to obtain the MOT steering certificate, required for them to progress their maritime career either through examination to the position of either efficient deck hand / able seaman, or to sit, after four years, the exam for his second mate's certificate of competency. That certificate, then was the first step to the heady position of master mariner and eventually his own command.

When Jack began his sixth hour at the helm he noticed that slightly off the starboard bow was the loom of a light. The third mate had temporarily relieved the second, the navigator, as officer of the watch, so that the second could have his dinner, and the third mate was running to and fro between the chartroom and the bridge wing repeater gyro compass, where he would take a bearing using the Azimuth mirror to reflect the light onto whatever course the vessel was heading, and from that deduce the position of the vessel as it approached the light.

The one-hour periods of steering the ship were undertaken after the boys' duty hours, and coincided with dinner, served at 19:00 hrs. As all masters in the Port Line were required to dine with the passengers, Captain Bailey was not usually seen on the bridge at the time Jack was on the wheel. So it was a surprise to everyone – except, apparently, the duty officer – when at about 19:45 hours the chartroom door opened and into the darkened wheelhouse strode Captain Bailey with a burst of light ensuing. His unexpected appearance caused the apprentice practising his signalling to lose his focus, and he made a proper mess of his signal. Bailey stood still but then pulled the chartroom door closed, returning the wheelhouse to its normal gloom. He took a very avuncular view of the youngster misspelling his signal, simply saying to him, 'Take it a little slower and your signalling will improve.' Turning to his third mate he continued, 'What instruction has this boy had?' indicating Jack with a nod. The duty mate told the master the extent of Jack's tuition.

Captain Bailey promptly told his officer that straight line steering did not teach the art of helmsmanship, and immediately enquired of the boy what he knew of compass quarter points, degree orders, helm points and the other things to be considered when complying with orders. He then emphasised that when steering to a given *degree* the vessel must be turned to that heading and held there until otherwise instructed, and when given *points* the helm must be turned to the required tell-tale point and then held there until ordered to meet her, when the swing of the ship would be stopped. Captain Bailey then ordered the boy to put into practice what he had just explained. The navigator almost had a nervous breakdown as he attempted to plot the course, 'after the Old Man had buggered up the chart by going over the entire ocean,' after, to his relief, the master had gone.

As the third mate went to the door a quartermaster appeared and walked towards Jack at the wheel: 'You're relieved.' Jack then told him the course to steer. He in turn repeated it to Jack, then the boy went to the officer of the watch, the third, and told him the course. The officer then said, 'You're damned lucky – all I had was straight line steering tuition. Don't think that every trick at the wheel will be as good as this one.' Jack, leaving the wheelhouse totally exhausted, realised that he had been on the wheel for almost two hours.

As a result of his more than usual association with Captain Bailey the boy never lost his admiration for him despite the occasional little 'difficulty' when the master came around to inspect the accommodation every second day at sea, except Sunday. Bailey, when inspecting, was very fond of flicking a card matchstick to land wherever a surface should be white. Should the matchstick be whiter than wherever it had landed, a severe verbal onslaught was guaranteed. The result would be the same in the cabins if papers were found under cushions or soiled clothes found in drawers. What with his matches and a large torch, nothing was missed by his inspection. He would be accompanied by his entourage of the purser/ chief steward, who liked to be called just purser, and the bosun in the sailors' accommodation. Captain Bailey in full dress with his cap at a slightly 'Beatty' angle brought fear to the peggy boys, not to mention the catering staff.

He was particularly rigorous with the galley staff; after all he was eating food prepared there, and he made sure they appreciated that fact.

One day, early in the morning, the bell to summon the deck crew to their berthing stations rang, and Jack went on deck on a most beautiful tropical morning, to take in the sights, sounds and smells of his first visit to a foreign port. Like many children of his age, he had been brought up on stories of the Spanish Main, pirates, privateers and men-of-war. Port of Spain: what images such a name could conjure in the fertile imagination of a young man! Here was the reality; the sight was of tropical trees and shrubs with American cars travelling at what appeared to be excessive speed with a seemingly total disregard for rules, animals and pedestrians. The sounds were principally of screeching tyres, incomplete exhaust systems and English spoken with the distinct Caribbean lilt and a slight American twang. The smells were a mixture of sweet perfume, rotting vegetation, tropical heat and exhaust fumes.

As the men trooped down to the mess room for breakfast the mail from home arrived. Homesickness had not bothered Jack since his first few days as a trainee – but with the arrival of letters from his mother, sister and current girlfriend the minutiae of life in north Somerset were set out before him, and the boy, despite being one of 80 men aboard the vessel, felt very strong pangs of loneliness. However, when after reading his mail he went out on deck, facing seaward, he witnessed a sight not to be forgotten for the rest of his life. Heading into Port of Spain was a full-rigged ship under full sail with the rays of the sun catching the white of the sails, giving an almost magical vision of a storybook scene. The ship was the Norwegian training ship *Christian Radich* on a courtesy call to Trinidad. Some years later, in Sydney, Jack saw a film about the ship, with a concert pianist among the crew playing Grieg's evocative music.

At about midday Jack was told to go to the purser/chief steward to get a 'sub' of the local currency, British Caribbean Territories dollars. This money, deducted from their final pay-off, was to allow the crew to go ashore and hopefully enjoy themselves. At 17:00 that first day Jack and the other boys were given permission to go ashore – but not until 19:00, and under the supervision of a chaperone. The boy ratings took this idea with very poor grace – but the supervisor, one Cuffy, taking them outside the dock perimeter gates, said: 'Behave yourselves and be back aboard by 22:00. And if anyone asks, I saw you back aboard, then I went ashore again.' He left the boys to their own devices and disappeared into the Trinidadian night. A little later it was the 'vices' part of the word 'devices' that turned out to be the operative word during their adventures in Port of Spain ...

Not too far away from the docks, Jack and his chum came across a brightly lit hotel. With the intention of going there for a soft drink the boys entered a bar area. The now very slightly homesick Jack was amazed to find, on a shelf above the barman's head, a very palatable reminder of home insofar as his house overlooked the Coate & Co. cider works. Sitting on the shelf were bottles of Coates Somerset Cider, with its familiar green label with yokels thereon, and the legend 'Coates comes up from Somerset where the cider apples grow'. Without doubt it was the best cider produced anywhere in Britain at that time. Jack went to the bar and ordered two bottles. He was quite taken aback to be charged 5s each, considering his pay was only £12 2s 6d a month. The fact that no one had asked his age meant that he was not too inclined to draw attention to the pair of them. But in fact he did draw attention, in that he remained at the bar, expecting to collect the cider. The barman, plainly knowing that these boys were greenhorns, gently explained to Jack that the drinks would be delivered to their table. When the drinks arrived via a salver-carrying waiter, paper doilies were put under the glasses and – may the Lord forgive the waiters for offending the boys' sense of propriety – the cider was served on the rocks. However, they enjoyed a good hour over two half-pints admiring the clientèle. Clearly this place was considered to be socially superior to those usually frequented by boy seamen.

When they finally finished their drinks the boys headed out and along the road which they thought would take them to town. The first shock of the evening – except of course the price of the cider – was the people sleeping on the streets. Not one or two, but dozens upon dozens. This was certainly very different to Somerset, and it was while navigating through these bodies that the boys became aware of about four rather large and, to the boys and their imaginations, menacing figures following them. The boys quickened their steps and decided to take the first turning on the left in the hope that this would lead back to the dock. As they turned into the street all the street lighting went off, so it really was dark. And while they had been unnerved a few minutes before by their followers, they were now truly frightened, as they could not see their followers but they could hear the sound of feet on the roadway. They were just about to run when a door opened on the other side of the street and the light from the building attracted them like moths to a flame. They needed no second persuading when a voice with a distinctly British accent invited them into the safety of what they believed to be a bar. Inside were tables with men and women sitting drinking, and a bar at the end of the room. Whilst to the boys it was a place of sanctuary, it could not remotely compare to the previous establishment patronised by them. The place appeared to be clean, but no waiter was likely to bring their drinks to the table – nor were they likely to find the cider of Redvers N. Coate & Co.

As Jack had brought the last round of drinks, his chum breasted the bar and ordered two beers. While he was at the bar two of the unaccompanied women at the other table smiled at Jack, and he with courtesy returned the unexpected gesture. With that, his chum returned with two beers, and the information that they were not going to stay there once they had drunk their beers because, 'These beers cost me about ten bob each in their money,' his features displaying the anguish of the transaction. Lurking assailants or not, the two decided that the option of leaving the expensive safety of the bar appeared to be the lesser of the two evils.

As they took their leave, coming in through the doorway was a senior rating from their vessel, who enquired, 'What are you boys doing in this place?'

'Don't go in there. They charge about 10/- for one small beer,' Jack's chum responded. 'Have you paid 10/- and only had a beer?' asked their shipmate.

'No,' replied the chum with no small amount of plainly hurt feelings. 'I've paid £1 or whatever in their dollars for the two beers.' The boys told of their great scare and enquired the way back to the ship. The sailor directed them on down the road they had taken, and as they emerged from the bar the street lights were on again – and, sure enough, down the road and around the corner was their vessel. The beautiful lines of the brightly illuminated *Port Brisbane* were never a more welcome sight as they went aboard – well before their time limit – and turned in, very grateful that they had returned from their first foray on foreign soil in one piece.

At breakfast the following morning the boys were stopped in their tracks when they overheard the senior rating they had met at the bar in conversation with his chums in the petty officers' mess room, regaling his messmates about his experience of going ashore in Port of Spain. The boys, out of sight, listened as the man said, 'I went up town and found this knocking shop, and as I went in the two boys, the peggies, were coming out. I couldn't believe my eyes and thought, what in the 'ell were they doing in there?' He burst out laughing and continued, 'The short one told me not to go in there 'cause they charged 10/- for a beer. I asked them what they'd 'ad, and the lad said he'd paid £1 for two small beers, and that was sheer robbery. They'd been chased into the bar and wanted to get back 'ere. I told them 'ow to get 'ere and I went in and got two free jumps with a smart piece of stuff for the quid they'd paid for 'er.'

The mess room erupted into almost uncontrolled laughter at the story. Then another voice said, 'Give 'em their money back, or you'll end up with a dose, I'm warning 'ee.'[3]

'I can't,' replied the seaman, 'I only got their dollars, and we'm sailing afore they could spend 'em. Waste of time.'

Jack was devastated by what he had just heard, but thinking back he realised it was a strange place. He was hurt that he was so naïve that he hadn't recognised a brothel when he was in one, despite all the warnings when he was in training about 'ladies of easy virtue'. His chum was mortified to think that in the first place he had been in a brothel, secondly that he had paid for the sexual pleasure of another man, and thirdly that everyone on the vessel would hear about it and laugh at his expense – in more senses than one. In the event the rating never paid the lad his £1, and sure enough, in Auckland the man was off to visit the pox doctor. He was definitely not laughing then!

Some of the gloom was lifted from the boys after breakfast at the sight of Cuffy, their erstwhile supervisor, visiting every pool of vomit looking for his false teeth. During the course of the voyage this performance became a ritual, yet he always found them.

The following day Jack was allowed an afternoon ashore. Port of Spain looked

---

3 A typical sailors' superstition.

so much better in the sunlight. It was colourful and interesting, and its people were most friendly. There were no people sleeping on the streets, either, for which Jack was relieved. As he searched for a souvenir he could afford he found a coconut carved in the shape of a head with the word 'Trinidad' carved into its hat. For many years afterwards, when looking at the coconut his thoughts turned to his unintentional intrusion into that Caribbean brothel.

Soon it was time to leave Trinidad and make towards Caracas Bay on Curaçao, a Dutch colony off the north coast of South America. There the *Port Brisbane* would fill her bunkers with fuel oil to power her until her return in four months' time. On entering the bay, to the right stood a headland bathed in tropical sunshine, and atop the small cliff which comprised the headland stood an ancient fortification tower. Jack was told that this fort had been built by Henry Morgan, the renowned Welsh 17th-century pirate from Bristol, who eventually became deputy governor of Jamaica. The cliff was called the Virgin's Leap, where allegedly nuns had committed suicide rather than succumb to the depravity of Morgan's men. Make-believe or fact? Jack, during his career and many visits to Caracas Bay, never established which it was, but the yarn suited the scene.

The beauty of the bay in Morgan's time was lost to the bunkering facilities and fuel storage tanks filling much of the land and the sparkling clear water. Going ashore in the bay meant a walk along the jetty to a grid over the water and under the Virgin's Leap. Here the boy stood amazed at the crystal-clear water and the many garfish twisting and turning a few inches from his feet. His souvenir from the waters of Caracas Bay was a small but to him fascinating lump of coral with the wonderful geometric designs put there by nature long before humans existed.

Ten hours later the *Port Brisbane* disconnected from the fuel hoses, took in her mooring lines and left with full bunkers heading for the Panama Canal: a wonder of the world.

South of the Line

The geography master at the school Jack had attended was one Geoffrey Bates. He was a remarkable teacher in the lash-and-flog-'em era of 1950s education, in that he was the only

Caribbean Dollar Note (Front and Back)

master capable of achieving obedience from his pupils without using a cane. While the rest of his colleagues were liberal in administering corporal punishment, often to the wrong pupil, they did not obtain the same measure of obedience. Geoffrey could, however, tongue-lash pupils to an extreme which could reduce the largest sixth-form bullies to tears. In this field he was quite merciless, but when the tongue-lashing, usually in front of the class, was completed, he would treat the miscreant exactly the same as the rest of the boys, with a kindness and understanding that was genuinely appreciated by his pupils.

Geoffrey Bates had been a pre-war naval reservist and had become a Wavy Navy lieutenant commander when he went to war in 1939. His ability to exact obedience at school simply by dishing out a verbal onslaught was ascribed to his training by His Majesty's Navy – as Jack, later in his sea training, could well understand. To be on the end of a tongue-lashing by Geoffrey Bates, or from his former Whale Island gunnery instructors, was an experience in itself.

One of the O-level geography topics in Mr Bates' class was the West Indies and Central America, their resources, trade etc. During his war service he had served in the Caribbean and had transited the Panama Canal on a couple of occasions. The subject in question was grist to the mill as far as Jack was concerned. Geoffrey waxed quite lyrical, as the normal, sometimes boring, studies of various parts of the world were of minor importance to the boys unless it was exam time. The class appeared to spend an unusual amount of time discussing banana boats and the Panama Canal. At the time, Jack had, as a prospective mariner, taken notice of both the banana boats and the tales of the Panama Canal; Mr Bates would explain how towing in the canal locks was carried out by mules, and how first-timers to the canal, particularly boy ratings, would be told to collect bread crusts to feed to the mules. This they would obey, only to find when they appeared on deck with a sack of crusts, to the considerable amusement of the crew, that the mules were in fact mechanical tugs.

The sailors told Jack and his chum the bread-for-mules story. In the quiet of their cabin Jack explained to his chum what nonsense it was, although in fairness his chum was just as wise to the ruse. But then they heard two of the first-trip catering boys talking how they were going to prevent the peggy boys from collecting the bread as usual; the galley boys would collect it instead, and deliver short measure to each mess, then keep a stash aside for the Panama mules. For several days Jack and his chum made a great play on the fact that they were denied access to bread, and the galley boys could not contain their glee that they thought they had one over on the peggy boys. It was quite clear that the second-trip catering boy was going to allow his junior colleagues to make fools of themselves, probably as he had on his first voyage.

Unlike almost anywhere else in the maritime world, the Panama Canal Authority would not allow ships to put a pilot ladder over the side for their ship's pilots to board the vessel. They insisted that the ship's starboard gangway should be lowered, This enabled the pilot, like the important person he felt he was, to swagger up the gangway, cigar clenched firmly between the teeth, with a stetson hat and bootlace tie, as seen in all good all-American films. This scene was a matter of wonder to Jack, but what impressed him most was the motor launches, similar to the wartime motor torpedo boats; the deep throb of their engines was most impressive as they roared away from the ship. That particular bit of Americana was acceptable to Jack's conservative mind, even if the speed was more a case of showing off rather than a necessity.

For the transit of the canal all the awnings were rigged including the fo'c'sle head as for those who had to be there it was extremely hot, but the wires from the mules to the ship were handled by employees of the Canal Authority, so most of the crew had a day off. It was also a requirement of the Articles of the MOT for lime juice to be offered to all on board in these climes. No one drank it, but it was used by Jack and his messmate to clean the fiddles on the mess-room tables. The fiddles, which kept items on the tables during rough weather, came up quite white, which impressed Captain Bailey when he did his inspection after the ship reached the Pacific Ocean. He might not have been so pleased had he known what the expensive gallon of lime juice had been used for. On the other hand, when he was a boy he might have done the same thing.

As the vessel was hauled into the Gatun locks, the sailors asked Jack where his bread was for the mules. He told them that the mule, indicating the electric locomotive, would be hard pushed to digest any bread. They were none too pleased that he had not fallen for their joke: ' 'E's a right little smartarse, ain't 'e?' The only offence that the boy found in the statement was the word 'little' – after all he was 6 feet tall now, rather taller than most of the sailors. Whilst he was considering his position relating to the men now on the foredeck, the door from the galley store room opened and staggering through came the two catering/galley boys carrying sacks of bread. The appearance of these boys concentrated the minds of the men onto the galley boys rather than Jack. When the laughter subsided, the older and wiser sailors patiently disabused the boys. Their look of pure hatred was a sight to behold as they realised that they were the butt of the joke – and worst of all, that Jack and his chum had been in on it all along. They never forgot that incident, and many years later, in another vessel the assistant cook/ second baker was one of those boys. When he saw Jack, by then a senior rating, he became quite paranoid throughout the voyage about the slight of so many years ago; all Jack had to do was either smile or perhaps laugh in the presence of the assistant cook for him to take such mirth as being directed towards him and cause a scene, making sure that he was behind the grille partition, safe from retribution, before he sounded off. When the crew discovered why he had such vitriol towards Jack they nicknamed him 'soft crust', causing him even more angst.

Apart from his admiration for the American pilot launches, Jack was not overly impressed by his American cousins, and the sight of the brash pilot boarding the *Port Brisbane* only went to increase his prejudice. However, as the vessel proceeded through the Gatun Lake and on through the Gaillard Cut, Jack could not fail to be impressed by the wonderful and very skilled engineering by the American Corps of Engineers; perhaps not all the Yanks were like the film actors and the pilot.

Soon they had made the complete transit of the canal, and down came some of the awnings as the vessel headed into the Pacific Ocean for the long voyage to Auckland. As the vessel crossed the Equator, everyone who had not been across the Line had to meet King Neptune at the ship's canvas swimming pool. There Jack and the rest of the first-trippers were baptised with a concoction believed to be a mixture of flour, jam and perhaps custard; unsurprisingly the crew, both officers and men, received much rougher handling than the passengers.

For the next 13 days the ship's routine went smoothly. The two galley boys were still very unhappy with Jack and his chum, but as the galley boys were not up to giving the pair a good hiding they allowed their hatred to be reflected in their attitude to all the deck ratings. The posturing by the galley boys did not appear to have the slightest impact on the sailors, until one day an AB found a Green Gilbert – sputum – under his fried egg. He was displeased, and out of sight of anyone in authority – but certainly known about by said authority – both galley/catering boys were shown the error of their ways by a thorough and rather bloody reprimand from the sailor concerned.

The issue which taxed the brains of the rest of that mess was just how many times since Panama this adulteration of food might have occurred without anyone noticing. For many weeks afterwards the occupants of the sailors' mess room examined their plates very closely.

Just off the coast of New Zealand a Southerly buster struck the vessel, and Jack had his first taste of a severe storm powered by a deep depression from Antarctica. Metal deadlights, shutters, had to be secured over the cabin portholes in case of the glass breaking, even though it was very thick. The vessel, although renowned as a good sea ship, rolled and pitched in the huge swell and enormous waves. The storm raged for two days, keeping all but the watchkeepers off the open decks. As soon as the wind and waves decreased, there was a concerted effort by the deck crowd to rig the cargo-lifting derricks with their guys and preventers: they also had to get the mooring lines up from the forepeak for the forward moorings and up from the tonnage hatch for the after lines. After a very hard day's work, Jack took to his bunk, a very tired boy by any measure.

The following morning he was put on call at 06:30, and looking out of the cabin porthole as the ship glided through the Hauraki Gulf, Jack saw, for the first time of what was to become many, the wonderful city of Auckland bathed in beautiful sunshine,. The city looked colourful and bright, with all but one of the jetties extending at right angles to the quay walls, and with what appeared to be many ships alongside. After a very quick shower and shave Jack went on deck to see Rangitoto Island, an extinct volcano and Auckland's distinctive landmark, on the starboard side. Turning under the control of the pilot, coming in adjacent to the Royal New Zealand Navy base, Devonport, with the cruiser HMNZS *Royalist* alongside, the *Port Brisbane* moved slowly to her allotted berth, almost at the end of Queen Street, Auckland's commercial centre.

After Jack's experience of docks in Britain, he was totally amazed by the clean quay walls, the very tidy transit sheds and the lack of filth on the docks. At 8:00 the dockers and stevedores appeared for work. This was to be another total revelation to the boy; all these men wore clean clothes – a tidy shirt, shorts, socks and shoes. Almost all had a trilby hat and a small brown leather case. They went into the transit shed and emerged in working clothes. Even their working clothes were clean and in good order. How very different to the unkempt dockworkers on the British quay walls. However, in the defence of the British dockworker, their management and port authorities had made absolutely no effort to improve the lot of the employees or casual workers since the 19th century. In those days only lavatories were provided for British dockworkers, and they were always filthy: if cleaned at all it was by a hosepipe from the doorway. The one thing that these New World dockworkers and the British ones shared was their religious following of a messiah in the form of trade unions, and their propensity to call a strike at a moment's notice, often for the most petty and ridiculous of reasons.

As soon as Jack's duties were over and he had some New Zealand currency in his pocket, he headed towards the main post office, situated not too far from the dock gates, to post a letter home telling of his Pacific crossing and the storm. On entering the – very plush – post office, he was again surprised to see all the clerks wore a uniform: shorts, regulation socks, and shoes. Everything was bright, and above all clean. When he asked for air mail stamps and stickers, they were passed to him and, lo and behold, what should be depicted on the stamp but his ship, the *Port Brisbane*, accompanied by a lamb! It had been issued to commemorate the 75th anniversary of the New Zealand lamb trade. His first reaction was to be very proud that his ship was on a postage stamp – but it soon dawned on him that it was unusual that a New Zealand stamp depicted the *Port Brisbane*, named after an Australian city, the capital city of the state of Queensland, when her near-sister ship was the *Port Auckland*, with a name much more suitable to commemorate such an anniversary in New Zealand.

As he walked down the steps from the post office little did Jack realise in years to come just how important these steps would become to his love life. Over the period of his visits to Auckland at least three Auckland girlfriends would arrange to meet him 'on the post office steps at 'siven to tin paast'. He was smitten by the female Kiwi accent, and that captivation too would endure to his old age.

To Jack, the highlight of this first visit to Auckland was his trip to the Civic cinema at the top end of Queen Street. This cinema was a superb venue with luxurious seating, a Hammond organ and a ceiling decorated to reflect the sub-equatorial night sky. At first glance it was as if the roof had opened to the sky. It was all quite mesmerising for the young boy.

A couple of days after the ship's arrival the local padre turned up. The Flying Angel was the logo used to represent the Anglican Mission to Seamen; this was an organisation created by a Church of England clergyman in the 19th century at Clevedon in north Somerset. Its original purpose had been to minister to the spiritual and temporal needs for seamen on sailing ships anchored in the Bristol Channel. Padre Brown ran the Auckland branch of the Flying Angel Mission to Seamen – colloquially spoken of as the Flying Sea-boot – like clockwork. He was a man who stood for no nonsense from his clients, and was more than able to look after himself should the need arise.

Because of the boys' limited financial funds, the Mission was a favourite destination for them and junior seamen, and all manner of activities was arranged for visiting seamen from any ship and any nation. This organisation, like so others such as the British Sailors' Society and the Catholic Stella Maris, owed its existence to the numerous ladies, often of a certain age and social standing, who took it as their duty to support organisations, both financially and materially. These ladies took a motherly interest in the boys far away from home, and presented their daughters, nieces and the like as partners to the visiting seamen for the weekly dances at the Mission. Jack very much enjoyed these dances and, despite his girlfriend at home probably not approving, took a lot of interest in a particular young lady from the suburb of Howick. However, the girls and young women made sure that for their part there would be no romantic attachment, and Padre Brown would sit watching the couples; should he see any activity which he saw as improper or likely to become so, he would wag his finger. Nonetheless the dances were welcomed by the boys and kept them in touch with the nicer female company, if for only three and a half hours a week.

After a fortnight discharging general cargo the *Port Brisbane* sailed for Wellington, the capital city of New Zealand. The city is at the southerly end of the North Island, with the Cook Strait between the two islands, and it has the well-deserved title of Wet and Windy Welly; whilst there were many lovely spells of weather, it was just like being in Britain but slightly warmer, as Jack would find out one Christmas Day in the years to come.

Wellington was the headquarters for Port Line in New Zealand, so there was always a surfeit of superintendents and captains coming aboard, along with others claiming to be of importance to the welfare of the company.

The view on arrival at the capital city by sea was far removed from the attractiveness of Auckland. In Auckland there was a wealth of colour and many public park areas, including the verdant Domain Park with the truly impressive white War Memorial museum overlooking the harbour and city. But Wellington resembled the sometimes dour appearance of many British port cities. However, there were some fine parks, open spaces and beaches in Wellington.

It was in this city that Jack and his messmate were detained for allegedly smuggling beer. The story began when the *Port Brisbane* ran out of beer and some bright spark

The Wellington waterfront

rang up the purser/ chief steward of the vessel *Port Lyttelton*, berthed a few jetties away, and arranged for a dozen or so cases of beer to be purchased from the ship for the wholesale price – plus a donation to the purser's funds, naturally. Jack and his messmate were dragged from their cabin, and with the money in their hands were sent to the *Port Lyttelton*. On arrival they were met by the second steward and in their innocence asked to see the purser, only to be rather snootily told that, 'The purser's not likely to bother himself with the likes of you. You've come for beer, and subject to the cash being right you'll get it.' They went to the store and gave the steward the money in the hope that the purser would get his cut of the cash. But it soon became apparent that they could not possibly carry the cases of beer to their ship, so they commandeered two sets of sack trucks, loaded up their beer and set off to the *Port Brisbane*.

When nearing their vessel they were accosted by two men in civilian clothing who told the boys to stop – a heart-stopping moment for the lads, as they thought they were about to be mugged. The men, with a flash of some card or other which showed nothing in the dim light of the quay wall, announced that they were customs officers. They demanded to know where the boys were going with the beer. The boys told them that the beer had come from the *Port Lyttelton* to which the men replied, 'We know that. We were watching you. We asked you where you were *going* with the beer.'

Jack's chum, full of bravado – which, to be quite honest, stemmed from the relief that they were not going to be mugged – said, 'It's quite all right, Sir – we're taking the beer from one vessel to another.' The first customs officer appeared to be incredulous

MV *Port Lyttelton*

that a whippersnapper of a youth should speak with such apparent authority, and replied with a rather heavy hint of menace, 'We decide if it's all right – and in this case, son, it's *not* all right.' Jack could have cheerfully killed his chum when the boy, very stupidly, continued, 'Perhaps you're mistaken, Sir.' Red rag to a bull could really not equate to the temper displayed by the customs officer at this cocky Pommie bastard of a child. The boys were taken a gatehouse and questioned. This resulted in further enquiries involving those aboard the *Port Lyttelton* and the seaman from *Port Brisbane*. Then the beer was confiscated, as duty had not been paid on it.

Judging by the reaction when the boys rejoined their vessel, the seamen were less than pleased – though they were delighted that the chief and second steward of the *Port Lyttelton* had found themselves in hot water with Her Majesty's New Zealand Customs and Excise men.

Before the *Port Lyttelton* left Wellington it was the avowed intent of the short-changed sailor to recover his beer money from the steward of that vessel. Whatever he used as method of debt recovery, it worked. Jack and his chum had visions of the steward's blood and guts spread wide, but according to the soothsayers of the sailors' mess, there was no violence; simply the sight of the *Port Brisbane* sailor approaching the *Port Lyttelton* promptly produced the money owed via the duty quartermaster, before the aggrieved sailor could fully ascend the gangway. Yet again the grey-bearded mess-room predictors had ruined the two boys' more basic fantasies, that yet again the deck department had kept the catering department where they belonged – at the bottom of the pecking order.

The next morning the boys were summoned to the master's day room. With some trepidation they were taken there by the first officer and stood before Captain Bailey. He looked at each of the boys and said, 'I've been told of your escapade. Let me tell you that the only errands you'll carry out ashore will be ones that the first officer or I order you to carry out. Do I make myself quite clear? I accept that you were simply helping the seamen's mess, but look at the problems it's caused with the authorities. This is your first and last warning.' With a wave of his hand, he dismissed Jack and his chum.

For the rest of their stay in Wellington the boys kept a very low profile. Soon – and for the boys none too soon – the ship sailed for Lyttelton, the port for city of Christchurch, in the South Island.

The *Port Brisbane* sailed out of Wellington Harbour, also known as Port Nicholson, and slowly gathered way. At the same time the inter-island ferry left for the overnight trip to Lyttelton. The ferry, *Maori*, was an attractive vessel of about 8,000 tons, and without the need for a harbour pilot she swept by the *Port Brisbane* as the two vessels made their way into the Cook Strait, passing the Barrett Reef, sometimes known as Wanganella Reef. This was not the official name for the rocks, but in 1947 the *Wanganella*, a large vessel used as a ferry regularly trading from Australia to Wellington, had run aground on it. Whilst this was a disaster for the vessel – and in particular for her elderly, but very experienced, master – the gods of meteorology smiled on the incident. Deep depressions in the Tasman Sea create the appalling weather regularly experienced in Wellington and the Cook Strait. For several weeks the *Wanganella* was stuck on the rocks, and should a storm have arisen she would have been completely wrecked. In the event, fair weather held out until she was salvaged and towed into the safety of Port Nicholson. From that incident any prolonged period of fine weather in the Cook Strait was called Wanganella weather.

By the time the *Port Brisbane* arrived at Lyttelton, having passed the *Hinemoa*, the *Maori*'s running mate, on her way from Lyttelton to Wellington, *Maori* had completed the discharge of the passengers' motor cars onto the jetty. As the *Port Brisbane* manoeuvred towards her berth, Jack saw that she would share a jetty with her near-sister vessel the *Port Auckland*, both vessels stern to shore. From the shore the stern view of the two ships, apart from their funnel shapes and their names, were identical.

Lyttelton was not the most sophisticated of towns in New Zealand but nonetheless had a charm often associated with such settlements in New Zealand and Australia. The port town was simply the gateway to the beautiful city of Christchurch, no pretence at being anything more. Jack was fascinated by the cinema– it was as far removed from the splendour of the Civic cinema in Auckland as it could possibly be. The green fabric on the seats was almost threadbare and to Jack the uniqueness of the cinema was not that it was known, quite inaccurately, as a fleapit, but that it was equipped with courting

Wanganella in her dotage

seats; in the back of the circle a row of double seats where a couple would sit and often ignoring the film, spend their time kissing, cuddling and perhaps a little bit extra. The little bit extra was often, but not always, lost in the gloom of the grand circle. In those times New Zealand, quite refreshingly, was not known for the hypocritical attitude to certain morals, as were the often very two-faced buttoned-up British.

Apart from the courting seats, Jack witnessed another difference between the carnal activities aboard the *Port Brisbane* in British waters as against New Zealand waters, where these activities involved young women who for some unknown reason were known as Ring Bolters. When the ship arrived in New Zealand, various women came aboard on an official boarding pass. These women, as Jack later found out, would remain on board throughout the vessel's stay in the country, living with whoever had obtained their pass. The fact that these passes were for one day only was apparently of little interest to the women, or to their sailors, cooks and engine-room ratings.

Apart from satisfying their men's sexual needs, these women cleaned the crew's accommodation, washed their clothes and, in some of the mess rooms, served the meals. For the peggy boys this was pure heaven, leaving little for them to do. In port and on the coast the crew accommodation inspections, usually carried out by the first mate rather than the captain, took place only once a week. When inspection day arrived, these women, most of them quite tidy in dress and looks, would run from one side of the accommodation to the other, depending on where the mate was at any given time. The other place Jack found them hiding during inspection was in the tonnage hatch, mostly used to store deck equipment. The fact that these women were aboard was well known by the officers, but ignored as long as they did not see them or officially know about it; they chose to ignore their existence, as it was believed that their presence kept the men in order to some degree. This was to a large extent true, but sometimes the sharing of their favours between more than one sailor could provoke disputes. However, the resourceful men usually overcame this difficulty by agreeing to share the woman not furtively or behind locked doors, but openly and in front of each other, so that jealousy would not rear its ugly head. This side of the Ring Bolter's life was an eye-opener for Jack. As the ship left her last port in New Zealand, the ladies of both day and night would go ashore, to join a new arrival.

It was in Lyttelton that Jack and his 'pauper' boy rating shipmates discovered shore pay. When there were a lot of vessels needing loading or discharging there were sometimes not enough dockworkers to man the holds of the vessels requiring them. The dockworkers' employers would then offer temporary work to anyone willing to apply. Jack and his shipmates were told that if they were 18 or over they could offer themselves for employment aboard the distinguished-looking *Tasmania Star* berthed on Gladstone Pier, which was discharging steel into railway wagons. As they had to work on their ship all day they offered themselves for night-time employment over a weekend. When asked their age, they all claimed to be 18. Even a half-wit would have reasoned that not all six boys would be 18, but it being New Zealand, and long before any 'elf & safety' legislation had been thought of, the boys were hired. Over that weekend they worked all night, some on steel and some on cased motor cars. The 'night' ended about 4:00 a.m., and they had a bit of time before they were put on shout for 6:30 aboard the *Port Brisbane*. By Monday they were just about dead, but waved the *Tasmania Star* farewell as she sailed away, to load refrigerated produce in another port.

To the astonishment of the boys they received the overwhelming sum of NZ £60 each for their efforts aboard the *Star*. Their regular pay being £12 2s 6d per month, this £60 was nothing less than a fortune to them. It would appear that because they worked at night and over a weekend their normal shore pay had increased in leaps and bounds, along with the bonus for working unsociable hours. It was to their eventual benefit that Lyttelton had little for them to spend their money on.

It was a Port Line policy that it would, as a matter of choice, employ sailors from the Hebrides, Shetland and surrounding islands, as these men were known for their hard work, maritime skills and the fact that they would work a two-year contract for the company on whatever vessel it put them on. While their skill and hard work was a fact, so was the undisputed fact that their hard work was complemented by hard, but sociable and – in most cases responsible – drinking. These Shelties and Stornowegians were men of almost monosyllabic conversation except amongst themselves in Gaelic, when for the most part they were very animated. In Lyttelton after closing time at the pub, it was quite common for the clientèle to move from the bar to a back room or two and continue drinking until either unconsciousness or the landlord's bedtime meant the end of a prolonged drink-up time for the alleged party.

On one particular day, the men from the Isles from *Port Brisbane* and *Port Auckland* decamped to the pub at 5.00 p.m. as usual. At 6:30 the following morning, the deck crew of the *Port Brisbane* were put on shake to turn to for work at 7:00 a.m. At first nothing seemed to be amiss as the sailors washed down the decks and prepared the hatches for the dockworkers to commence discharging the vessel at 8:00 a.m. This contented scene was to last until they left the deck for breakfast. As the men trooped past the petty officers' mess room, the boatswain appeared in the doorway, doing a double-take as the men went by, but saying nothing. After about 15 minutes the non-Islanders amongst the deck crew began to stare at their messmates. Slowly and surely it began to dawn on those who were not from the Islands that in the previous 12 hours some of their Gaelic-speaking crew-mates had changed. At about a quarter to nine the bosuns of the two Port Line vessels appeared in the seamen's mess room, and the one from the *Port Auckland* began to identify which men in the mess belonged to his ship, telling them to get back aboard. As they got up to leave the bosun of the *Port Brisbane* slowly – oh so slowly – realised that he was short of at least four of his sailors. Within minutes, the noise of feet coming down the companionway could be heard as the missing men arrived without a care in the world, having been chased off the *Port Auckland* by its bosun.

Much to the amusement of Jack and the other men, the Islanders, on returning from the pub about midnight, had gone aboard what they had believed to be their own ship. Both ships, as explained previously, looked almost identical – certainly to alcoholic eyes – from astern. The men had stumbled aboard, gone to their cabin and turned in. When they were put on shake in the morning they dressed (or not), some in working clothes and some in shoregoing clothes – little apparent difference – and reported for duty at 7:00 a.m., some of them on the wrong vessel.

This caused much amusement amongst those not involved, and was decreed by some wag to be worthy of a music-hall turn. The men concerned did not take lightly to the almost constant teasing from their colleagues, but nonetheless it was of note and should be chronicled in the history of both Port Line and the Islands. The incident rather limited the enjoyment of the after-hours pub delights of Lyttelton for some of the deck crews from both vessels concerned, but it most definitely improved the sight in many alcohol-influenced eyes.

It was in Lyttelton that the small brown cases carried by almost every male, noted by Jack on his arrival in Auckland, revealed their secrets to the boy. As the pubs closed their doors at 6:00 p.m., the menfolk of New Zealand would take two demijohns out of the case just before closing time, fill them with beer and then, returning the jars to the case, make their way home. It was almost a trade mark of the New Zealand male, and unique as far as Jack was concerned.

Also Lyttelton revealed yet another pleasing streak in the character of New Zealanders. The country's seaports were open to the public. At that time only Wellington and Auckland docks had gates – which were never closed. At weekends all the piers, quays and dock walls were very busy with the general public strolling along – mothers, fathers and children taking in the sights of the vessels alongside. In the case of Port Line and perhaps other companies, the ships would be open for a couple of hours to the general public. Although some of the visitors were third- and fourth-generation New Zealanders they still thought of Britain as home, and they would refer to British vessels as home boats. On many occasions, these visitors liked nothing more than a chat with members of the crew of every rank. These chats could, and did, result in invitations to visit the homes of these families and enjoy a meal. In many cases, these ship visits led to lasting friendships which endured over many

Above: *Tasmania Star*
(Courtesy FotoFlite)

Right: Lifebuoy

Port Chalmers

pleasant years. New Zealanders are the most hospitable of people, and a credit to their nation.

When the discharge of cargo was completed at Lyttelton the *Port Brisbane* sailed for Port Chalmers, the seaward port for the city of Dunedin. Dunedin has its own waterfront, but Port Chalmers is a deep-water harbour for the larger vessels to berth, and unlike many New Zealand ports it had its own dry dock capable of accepting the bigger vessels; at that time it was mostly used by the cargo ships of the Union Steamship company of New Zealand. Jack noted that these vessels carried the same funnel colours as the Port Line vessels, even though there was no commercial link. The Union's coasting vessels were workhorses and looked like it, their accommodation a muddy brown with a black hull. Jack had seen a model of the beautiful pre-war Union Steamships liner *Awatea*, with her dark green hull and white superstructure, and he thought it bizarre that she could belong to the same company as the smaller, rather grubby, cargo vessels.

At Port Chalmers the remaining cargo was discharged and the hold cleaning began, ready for the first cargo of lamb from Canterbury or Otago.

Homeward bound

Cleaning the cargo holds was particularly dirty work, and the boys and the apprentices had the worst of the jobs. In a vessel designed for frozen and chilled food, the cargo holds are divided from the deck downwards into the shelter deck, upper 'tween deck, lower 'tween deck and lower hold. In the 'tween decks would be lockers for chilled products rather than frozen. The largest hold was the lower hold in all the hatches, and its bottom was known as the floor. (As almost every other horizontal walked-on surface in a vessel is known as a deck, the word 'floor' does seem a bit odd.) On each side of the floor ran the bilges, set into the underwater curvature of the vessel's hull. The bilge was designed to collect any water or other fluid which might find its way to the internal part of the hold: vital for the safety of the vessel in the days of wooden ships when water seepage was common, but in metal vessels, the bilge was not quite so necessary other than in, for example, damage from collision. However, the bilge was still a stinking watery hole by any standards.

To remove the water there was a bilge pump. At the end of the pump shaft was a piece of apparatus known as the strum box, for filtering out items which might block the pump shaft. In this box collected all manner of unpleasant and very odorous items. The boys and apprentices, who in the lower holds of vessels were known as bilge divers, were sent into these dirty and extremely confined areas to clean the bilges and the strum box. While Jack and his chum took an instant dislike to the job, the apprentice mates thought it below their dignity even to contemplate such a degrading task. Whilst their opinions did not change, their reluctance did, as their boss, the first mate, made it quite clear that whilst Jack and his chums were to do one bilge the apprentices would do the other, for his inspection later. After the apprentices had finished this bilge duty, much against their will, they were told to replace the limber plugs (insulated wooden plugs that isolated the bilge from the hold). The barely-concealed petulance in these would-be officers was intensified when the mate told them that they had four other holds to 'practise their bilge diving skills in' before they were finished.

Once the hold was washed down with non-contaminating disinfectant, the New Zealand Meat Board inspectors would either pass it as fit for food or demand that it was washed again. After that, timber dunnage was fitted, allowing cold air to circulate around the cargo. Eventually the holds were passed by the Meat Board, the Butter Board and just about every conceivable official, and the *Port Brisbane* began to load its refrigerated cargo for Britain. The difference between the care taken to load the refrigerated cargo and the indifference displayed in the discharge of general cargo was very obvious, as was the difference to the almost obsessively hygienic loading in New Zealand and the disgusting habits of the British dockworker – particularly some of those in Liverpool – when discharging the same cargo for human consumption.

As the railway trucks brought the cargo of lamb alongside the vessel, each carcass would be landed on boards, then put into a rope and canvas strop and lifted by derrick or shore crane into whichever hold was working at that time. There the carcass would be carefully stowed, ensuring the circulation of cold air where it was required. The crates of cheese or the boxes of butter, requiring a different temperature to the lamb, were stowed separately. The wool and the bagged casein – general cargo – were brought in by lorry, and stowed in the non-insulated part of the hold. The wool in particular was a valuable cargo, and its price would be affected by its arrival time in the United Kingdom and whether or not it coincided with the wool sales auctions.

While the senior ratings spent their recreation time in Dunedin, Jack and his shipmates, constrained by their financial condition despite the £60 earned at Lyttelton, confined their run ashore to the Port Chalmers milk bar. Here they enjoyed the variety of flavoured milk shakes and the platonic company of local girls – innocent fun, but enjoyable nonetheless.

It was at Port Chalmers that Jack witnessed some of the Ring Bolters sneaking off the vessel to visit the local shops or those at Dunedin. They would leave the vessel before work started and return late the same evening, looking, in most cases, very pleased with themselves. Their day ashore had an effect not only on the pockets of various sailors – the ladies' keepers – but also on Jack and his chum, as the boys had to resume their duties as mess-room peggy: serving, scrubbing and dusting.

Soon it was time for the vessel to return to Lyttelton for more lamb and wool. This time there were no offers of shore pay, so the boys' recreation time was spent in cinema or milk bars. Fortunately for the Gaelic speakers in the seamen's mess room, the *Port Auckland* was no longer alongside, but the after-hours pubs were, as usual, well patronised by the Island men, even if the after-hours party was in the more private ladies' lounge, a traditional part of Kiwi pubs. One of the amazing things witnessed by the boys at Lyttelton was the sight of some of the men accommodating the Ring Bolters in their bunks arm in arm with another woman, doubtlessly furthering their romantic and probably sexual appetites. Such strange behaviour by the men, and the conviction by the boys that their seemingly normal colleagues must be a type of Adonis in the field of charming the clothes off the ladies, was strengthened at the sight of two middle-aged former lady passengers boarding the ship. The boys, expecting them to go up to the officers' quarters, were very surprised to see them in the crew's recreation room. Then 'Bugger off' from an AB made it quite plain that boys were not allowed in the room with these ladies present.

But as the boys' cabin was next to the recreation room, the noise could be clearly heard; part of the loud proclamations from one of the ladies was, 'Stop frigging in the rigging.' This was followed by the same voice saying, 'No, keep going– I've changed my mind.' Jack and his chum were almost beside themselves with curiosity about what was going on next door, when suddenly all was silent until they heard a distinctively authoritative male voice: 'I'm afraid you're not allowed down here, Madam. I must insist that unless you have a pass you must leave the ship now.' This was followed by the sound of feet on the companionway at the back of the boys' cabin. Surreptitiously Jack's chum peeped out of the cabin door to see the second mate disappearing up to the next deck. There was almost dead quiet from the recreation room, with the occasional expletive directed towards the officer, and soon they heard the sound of many feet going up the companionway and one of the women saying, presumably to her escort, 'Stop frigging in the rigging – the fun's over for now.'

All this association with ladies by the sailors was enlightening the boys' previously rather naïve attitude to the various manifestations of sexual gratification, none of it particularly endearing – but that appeared to be life at sea, or rather ashore, in the 1950s. When Jack's chum went to clean the recreation room the following morning he was helped by a Ring Bolter, who found two pairs of briefs and a large bra under the cushions. From her reaction it was pretty obvious that she was not too pleased to find evidence of another woman and that she had not been told of the party – or, worse still, had not been invited.

Sailing from Lyttelton, the *Port Brisbane* made her way back to Wellington, where Jack and his chum were in no hurry to go ashore in case they ran into the customs man again. In the event, they were sent on several errands to the Port Line head office, and they had no difficulty with customs men or anybody else. However, they were still very cautious. The incident with the contraband beer dominated their thoughts and to a large extent their actions while they remained in Wellington.

From Wellington the *Port Brisbane* sailed up to Auckland again. Here the boys felt very much at home. Although it was now autumn in New Zealand, it was very balmy, and delightful just to look out over the harbour towards the naval base at Devonport. From the base there was an almost constant naval launch service to the steps at the bottom of Queen Street.

The purser/chief steward of the vessel was a keen fisherman, and while the vessel was berthed at Auckland he could be seen fishing from the stern. Not too surprisingly, he caught many fish from the waters of Auckland harbour, and in due course the crew was regularly offered red snapper for dinner. This was a delicious fish, and a lasting memory for Jack from his second visit to Auckland.

In a different life, many years later, he was closely involved with the sad story of the submarine HMS *Snapper*, sunk by the enemy during the Second World War, and he produced articles on the subject from the magazine *Sea Breezes*. While dealing with the peripheral matters relating to the submarine and her connection with his home village of Wraxall, he was always reminded of Auckland, and particularly the snapper meals he had enjoyed there, as he painted the carved *Snapper* on the commemorative teak seat in Wraxall churchyard.

With *Port Brisbane* now full of cargo, her passengers aboard and the vessel battened down ready for the long trans-Pacific crossing back to Panama, she left Auckland. Despite his brush with HMNZ Customs, Jack had fallen in love with New Zealand and what he had seen of its way of life, and the apparently seamless social mix between the original Maori with their culture and that of the incoming British settlers. The New Zealand culture may have been British at its core, but the wonderful sense of freedom from the restrictions of birth, breeding, school, privilege, social rank and titles found in Britain was never forgotten by the boy as he waved farewell to the people watching the vessel's departure from the end of the jetty.

The vessel made her way through the Rangitoto Channel and, passing the island of the same name, entered the South Pacific Ocean bound for the Panama Canal. As the passengers settled in, all the cargo working gear was overhauled and stowed below decks. The timber and canvas swimming pool was erected, although judging by the age of the passengers they would not be regular users of it. Jack was amused to hear the opinion of the sailors, Roy, in particular – a very opinionated able seaman – gave his verdict on the subject : 'They'm either old buggers going out to the Colonies to see their kids and grandkids for the last time before they kick the bucket, or else they'm going 'ome to see the Old Country before they snuff it.' He then brought into the conversation the lack of younger females amongst the passengers with the observation 'the youngest bird we get 'ere is about 60,' with a look defying a challenge to his views. The first opposition to Roy's views came from his table-mate who, quick as a flash, said 'Sixty eh? Should just about suit you. What are you moaning about? You couldn't do anything about it anyway, even if she dropped 'er drawers in front of you.' Roy looked daggers at his table-mate and opened his mouth, then changed his mind and clamped it shut with a clash of teeth when he saw the rest of the mess-room occupants smiling at him rather than with him. Young Brian, a junior ordinary seaman, took quite a chance at joining in the conversation, asserting, 'There was a young bit aboard on the way out, and she was in her twenties.' Roy saw another chance to air his views, and was quick enough to pontificate on the subject with the observation, 'She looked like a bloody 'orse, although the longer the trip took, she did look a bit better every day until the time we arrived in Kiwi.' The men got up and made their way along the alleyways towards their cabins. Jack, clearing away the remnants of the meal, could still hear the faint sound of Roy trying to justify his opinion. He was silenced by someone telling him to shut up and bugger off.

After overhauling the deck working gear, the men turned to the twice-a-voyage job of painting the ship's upper works: a light buff for the derricks, the mast and most of the Samson posts (which anchored the foot of the derricks and provided another anchor point for the blocks at the top that carried the wires to raise and lower the derrick). The Samson posts at No 4 hatch were painted white, as were the bulkheads of the accommodation. But the most important piece of painting, other than the funnel, was the forepart of the bridge, from the top of the wheelhouse down to the deck level at the after end of No 3 hatch. When the wind was astern the sailors would rig two-man painting stages off metal poles secured through the wheelhouse windows. Then they would lower themselves, first of all to *sugi mugi*, wash the paintwork (this name was believed to have come from India). The men also cleaned the exterior of the forepart windows before they hauled the stages back up to the top. On their second trip down the forepart they would have buckets of white paint and 4-inch brushes, the best that Lampy could supply. All the accumulated skill from years of painting would be used in this most vital of tasks. No excuse would be accepted for 'holidays' – the places where no paint had been applied – or 'curtains', where the paint had run because too much had been applied and not stroked in properly.

It was not unheard of for a sailor to be sacked from a vessel because he had made a mess of painting the forepart or the funnel or both. The first mates of Port Line vessels, particularly these two senior officers of the *Port Brisbane* and *Port Auckland*, had much to fear from the marine superintendent if the vessel arrived, particularly in London, with a less than immaculate forepart and funnel.

The men on the outboard stages were out over the sea when painting the forepart of both vessels, and should they let go of the securing line they would fall in – this was long before they were issued with a harness to prevent that happening. This time, the job was done by 16:00 hrs. The paint and brushes were returned to Wally the lamp-trimmer, and the stages returned to the tonnage hatch, along with the metal poles. The mate and the bosun inspected the job, appeared to be satisfied with the handiwork, and assured themselves that the marine super would be very happy with the vessel's appearance on her return to London.

Several days before the *Port Brisbane* arrived at Panama, Jack became aware that all was not in order relating to the pristine forepart by listening to the bosun discussing a difficulty with his colleagues in the petty officers' mess room: 'There's shit all down it, and it's only just been painted. The mate's going to be mad as hell when I tell 'im.' The engine-room storekeeper said, 'Shoot the bleeder.' The bosun thought deeply for a few seconds and, reasoning that the storekeeper meant the bird not the mate, declared, 'Can't do that – the passengers might see it and some of 'em are funny blighters where birds are concerned.'

It transpired that a large eagle-like bird had taken to roosting overnight on the port yardarm, and had been discharging the contents of its bowels all over the newly painted forepart of the bridge and the deck. The first mate and the bosun studied the offending, running, odorous matter, then looked behind them at the bird perched on the yard. It twisted its head to look down on them. After a sailor was sent over the bridge wing on a bosun's chair with a bucket of sugi mugi to remove the brown, in some places green, filth, a positive decision was made; they sounded the electric klaxon to frighten the bird off the yard. But the bird made no effort to leave its perch. The next bright idea was to send a sailor up the mast to scare the bird off. Sure enough, the bird took to the air, and life aboard the *Port Brisbane* returned to normal. However, a fact to emerge from the sailor's ascent to the mast table was that the bird had claws rather than the webbed feet normally expected of a seabird.

The following morning at breakfast, the bosun was missing from the petty officers' mess room. His colleagues told Jack that the mate had called for him at 07:30 and they had gone for'ard. With that, a sailor came down the alleyway rejoicing in telling his chums, 'The bird's back and has shat all down the forepart again.' There was a mad scramble of men leaving the mess rooms for the fore end of the vessel. Jack reasoned that for the men to leave their breakfast to get cold the matter must be important. Perhaps, as there was no one in the mess, he could also head towards No 3 hatch, the deck between the mast and the forepart of the accommodation – the place of possibly considerable action.

Like other vessels, the *Port Brisbane* was fitted with a rarely-used steam whistle. It was toned to the same pitch as that of the Cunard Queens, a beautifully deep-throated roar. Whilst the seamen and the passengers watched, although the passengers in their lounge could not see the results from the bird's digestive system, the brains of the first mate and the bosun came up with an even better idea than sending a man up the mast. Operate the steam whistle, they thought. No sooner thought of than put into practice. In response to a long and wonderfully deep blast from the funnel the bird rose into the breeze, then headed off in a north-easterly direction. Over the bridge wing went a sailor again to clean the foul-smelling filth from the almost new white paint. Yet again, the easy pace of shipboard life continued as the crisis was resolved, with Panama looming ever closer.

But the following day the bird was back again, roosting on the same port yard, and again soiling the paintwork. Despite Captain Bailey's low opinion of the mental ability of his bosun, said bosun suggested a unique way of not only getting the bird off the yard but inflicting pain on it – hopefully reminding it that its presence was not welcome aboard. The new and quite revolutionary plan was, since the bird was perched immediately above a halyard block, to use a signal halyard running through the block under the yard. To this halyard a broom would be attached, head up – 'up' being the operative word. With the anguished features of Wally the lamp-trimmer – no doubt mindful of the fate of so many of his brooms in the rat pantomime – watching his beloved broom secured to the halyard, the first mate took station on the port bridge wing. Here he could command operations from this great height suitably adorned in his tropical whites and glistening epaulettes in the early morning sunshine. The broom began its ascent.

Up and up went the broom, and to the bosun's eternal satisfaction it struck the bird with a mighty thump. At first it did not have the opportunity to take off sedately, and the thump sent it tumbling until it regained its senses and spread its wings. Then up it swept above the mast, and as a final insult to the vessel it discharged the contents of its bowels which, in almost slow motion, descended to yet again adorn the paintwork – and allegedly soil the epaulette and shirt of the officer directing operations from the port bridge wing.

The men on the deck could not see the mate's distress, nor could they have witnessed the joy of the bird as it circled around to look at its revenge after the ignominious, and perhaps painful, ejection from its place of rest. The stifled mirth of the quartermaster as he saw the mate raging at the bird was soon brought under control as the watchkeeping officer told him to clean up the mess on the white teak deck before it dried into the woodwork under the tropical sun.

Back on the No 3 hatch cover, the assembled men drifted away as the broom was lowered to the deck, where Wally the lamp-trimmer clutched it to his bosom and disappeared into the gloom of his store, no doubt grateful that in this encounter with a wild creature – in contrast to the hunt for the rat – his broom had been returned in one piece. The sailor was again lowered over the bridge to clean the excreta from the forepart, and it was claimed that the mate on the port bridge wing discarded his shirt and epaulette over the side into the Pacific Ocean.

Later that day, a brave able seaman who had previously sailed with the mate said to his superior when they met on deck alongside Jack, 'If a bird dropping on you is a sign of good luck, you certainly had a bucketful of luck today. It should last the rest of the voyage.' The officer glowered at him, and plainly the sailor thought that he had touched a nerve, because he added as an afterthought (and a parachute for his career) 'Sir.' The mate looked at the sailor for a seemingly long, quite disconcerting, time before saying, 'You're treading on thin ice, and it may well be you who'll need the luck, not me. If the bird returns it'll be you cleaning the forepart.' The sailor took every word to heart, and within seconds went from looking pleased with himself to looking, and probably feeling, rather deflated. As he turned away the officer, with his finger wagging at him and a smirk on his lips, told him, 'In future *I'll* do the jokes and *you'll* laugh. Is that clearly understood?'

Jack said to the sailor, 'That was a near miss.'

With bravado the sailor replied, 'Nah. We get on all right – he's better than most, and he kicks the bosun's arse regularly. That suits me.'

On the following morning as they approached Panama there was no sign of the bird, either as an addition to the port side yardarm or on the front of the forepart. The bosun, for all that Captain Bailey might have thought of him, had at last triumphed.

On arrival at Panama it was noticeable that the catering/galley boy was keeping a very low profile, but still, to his eternal disgrace, Jack was with his fellow boys shouting up and down the accommodation alleyways, 'Bread, bread, who's got the bread for the mules? Galley boy, bring bread for the starving mules. Where are you hiding with the bread?' Not a sighting nor a sound from the boy was apparent until the vessel, after taking on fresh water, had left Colon, heading again for fuel at Curaçao before returning to London.

The voyage across the Caribbean and the Atlantic was uneventful, and when the vessel entered the Western Approaches, Jack was quite taken aback by the repartee between the crew, including those who'd had little social intercourse previously. Even the catering/galley boy sometimes had a very slight thin-lipped smile on his face. This change of character, light-hearted banter and goodwill towards all men was popularly known as the 'Channels'; it appeared to stir the souls of the crew in all British ships as they approached the end of the voyage.

About 07:00 Jack looked through his porthole to see the green fields of Devon as the *Port Brisbane* turned towards Brixham to pick up the Channel pilot. Although a pilot was not compulsory, Port Line's policy was that its ships would have a pilot aboard for every voyage up the Channel before entering the compulsory pilotage for the Thames. It was a strange sensation for Jack to see the beautiful green of the fields after so many weeks at sea – and to his surprise, for the second time in the voyage he felt a pang of homesickness. He had gone up on deck to get a better view of the green pastures, but was soon brought down to earth when he heard the dreaded words, 'Oi, Peggy, get on with your work. You ain't paid off yet.' He turned to see the bosun indicating the companionway to the mess rooms. Through the boy's mind went the thought, 'Not much of the Channels in him.' The voyage up-Channel, before shipping lanes were made mandatory, took *Port Brisbane* near the English coast and past the busy port of Dover. On she went, past the Downs, past the North Foreland light and into the Thames Estuary. Soon she was passing Gravesend and into the King George V locks, then she was alongside at her berth.

The next day was pay-off day. By 10:00 a.m. Jack, along with the rest of the men, had collected his pay-off sheet, detailing his income and expenditure during the voyage and the accompanying cash lump sum. It was customary at this point, or some days before Pay Off, for the chief mate to ask the seamen and boys he wanted for the next voyage whether they were willing to return to the ship. Jack and his chum had not been approached concerning their further employment by Port Line, and at the pay-off desk Jack's nemesis, the crew manager, told them that the ship was to go for a three-month refit, so, like the rest of the deck ratings, they would not be required. With their Pay Off in their pockets, their bags packed and their MOT steering certificates they set off for home, not knowing what the future held. However, they could, at least in theory, steer the *Queen Elizabeth* with their newly acquired steering certificate, signed, along with their discharge book, by their redoubtable yet highly respected first deep-sea master, Captain Francis W. Bailey.

Jack's next stop was Paddington station, and home to Somerset. There the boy returned to his old school and regaled his friends and classmates with the stories of derring-do. To his considerable embarrassment his former headmaster accorded him the accolade 'Salt of the Earth'. His classmates, not to be outdone by the headmaster, then good-naturedly – as any boy would – titled Jack: 'Creep from the Deep'. However, they were only too pleased to sit in the pub and hear his yarns.

3

MV *Port Lincoln*

First voyage

The telephone rang, and when Jack reached it he found the caller was his shipmate from the *Port Brisbane* to tell him that Mr Lofthouse, the crew manager at head office, would be sending him a rail warrant to join a ship in Liverpool. Sure enough, the following day a telegram arrived at Jack's home, instructing him to join the *Port Lyttelton* in Huskisson dock, Liverpool, in seven days' time: the warrant would arrive by post. After the palaver in Wellington relating to the *Port Lyttelton* and the beer, Jack was less than happy with his new appointment, and was in two minds whether to return to sea at all. However, rather than let his chum down, he headed north via Crewe railway station, which he had last visited as a five-year-old going to Edinburgh, until he arrived at Liverpool's Lime Street. This was to be the first of many visits to that station.

A walk down the dock brought him to the dreaded *Port Lyttelton*, and he made his way to the first mate's cabin. The mate noted his name, examined his discharge book and sent him to see the bosun. That officer directed him to the deck boys' cabin which, unlike his previous vessel, was on main deck level, with the starboard alleyway outside the cabin porthole. In the cabin Jack met up with his chum, who acquainted him with his duties: less peggying and more on-deck work. The boys had to serve at sea for a minimum of nine months before they could be promoted to the rank of junior ordinary seaman and see the last of peggying – and then lord it over new boy seamen.

The *Port Lyttelton* was a single-screw vessel of 7,413, grt with a speed of 15 knots, built by H. & W. Hawthorn Leslie & Co. Ltd in 1947. This was only a year before the delivery of the *Port Brisbane* to the company, and a greater contrast in design could not be envisaged. Whereas the *Port Brisbane* was of a truly innovative and uniquely modern design, *Port Lyttelton* was neither as graceful as the pre-war ships of the company nor as attractive as the *Port Brisbane* and the subsequent post-war vessels, up until the 1960s and the advent of vessels with a more utilitarian appearance. This ship was of a basic, almost wartime, shape, and that was yet another reason for Jack to take a dislike to her, little realising the work-related disadvantages of the more modern design of future vessels.

On the following day, Jack carried out his mess-room duties and then reported on deck. The first mate approached him and said, 'You won't be required for the deep-sea voyage, as the previous boys will be returning to this ship. You're only required for the run job from here to London, and then pay off.'

Racing through Jack's mind was thankfulness that he only had to serve on this vessel for a few days and not the full five months of a deep-sea voyage. As he replied, perhaps rather indolently leaning on a cowl ventilator, his elbow disappeared into the top of the cowl. At that moment, while Jack was trying to find his feet and steady himself, he heard the officer say, 'Oh, bloody hell.' Jack and the officer, looking inside the mouth of the cowl, saw ragged edges of what appeared to be chart paper hanging down, his elbow hole letting in unwanted light, and possibly even more unwanted rain, in the event of the frequent rainstorms common in the Western Approaches. 'Crafty bastard' appeared to be the mate's opinion of his predecessor, who must have allowed this most unsatisfactory repair to be executed on the previous voyage. As the mate strode away, sailors gathered around the ventilator, one of them asserting that he would expect such a shoddy and in some circumstances dangerous practice to be the preserve of 'a bleedin' Greek tramp, not a sodding Port boat like this 'un.'

On inspection it was evident that the cowl had rusted through, and the ship's previous mate, instead of getting a new cowl top, had instructed that a sheet of cancelled chart paper should be placed over the hole and painted white. It was quite a deception by any measure: certainly enough to deceive the marine superintendent when he had inspected the ship on its return from New Zealand. This incident was yet another matter to join the list of reasons why Jack was never to forget his association with the *Port Lyttelton*. Within a couple of days she sailed for London, berthing there on 18 August 1957. At the pay-off desk from the two-day home trade voyage, Jack and his chum were sent to another of the company's vessels, *Port Lincoln*.

The *Port Lincoln* had been built by Swan, Hunter & Wigham Richardson in 1946 to a basic design, much the same shape (other than her poop deck), size and speed as the 1947-built *Port Lyttelton*, and this made the vessels near-sister ships. The *Port Lincoln* was named after the grain-shipping port of Port Lincoln in South Australia, famous in the days of sail. She was a single-screw vessel capable of making 15 knots, with accommodation for two passengers, who were berthed in what was known as the owner's cabin.

Jack and his chum spent a long time 'working by' the vessel. This was casual labour, not under Articles; they were paid a weekly wage for the duties they carried out, with accommodation aboard but no food. So, in the recognition that they had to eat ashore their wages were higher than usual. For the boys, this time aboard the *Port Lincoln* was not welcome because unless they were signed on Ship's Articles the time did not count towards the mandatory nine months of boy service required before they could be promoted and receive higher wages.

The day for the signing-on ceremony arrived, and as might be expected by now, the crew manager and Jack did not see eye to eye on the pronunciation of a certain name. The crew manager appeared to take further offence at the fact that his boss at Leadenhall Street had given the boys berths aboard the *Port Lyttelton* for the coastal voyage, and berths for the deep-sea trip aboard the *Port Lincoln*.

The next day, Jack was on his knees scrubbing an internal alleyway when he noticed a pair of trousers and two shiny black shoes on his still-wet deck. Looking up, he saw a diminutive man in civilian clothes. In a rather truculent tone of voice Jack told him, 'The deck's still wet; will you kindly go back? I've just scrubbed where you're standing.' Without a word the man turned and left, and aggrieved that no apology had been forthcoming, Jack started scrubbing again, including the place where the man had been standing, but with evil thoughts occupying his mind. Some two days later, he was again on his knees scrubbing the same cross-alleyway when in the distance on the by now dry part of the deck he saw again a shiny black pair of shoes and a pair of navy blue, smartly creased trousers. Before he could look up, an authoritative yet tempered voice urged him to 'Say Amen and get off your benders.' Jack looked towards the voice and he saw the man he had told off for walking on his wet deck. However, on this occasion the man was in uniform, with four gold bands on the sleeve of his jacket. The boy shot up straight, and in that instant thought his career was finished; this was his official introduction to his new master, Captain C.J.H. Gorley.

With a steady, almost disconcerting, stare Captain Gorley said to Jack, 'I did not object to your sentiment concerning my walking on your scrubbed deck, but I *did* object to the truculent tone of your voice.' He continued, 'You had no idea who I was. By all means remonstrate, but in a courteous voice. Had you known who I was, would you have spoken to me as you did?'

'No, Sir,' replied the boy in a hushed tone.

'Quite so,' said the master, and after the slightest of pauses continued, 'I might have been a director, a very important shipper or indeed just a labourer. If you wish to have a successful career under my command, speak to everyone as if they could be your captain or the owner.' He concluded, 'Courtesy costs nothing. Is that clearly understood?'

Jack nodded and just managed a 'Sir,' before his voice gave out.

'Put you in your bleedin' pigeon hole didn't 'e?' Several sailors who had been listening outside the accommodation door stuck their heads, one above the other – just like a comedy turn – around the door jamb, grinning at the shell-shocked boy.

Within days, with her loading complete, the *Port Lincoln* sailed from London for Cape Town via the Canary Islands, where she was due to refuel. The voyage began well for Jack and, other than the vessel itself, was little different to life aboard the *Port*

Brisbane a couple of months before. There were few 'characters' and more of a mixed deck crew than before, at that time only a quartermaster standing out as a very nice chap as far as the boys were concerned. This particular quartermaster heralded from the Shetland Isles, so was known as Sheltie. Officially, ratings were not allowed spirits on the vessel; they could have two cans of beer per day, but no spirits. However, Sheltie had a most distinguished wartime service with the company, and no one in authority was going to deny him his 'wee dram' as and when he wanted it.

It was a matter of fascination for the boys to witness Sheltie who, after several large glasses of whisky, begin to sweat on his rather large, sometimes almost purple, nose. The beads of sweat turned out to be a yet further distillation of the spirit. As if to prove the point, when the beads formed one large drip Sheltie was sometimes too slow to catch it in his handkerchief, and it would land on the Formica tabletop; within seconds the drip would evaporate, leaving a strong odour of whisky. During the voyage this phenomenon was observed time and time again, one of the seamen suggesting catching all the drips to provide a half-decent tot for the rest of the men.

In no time at all the vessel docked in the Canary Isles and Jack was surprised by two matters he witnessed there. The first was the Spanish navy. The vessels berthed in the naval yard were of First World War vintage, or even earlier; Jack had only seen pictures of such warships, never the real thing. The second incident related to the disposal of certain property of the Port Line. Jack went for a walk towards the fo'c'sle head in the late evening. Before he ascended the ladder onto the deck, he could see two men bending over. He went to the starboard side of the foredeck and on the quay wall saw several Spanish sailors coiling down a rope coming from the Port Lincoln's foc's'le. The boy again stepped onto the ladder and looked for'ard again, to make out the two men bending down. They were people of rank, and they were paying out a mooring rope to the sailors ashore. Jack decided it was time to depart the scene and, going to the mess room, casually mentioned to the sailors what he had seen. No one seemed in the least concerned, and he was informed that the two men were getting rid of worn-out mooring lines. In his naïvety concerning such matters the boy enquired, 'Why give the Spanish Navy old mooring lines?'

He was told, 'Give? give? Who said anything about giving? They sell them of course! I expect they'll get about £50 for them. It's normal. It's the perks of being who they are – perks of rank, so to speak.'

Within a year, Jack, splicing an eye into a new 4-inch mooring line, found running through its centre a narrow tape with 'Port Line, London' printed along its length. That simple but perhaps expensive tape must have ruined the perks of some personnel of the Port Line and probably other shipping lines – and thereafter, all the company's old hemp mooring lines were sold off by the company, sometimes to be turned into Bank of England notes and other long-lasting, oft-handled documents.

The *Port Lincoln* sailed south in the tropical weather, hot and calm, the boys

Port Lincoln

watching with great and perhaps perverted pleasure as King Neptune came aboard to baptise the virgin sailors as they crossed the Line with great ceremony – and with considerable amounts of flour and Mytilus grease as the baptismal fluid. Both boys noticed the effect of having no passengers: on the *Port Brisbane* the crew had been 'baptised' a little more gently than the unfortunates aboard the *Port Lincoln*.

Cape Town and Table Mountain came into view in the early morning, and the ship berthed not far from the lavender-coloured hulls of the Union Castle Line; this was an ancient line formed by the amalgamation of the Union and Castle Lines, which in recent times had been taken into the fold of the Cayzer, Irvine shipping empire.

When the dockworkers began working down the holds Jack had his first experience of discrimination between South Africans with white skins and those with black. In one particular hold he was amazed to see – in 1957! – a white overseer apparently whipping some of the African workers in the after end of the hold. However, to see such seemingly unnecessary harsh treatment of black Africans was quite an eye-opener, as the men, chanting while they worked, appeared to be moving cargo much faster than were their white British brothers. Jack's chum was so incensed that he shouted to the overseer, a Scot, but was given a mouthful of Glaswegian for his trouble. The first mate sent the boys packing, warning them not to interfere and interrupt the discharge.

The story was a little evened out in the evening when the boys went ashore and, as in Trinidad, they got lost. Unlike in Trinidad, though, there was no welcoming light available, nor even a brothel. Instead, in time they came to a galvanised fence topped with barbed wire, with a huge fire burning inside and the sound of chanting. There was no one on the streets, but as they approached the fence it turned out to be a huge compound, and dozens of native South Africans swarmed to the wire screaming through it at the boys. Such hatred towards them put such fear into the boys that they took to their heels and ran away as fast as their legs could carry them. Within minutes a police car pulled alongside them and they were abruptly told to get in. When the boys had caught their breath, instead of the police showing some concern or sympathy they severely admonished them for being in the neighbourhood, as it was reserved for 'blacks' – though another derogatory name was used – and the presence of 'whites' caused unrest. It was suggested, if not indeed ordered, that for the rest of the stay of the vessel they should stay aboard if they could not be trusted to stay in the city centre.

The boys were returned to the ship and handed to the mate by a bullying type of policeman, who intimidated the boys so much that they had no appetite for any further excursions ashore. Two days later the *Port Lincoln* left Cape Town and ploughed into the Roaring Forties. As she left Cape Town she began rolling in the ever-increasing wind on her starboard quarter. On the second day out Jack was surprised to smell a pungent odour coming off the ocean, and when he mentioned it to Sheltie the quartermaster replied with a distinctive look of wistfulness – indeed perhaps of nostalgia – 'Somewhere out there is a whale factory ship, and the smell is the blubber rendering.' It transpired that before the Second World War Sheltie, along with many of his fellow Islanders, had done a two-year stint as teenagers on the factory ships and the small but very seaworthy whale chasers owned by Salveson of Leith. In those days they used South Georgia as a base, and when returning from the Southern Ocean for a refit they often used the facilities at Cape Town. In those days the whaling industry was dominated by Norway and Britain, and Sheltie had served both countries aboard the factory ships and the whale chasers.

On the horizon just before the light faded the factory ship appeared, and that was the one and only time that the boy saw one. Little did he know that whale oil and the other by-products of the animal would shortly be replaced by synthetic products; they destroyed the whaling industry, but saved whales from possible extinction.

Within a further day the vessel, in the low Roaring Forties, had the wind and the sea right astern making her roll quite considerably and causing mayhem with the food in the mess rooms – and most of all in the galley. Sleep was difficult, too, unless you were wedged into your bunk with pillows and a lifejacket.

Until the vessel left Cape Town the seas of both the North and South Atlantic had been calm. But now the boys were to experience the full power of the great Southern Ocean in a vessel much smaller than the *Port Brisbane*. During that first voyage they had thought that the vicious storm off New Zealand was frightening – but during the next 14 days they really found out about the immense power of the sea; even on a well-found vessel it was not an experience to relish. Soon the enormous swell, generated by the severe gale to storm force winds constantly circling the Earth in these latitudes, began to lift the *Port Lincoln* as if she was a small boat. When she was rolling sleep was difficult, but now, with the 30–40-foot swell under her stern, the propeller was often out of the water as her bow plunged into the next swell. This resulted in an occupant of a bunk finding his head bouncing off its metal bar every few minutes as well as the rolling sometimes depositing him on the deck. Jack came off better than his chum in the top bunk, who had a rough time falling from it.

After a week of this atrocious weather a quartermaster played an evil trick. It was his duty to put the boys 'on shake' at 6:30 each day. One day he came into the cabin as the vessel took yet another roll and plunge, the propeller racing and vibrating. With his lifejacket on he said to the boys: 'Get up, lads, and take your lifejackets with you – and make sure you know which lifeboat you're in.' The boys needed no second warning. Without the aid of a vicious roll by the vessel they shot out of their bunks, grabbed whatever clothes were to hand and with their lifejackets made for the cabin door. As they got into the alleyway the quartermaster took his off and, laughing at the sight of the two terrified lads, said, 'That got you buggers up on time.'

The boys were livid that they had been tricked, and it took Jack until lunchtime before the dread receded. His chum, who was the peggy for the quartermasters' mess, heard the man who had frightened them laughingly telling the rest of the mess how he had put the breeze up the boys. But instead of getting plaudits for his joke there was silence, the only comment coming from the lamp-trimmer, who told the quartermaster, 'You're a Mark One bastard, and you should be bloody well ashamed of yourself. If the mate finds out, you'll be in the shit and I'll be the first to put the boot in.' For the rest of the five-month voyage the boys had no further trouble with that particular quartermaster.

Although at times the gales appeared to temporarily abate, the huge swells continued, and with them the discomfort. Jack almost got used to the plunging and sometimes corkscrewing motion. However, all the time the vessel was getting nearer to Adelaide, its first destination in Australia.

As the ship came out of the great southern circle and went through the Australian Bight, the swell and gales eased enough for the sailors to venture for'ard and rig the derricks, ready for arrival in port. And next day, when Jack was woken for duty, other than the noise of the engines there was silence: no storm, no gale, and the vessel was on an even keel. Peace at long last. When he went on deck it was to see the barren landscape of Kangaroo Island as the vessel turned towards Port Adelaide.

With the memory of his arrival in New Zealand and the attractiveness of Auckland, Jack had a very different scene to consider as the *Port Lincoln* went alongside. Adelaide was home to a branch of Jack's family, and his Uncle Victor, the senior member of his maternal family, had written a letter of introduction for him to take to his relatives when he visited them on his days off. Victor had also written to the family in Adelaide,

Port Lincoln in the Roaring Forties

to tell them of the arrival of his nephew. Jack thought that his relatives would come to see him aboard, but after a few days without any contact he decided to go into Adelaide and find them. After enduring the heat dressed in a suit with a collar and tie more suited to Britain than a sweltering South Australia, and with a Noel Coward song about the British abroad in tropical heat in his mind, he eventually found that his relatives were, according to a neighbour, most likely in but not answering the door. A very frustrated, if not a simply mad-as-hell, Jack returned to the *Port Lincoln* determined not to go ashore again – relatives or no ignorant relatives.

None too soon for Jack, the *Port Lincoln* left Port Adelaide for Melbourne, the capital of the state of Victoria. As far as the boy was concerned now, anywhere in Australia would preferable to Adelaide. The visit to Melbourne began with a transit through Port Phillip Bay, bypassing Port Melbourne, where the big liners berthed. Soon the vessel was in the River Yarra, which allegedly flowed upside down, in that the water was cloudy on the surface but clear below, but Jack never managed to establish the truth or otherwise of this remarkable statement. The main thing that attracted the boy as they went up the river was the remains of two sailing ships which in the 19th century had plied their trade from Britain to the colonial states of Australia. One of the hulks was used as a coaling barge, and in all probability so was the other. Eventually one of them, *Polly Woodside*, was fully restored to her former glory, and became a popular tourist attraction in Melbourne.

No sooner had *Port Lincoln* tied up than the local seamen's padre came aboard to recruit sailors to represent Great Britain in the Trafalgar Day celebrations. This representation would begin with a march-past starting at Flinders Street railway station, and finish at the nearby Anglican Cathedral of St Paul, where the Bishop of Gippsland would preach, and later mingle with the congregation. Jack, after a word or two with the bishop, reflected that within his limited knowledge of the Anglican hierarchy in England, such a person meeting and talking to the proletariat was not something easily, if at all, done by his Anglican colleagues of the House of Bishops and their like, and yet again, Jack was much impressed with the equality of class or social standing, albeit that common courtesy was often forgotten in pursuit of equality.

The mate selected two apprentices, the two deck boys and the two junior ordinary seamen for the march-past. When they reached the muster point they saw squads of men from the three armed services and other men from the British Merchant Navy who had come from the Orient Line passenger ships berthed at Port Melbourne. Jack was in his element with all the pomp; the last time he had taken part in such a ceremony was, on his training ship 12 months earlier, in 1956. He recalled the escapade when on the way back from that ceremony he and his chums had found their commander's car in the exclusive VIP car park. This little three-wheeler car, which had no reverse gear, was parked nose-in to the boundary fence, and was surrounded by Daimlers, Armstrong Siddeleys, Rolls Royces and similar classic motor cars. Jack and his chums, only thinking of their captain and his probably demeaning efforts to push his little car around to face the car park exit in such exalted company, simply picked it up, turned it around and put it down again, ready to leave. But this exercise in assisting Sir had not been appreciated, and had cost several of them, including Jack, early promotion.

Melbourne was reasonably cosmopolitan in its population, with many Greeks, Dutch and eastern Europeans living and working with the Australian population. This mix of nationalities was well represented in the city's restaurants and shops. Melbourne was also renowned for an art work to be found in a bar; it was a large painting, named 'Chloe', of a very attractive naked lady. Visitors from the various ships in Melbourne and Port Melbourne were encouraged to make a pilgrimage to see Chloe, and as Jack discovered, she was a sight worth seeing. Although it was an oil painting, the work was behind glass, as during the war an American had used his cigar to burn a hole in her crotch. Although they were under age for pubs, Jack and his chum were taken there by some able seamen, allegedly to see the painting – but in effect to get the boys, by way of a donation for their courtesy in taking them there, to buy them a round or two of beer. As the beer was served in schooners it was not too expensive, and in Jack's view was well worth the cost.

It was generally acknowledged that dockworkers in most English-speaking countries were, by the nature of their work and perhaps their background, a Bolshevik-minded, restrictive-practising, group of people. Melbourne also had to cope with the dockworkers in organised waterfront gangs. This fact had no particular significance for the visiting seamen, but as Jack was watching the dockworkers leaving the ship *en masse* for their refreshment break, he heard a popping sound. The workers stopped moving and gathered around something. The men of the *Port Lincoln* could not make out what the interest was until the sound of approaching sirens could be heard. The scene then became more akin to a film set when the group of men, probably 50 or more, simply faded away as an ambulance followed by a police car arrived on the quayside. Yet again, the men aboard the vessel could not see what was happening, as the ambulance was interrupting their view. More police vehicles appeared, and as someone was put on a stretcher then lifted into the ambulance the police spread out and examined the transit shed and the quay wall.

After their break time was over, none of the wharfies returned to the ship – they stayed away as a 'mark of solidarity' – but the policemen came onto the vessel and spoke to several men, though not Jack. When the policemen had left, Jack was told that someone had been shot: the popping sound had been shots, and the event had been a gangland retribution shooting. Whether or not the man was injured or dead Jack did not discover, but the police did not appear to take the matter too seriously, because shortly after arriving they all packed up and departed as promptly as they had arrived. Once the police had disappeared the 'mark of solidarity' evaporated and the 'brothers' returned to work. It appeared that the Melbourne waterfront was a tough place.

Of the Australian cities Jack visited, Melbourne was the most vibrant and interesting, but in no time at all the vessel was slipping back down the Yarra, past the black and derelict coal hulks into Port Phillip Bay, then through the entrance into the Bass Strait en route to Sydney. The first notable object that Jack encountered outside Sydney Heads was the large, old-fashioned pilot vessel with the name *Captain Cook* painted on an equally old-fashioned counter stern. The vessel, in immaculate condition, was wallowing in the moderate swell as its tender left its side to take the Sydney pilot to the *Port Lincoln*. When safely aboard, the pilot then took the vessel through the dramatic Heads into Port Jackson, also known as Sydney Harbour. The skyline was impressive; multi-coloured homes came down to the shoreline with many green spaces and lots of trees making the areas look most attractive. Into sight came the world-famous Sydney Harbour Bridge, a magnificent structure by any standard.

For Jack, stationed on the ship's bridge, this was the first time he had been aware that Captain Gorley could not see over the dodger. An apprentice carrying a small stool accompanied the master; whenever the captain stopped, the apprentice would place the stool for him to stand on. As the vessel approached the harbour bridge, with the green-hulled ferry boats dodging her on their way to Manley and other destinations, Captain Gorley, pointing to Sydney Bridge, told Jack and the apprentice that much of the steel for the bridge had been carried out to Australia in Port Line ships from the Dorman Long works at Middlesbrough. The bridge then took on an even greater significance for the boy.

When the *Port Lincoln* had gone under the bridge, into view hove the piers of Pyrmont. On the end of the transit shed was the legend 'Port Line Ltd'; to Jack it almost felt as if the vessel was coming home. She tied up at the adjacent jetty as the Orient Line passenger liner *Orsova* was leaving. This was the first time Jack had witnessed a large passenger vessel leaving a berth, and he was startled by the huge number of people running along the jetty with paper streamers connecting them to the passengers on the vessel. As the *Orsova* turned at the end of the pier she had a distinct list to starboard from the weight of the passengers on that side of the upper decks.

When the time came for Jack to go ashore he went via Pyrmont Bridge into the centre of the city, to find all the facilities that could be expected of such a city in the 1950s. Sydney was the first city in Australasia where the boy did not attend the Seamen's Mission, and the local padre made no effort to visit the ship. In fairness to the padre, though, Sydney was a very busy place for shipping, and no doubt the chap was rushed off his feet. In the absence of visits to the Mission, Jack spent many hours in the local city centre cinemas.

The boy's outstanding memory of Sydney was the conduct of the men attending the cinema or a restaurant with their ladies, married or otherwise. Female Sydneysiders would be dressed in all their finery for a night on the town, whilst the men were usually dressed in khaki shorts and shirts, open half-way down the chest, and topped by an often very greasy trilby hat. In almost every case the man would not hold a door for the lady, but barge into the cinema or whatever, allowing the doors to swing back into her face without any apology or any inclination to accept that his conduct was extremely rude. In the fortnight that Jack and his chum witnessed such total lack of common courtesy, not once in their hearing did the women complain. There seemed to be no defining age for this rudeness, the only difference being that the younger generation did not wear a trilby.

So Sydney, even with its natural and man-made physical attraction, did not commend itself to Jack, mainly because of the general attitude of the population he witnessed during his excursions ashore. The boy enjoyed himself on the ferry boats, on a trip to Launa Park amusement complex and in simply looking at the spectacular harbour. But although Sydney was only the capital of New South Wales, it reminded Jack of the impersonal atmosphere of London or a like metropolis.

With the cargo from Britain now discharged, he was not too sorry to sail down Port Jackson, under the bridge, past Fort Denison, through the sparkling waters of the magnificent harbour and out through the Heads to the classic boat awaiting the pilot.

From Sydney the *Port Lincoln* turned south towards Tasmania and the area known as Beauty Point, to collect fruit, mostly apples. The major town in the area was Launceston, with the River Tamar running from there past Beauty Point into the Bass Strait. When the vessel was navigated along the Tamar, Jack was reminded of his west country origin as the verdant pasture came down to the water's edge and, for seemingly many miles, rows upon rows of fruit trees and bushes making avenues towards the river. The beauty of it all was to be a lasting memory for the boy; the point certainly lived up to its name. When alongside the wharf, the vessel began loading the first part of her cargo for Britain, and the crew continued to clean her holds for more cargo as the loading ports were announced; after Beauty Point the vessel would visit Brisbane, the capital of Queensland, for refrigerated beef carcasses, and Townsville for more refrigerated cargo, and aluminium bars known as pigs, along with various other metals.

While at Beauty Point, Jack met some interesting dockworkers. There appeared to be no regular workers, and 'as and when required' was a fitting description of the men loading the cargo. When a vessel arrived the men of the local population appeared to become temporary dockworkers – or it may have been that their other work was only temporary. Whichever the case, these pleasant people made the crew most welcome, in

Strathnaver in transit through the waters of Port Jackson, passing Fort Denison, with a Port boat under Sydney Bridge. From a painting by Robert Blackwell by courtesy of Mrs Heather M. Nickell.

that any of the crew could use the community premises for their own purposes or mix with the locals in whatever they were doing.

Jack, particularly after Sydney, was very impressed by the hospitality of these Tasmanians. In conversations with them, he discovered that the ancestors of this local population appeared to be Cornish miners and others brought to the area in the 19th century for stone quarrying, hence the names Launceston and Tamar. The hospitality of these people reminded him of the smaller ports of New Zealand, the yardstick by which he judged all other Antipodeans.

Leaving Beauty Point, the vessel made her way up the coast of New South Wales towards Brisbane. One day at nightfall, Jack could see huge forest fires ablaze on the clifftops, in some places coming down to the shoreline. Although he was well aware that Australia suffered from such violent conflagrations, to see one not in a Pathé newsreel but in front of his very eyes was awe-inspiring. As the evening wore on, the entire crew came on deck to witness the spectacle, and Captain Gorley appeared on the bridge. As he came down to the boat deck he told the men, 'It's a typical bush fire, and if no habitation or people are involved no effort will be made to put it out. It'll be allowed to burn itself out in due course.' As the evening wore on, and the vessel had sailed many miles to the north, more fires could still be seen. Such destruction was almost unbelievable with, seemingly, no risk to life other than wildlife. This was one of the burdens Australia has had to carry since time began, and presumably it will continue until time ends.

The voyage up the Brisbane River was not as spectacular as going through Port Jackson or, for that matter, the trip through Port Phillip Bay and up the Yarra to Melbourne. However, there was a certain tropical air to the place. The riverbanks had several meat-processing plants and, most colourfully, the blue blossoms of the jacaranda trees. The *Port Lincoln* was destined for Hamilton Wharf, just below the city of Brisbane. As in so many ports, the colourful wooden houses really made the place look attractive, aided by the bright, sunny weather.

Part of the mooring process of a vessel is the use of wires called springs. The vessel's forward spring leads from the bow aft to a bollard on the quayside, and it is mirrored by the after spring, from the stern leading forward; these prevent the vessel from surging either way. In the strong currents of the Brisbane river, it is vital to get the forward spring eye ashore swiftly, in order to bring the vessel alongside with the minimum effort by engines and rudder. Jack was one of the three men stationed by the forward spring. Their mission was, when ordered by the bridge, to get the heaving line ashore for the hobblers ashore to throw its eye over the bollard. On deck, Jack and his men would then quickly take hand-turns of the wire around the mooring bitts, and then, by controlled slacking and tightening, ease the vessel alongside. With much shouting of 'Ease the spring!' or more often 'Hold the spring!' from the bridge, the ship was soon moored roughly where the pilot wanted her.

The art of being a successful team on the forward spring was to avoid parting, or breaking, it. This was no easy task as when told to hold it, some bright spark in the engine room would invariably push the vessel ahead with a turn of the screws, so holding the spring or breaking it was solely in the skilled hands of a sailor, who was acutely aware that a broken spring – a wire now under tension – could flail about and cause injury.

This, Jack's first visit to Brisbane, was indelibly printed in his mind for both the beautiful jacaranda trees at Hamilton Wharf and the use of the spring to bring the ship successfully alongside. In his later career with Port Line, on every occasion that his vessel berthed at Hamilton Wharf, Jack would, much to his chagrin, be stationed on the forward spring.

One of the ordinary seamen, from the Isle of Lewis, was very fond of rock and roll, and indeed everything relating to Cliff Richard. He was so obsessed with his idol that he would turn up in an iridescent suit, presumably imagining he was Cliff. The hilarity that Mac and his suit gave everyone – men and officers alike – was hard to conceal from the young man. However, to Jack it was a manifestation, and a very welcome one, too, of an interest by a man of the Isles beyond that of monosyllabic conversation, work and drinking.

Whilst the *Port Lincoln* was at Hamilton Wharf, Mac surpassed himself when at about 9 a.m. one day he appeared alongside the vessel. The dockworkers stopped work to stare, the canteen ladies pointed and laughed and, by a stroke of bad luck for the deluded Mac, the first mate and other officers, along with the bosun and his men, including Jack, were leaning over the rail overlooking the wharf. Seemingly without a care in the world, Mac, with his long spindly legs, marched purposefully along the wharf to the ship's gangway and ascended it. On arrival at the top, amongst the howls of laughter from the men and women ashore, he came face to face with the mate, who appeared less than pleased to see one of his sailors late for duty but also inappropriately dressed. The almost one-sided conversation with the first mate went along the lines of:

'What in *hell* do you think you're doing?'

The errant sailor, looking genuinely surprised, replied, 'Sorry I'm late, Sir, I was detained ashore.'

'Detained? *Detained*?' the mate queried. 'You should *be* bloody detained.' Stopping for a short breath, the mate, probably more in exasperation than temper, then said to the now silenced sailor, 'Just *look* at yourself, man! You're a disgrace: a total disgrace. What in *hell* are you thinking of?' All this time Mac had his back towards the people on the wharf. Amongst the sounds of loud laughter from ashore a woman's voice could be heard shouting, 'Turn around, please turn around.'

The officer, by this time incandescent with rage, continued, 'I can't believe you still don't understand your condition. Your act of stupid ignorance is bordering on insubordination.' Finally, he ordered the seemingly bemused sailor, 'Get below before I log you, you half-wit.' The sailor disappeared.

The laughter from the onlookers and the mate's temper was because as Mac had marched down the wharf, he had mislaid his trousers and underpants.

Within 15 minutes Mac appeared dressed, including his nether regions, but despite much enquiry as to the reasons for his costume shortcomings, he said nothing all day. In fact, he adopted the character of his Gaelic peers, only speaking when he needed to, and very briefly at that. After work he was seen slipping down the gangway, heading ashore again. The question amongst his messmates was where he was going and why. Within the hour he had returned to his cabin – to the relief of his colleagues, with his nether regions still covered.

But the story was not over. The following morning Mac was over the ship's side on a painting stage hanging over the edge of the wharf. The dockworkers must have recognised him, and to the sound of ribald mirth one of the young canteen ladies appeared, walking through an avenue of workers until she was almost under Mac on his stage. She stopped and held up a pair of trousers and a pair of off-white Y-fronts. In a broad Australian dialect she invited Mac to retrieve his clothes, which she had found 'in two trees in the park'. Mac ignored her, unlike at least 30 of the vessel's crew, including all the deck officers. The girl folded Mac's clothes and placed them on the wooden abutment under his stage; the men returned to their work and the girl returned to the canteen.

Further calamity was to follow as when the time came for Mac to climb up the Jacob's ladder back up to the deck he promptly put his size 11 boot in a paint kettle full of Port Line Topside Grey paint, splashing it all over his neatly folded trousers and Y-fronts. (The paint-splattered garments were still in situ when the *Port Lincoln* sailed to Borthwick's abattoir, further down the Brisbane River.) But Mac's agony was still not yet over, as when he ascended the Jacob's ladder the paint from his dripping boot splattered over the white apron of the port bow, and then, as he reached the deck he promptly put his wet, now grey, boot on the red deck paint of the fo'c'sle head. Although no longer a surprise to Jack, the language then expressed by the bosun would have brought a blush to even the rough-hewn cheeks of a navvy.

The bushes from which the girl had retrieved Mac's clothes were near the end of Hamilton Wharf, not too far from the stern of the vessel. The general consensus was that it was most unlikely that Mac had had a sexual encounter, and there appeared to be no common thread to his removal of clothes and his total lack of obvious concern at marching half-naked through groups of workers; in short, a mystery worthy of Agatha Christie. For the rest of the voyage Mac did not disclose any reason for the episode, and after that voyage Jack did not see him again. But Jack most certainly never, if only for the Hamilton Wharf entertainment, forgot Mac, the would-be Cliff Richard of the Isles, *sans* clothes.

Five days after arriving at Hamilton Wharf, the *Port Lincoln* moved a short distance to Borthwick's Morton works. This was an abattoir located on the riverbank, with its own quay to load vessels directly. The beef cattle were herded into the slaughterhouse early in the morning, and by late afternoon they were frozen cut carcasses, ready for loading.

It was of lasting fascination for Jack to see the most beautiful flight of eight or more pelicans in close formation lazily gliding towards the vessel and landing in the river like a flying boat touching down. But it soon became apparent why these ungainly birds chose to visit the vessel in the late afternoon and early evening on a falling tide; it was the discharge of all the offal, blood and detritus from the slaughterhouse. It would appear that this applied to other riverside livestock processing plants, so the Brisbane pelicans were undoubtedly the best fed anywhere.

Whilst Brisbane did not have the cosmopolitan air of Melbourne or the scenic location and attractions of Sydney, it was a very clean place with the friendliest of people, and almost the atmosphere of a village. To Jack, Brisbane's sub-tropical heat, flora and fauna made it one of the finest locations of mainland Australia, and he never tired of the city.

With four of the vessel's lower holds loaded with beef carcasses, the *Port Lincoln* sailed for Townsville, near the Great Barrier Reef. Arriving at Townsville in the early morning, Jack, like the other officers and deck crew, were greeted by sandflies – tens of thousands of them – that apparently delighted in biting any exposed human flesh. From the crack of dawn until sunrise the men would dance like banshees in an effort to prevent the flies from biting them: they were unsuccessful in almost every case. As the sun rose its heat diminished the attacks, and the less than polite language of the sailors on deck was much improved. Jack was, like all first-time visitors to Townsville, less than impressed by the painful welcome.

Townsville, to Jack's eyes, had the appearance of a tropical town with wide streets and covered verandas on the premises lining the main street. On his runs ashore he enjoyed the local milk bars and the female company such places attracted. Although widespread tourism had not been invented, many of the shops were selling typical tourist souvenirs of that part of Australia: chunks of the coral from the Great Barrier Reef, Aborigine-carved boomerangs, and many other native Australian items. Jack bought his mother a display of coral and, for his own use, a boomerang. Whilst later he had no luck in killing any magpies with it, he did find that it could decapitate cabbages quite easily until a very irate mother, on behalf of a cabbage-less and timid neighbour, put paid to such fun. This was undoubtedly the first – and last – time that a boomerang was used to harvest cabbages in Wraxall.

Within days of starting loading at Townsville, a rumour spread through the vessel that the *Port Lincoln* was bound for New York to deliver sides of beef before arriving in Britain; someone had seen a copy of the bill of lading, and clearly thereon was printed 'New York'.

New York was surely the Mecca of every film-watching boy, and Jack was no exception. Not all of the men, though, were too excited about their North American sojourn, particularly in midwinter. Within a short time the rumour was confirmed: *Port Lincoln* was going to New York, via the Panama Canal.

With loading complete the vessel left Townsville without a further attack of sandflies, and made her way across the Pacific without incident – and initially without much enthusiasm for setting up the first-trippers for the bread for the canal donkeys ruse. Old traditions die hard, though, and a couple of days before arrival at Panama the catering staff decided to tell the catering boys about the need for bread. The collections of stale bread began, but on arrival the chief steward decided that as his boys were the only ones being taken for a ride, and he was not inclined for his department to be ridiculed, he told his boys of the planned incident, much to the disgust of the perpetrators.

For the third time Jack was fascinated by the Panama experience. As they went into the Miraflores lock system the New Zealand Shipping Company's passenger liner *Rangitane* was exiting it in the opposite direction and despite his desire to go home, the sight of the liner on her way to New Zealand tugged at Jack's heartstrings. These thoughts caused a quite unsettling couple of hours for the boy until the splendour of the Gatun Lakes occupied his mind – not quite displacing the New Zealand thoughts, but certainly helping them diminish as the day wore on.

After taking on fresh water at Colon the *Port Lincoln* headed towards Curaçao, to refuel at Caracas Bay. A unique and unexplained incident on this particular visit made it rather different for Jack, memorable in comparison to his many other visits to Caracas Bay. The deck crew knew that arrival at the bay would be about 06:00 hrs and that the non-watchkeepers would be put on shake at 05:30 hrs, ready for berthing the vessel at one of the oil jetties. When Jack took to his bunk that evening it was secure in the knowledge that he would be up rather earlier than 05:30, so that the rest of the sailors could have a mug of tea before going to their harbour stations. But in the night he was woken by his bunk, the items in his cabin and indeed the whole vessel vibrating violently, while the alarm bells sounded. The sound of running feet dictated a speedy exit from his bunk and the quickest application of underpants, shorts and shirt the boy's frame had ever experienced. With the rest of the deck crew he emerged from the accommodation as the vessel stopped vibrating. The engines had been trying and had eventually succeeded in stopping 7,000 tons of vessel dead in the water.

With the others whose station was at the bow, Jack ran forward, exchanging comments such as 'What in the bloody 'ell's 'appening?' and 'Somebody's made a right balls-up.' When the men approached the fo'c'sle the only person there was the carpenter. As the men rushed up the port ladder the mate ran up the starboard ladder and spoke to the carpenter. Probably because of Jack's lowly rank, he was never able to accurately piece together the circumstances leading to the situation in which the vessel now found herself as the star attraction for all and sundry. Looking over the bow, he could see that the end of the oiling jetty was damaged and the starboard anchor cable was leading astern, bar-taut against the side of the vessel. He walked over to the port bow and there too the port anchor cable was leading astern – also bar-taut.

Under usual circumstances a motor vessel entering Caracas Bay would begin to reduce revolutions at least 20 minutes before stopping, a mile from the entrance, to pick up a pilot. But it appeared that the *Port Lincoln* had been under full power when she swept past the pilot vessel and turned into the bay. There were several accounts as to who was responsible for her turning into the bay at speed without a pilot. Scuttlebutt (gossip of a nautical nature) had it that for reasons unknown the duty officer had failed to carry out his orders and thereby endangered the vessel. The helmsman claimed that he did not see Captain Gorley until collision with the jetty was imminent. The hypothesis seems very unlikely, but clearly something *did* go wrong. Thanks to the efforts of the engineers turning the engines from ahead to astern within a very short time, the vessel was slowing, and as the carpenter, who had fortunately got up early to clear away the anchor cables, had taken it upon himself to let go both anchors, this had avoided the vessel slicing through the jetty completely. Eventually order was restored, and with a pilot aboard the vessel used her anchors, already laid out, to pull herself out of the end of the jetty. She was then berthed at an undamaged jetty to take on her fuel oil. The Lloyd's surveyor came aboard to inspect the damage to the vessel, and decreed that she was seaworthy.

This incident was to be the centre of interest in the mess room for weeks to come, the general opinion being that the officer of the watch was in the shit up to his eyebrows and that the Old Man would use the offending officer's guts for rope yarns. As is so often the case, the basic mess-room principle was 'never let the truth ruin a good story' – an undoubted truism by any measure.

As the *Port Lincoln* made her way through the Caribbean and up the east coast of the USA the temperature dropped considerably, until on arrival at New York it was freezing. Nevertheless, Jack was eager to see the spectacular places he had only ever seen on a cinema screen. The sheer bureaucracy involved in allowing him to go ashore in the USA made all the illogical regulations in Britain seem puny in comparison, but eventually he got ashore and wandered along Fifth Avenue, reaching Times Square. What a disappointment for the young man! He had gone there to see a film, but was astounded to view the mountains of newspaper and rubbish blowing around in the freezing wind. This had not been on the silver screen. The New York he had presumed immaculate was, probably excluding Fifth Avenue, a filthy place by any standards – and the dockworkers were even worse than some of the British variety.

Before being allowed ashore the crew, particularly the boys, were warned of the gang hazards of the city, and were urged to hand over whatever a gang demanded otherwise a knife in the ribs would be the likely outcome of any encounter. The introduction to a gang would probably be an invitation to 'give me a light, man'. Failure to comply was most dangerous, Jack and his chums were told by the Mission's padre.

Most vessels have one or two 'characters' amongst the crew, and this vessel was no exception to the rule. Apart from Mac the trouserless, there was an ordinary seaman nicknamed Coo-ee because he would shriek 'Coo-ee' whenever he was ashore, preferably in a confined space such as a shop or a restaurant. On the outward voyage, this article of humanity almost had Jack and his chums thrown out of a cinema in Cape Town; Jack and the others had seats in the auditorium while, unbeknown to them, Coo-ee was in the gods, and must have spotted them taking their seats below. The film had just started when the enjoyment was pierced by a deafening 'Coo-ee!' One of the boys in the auditorium stood up to remonstrate with him, and the security guards tried to evict the boys as trouble-makers. The boys protested their innocence and were supported by those sitting by them – who, in retrospect, had probably only supported them in order to see the film in peace. Everyone settled down to enjoy the rest of the film, even though Coo-ee was still at large in the gods. During the interval Jack and the rest of the party sought out the troublesome sailor, and laughing loudly he dismissed their protest with a rendition of 'Coo-ee' which caused some consternation amongst those patrons near him but unfortunately did not wake the security guards.

After the interval everyone returned to their seats, the film restarted … and about a quarter of an hour later, as the hero and heroine of the story were in a passionate embrace, a piercing 'Coo-ee' rang out again. This time, Jack and his chums did not respond.

Then seconds later, another 'Coo-ee' came – but it ended in a quieter, strangulated sound. After the film ended, when the boys left the cinema they found Coo-ee on the pavement, dishevelled and with an increasingly blackening eye. It appeared that the security men had quietly eased themselves into the row behind him and as he was about to let off another shriek they had grabbed him. As he struggled, an arm tightened around his neck, and a fist in the eye clearly indicated that to struggle further would at best invite yet another fist in the other eye, and at worst he would surely be strangled. He surrendered.

However, in the cold, dark depths of the New York waterfront Coo-ee's disposition proved most useful. As the group from the *Port Lincoln* walked back to their vessel, Coo-ee and several others stopped to light cigarettes. Then Jack and his chum saw a collection of men of varying colours but all of large build bearing down on them – a striking similarity to their experience in Port of Spain. With the padre's warning in their ears, they were surrounded by this mob, who demanded a light. Coo-ee just looked and laughed at the largest villain, who repeated the demand for a light as he waved a cigarette under Coo-ee's nose.

The sailor took a large puff on his cigarette, blew smoke at the fellow, and said, 'Don't smoke, mate.' At this point – only seconds from the start to the implied threat to the sailors – Jack's bowels were stirring, whilst the thug and his men were transfixed to the spot. Coo-ee turned and barged through the mob while shrieking his 'Coo-ee,' quickly followed by Jack and the rest of the fraught group. As they moved a few yards away with no small amount of relief, their hearts promptly sank again as Coo-ee called to the thug, 'Catch!' and threw him a box of matches. As the group swiftly made their way to the dock gates and safety they did not look back.

That night Coo-ee was forgiven for all his misdeeds in the previous months. But other than his totally casual response to the obvious challenge posed by the thugs, just what else had stopped them from robbing the sailors? Jack was very disappointed by New York and its filth, and the episode with the gang ensured that he would not go ashore there again.

The boy was pleased to leave the intense cold of New York, although moving *Port Lincoln* was not the easiest of tasks as the mooring ropes, solid with ice, had to be sledgehammered in order for them to bend enough to go around the windlass and be hauled aboard. Jack felt that the agony of the extreme cold was well worth it, though, to see the stern of the *Queen Mary* as she berthed after a stormy Atlantic crossing.

All too soon the North American cold was replaced by a North Atlantic Ocean blow, the blow turning into a near-hurricane. The crew's discomfort was much the same as in the Southern Ocean. With the wind and sea on both quarters, the *Port Lincoln* was dancing a merry jig, and the deck crew were having to deal with the problems created by the storm. While those in the engine room may not have had the wet and danger faced by the deck crew, they were faced with having to regulate the engine, as every few minutes the screw would lift out of the sea before dropping to 26 feet below the ever more mountainous surface. The men of the catering department, whilst neither in the wet nor trying to constantly regulate an engine as the vessel twisted, turned and plunged into a boiling sea, had to contend with trying to prepare meals as the galley stoves swayed with the rolling and pitching of the vessel, making their task more than usually dangerous.

When the vessel left the comparatively shallow waters of the continental shelf the rolling and pitching slowed, but as it was still severe the weather decks were still closed to all but the sailors on watchkeeping duties. Three days out from New York, the helmsman came into the mess room to inform everyone there, 'Summat's wrong with the steering. She ain't answering the 'elm very well. I think she's down by the 'ead, but in these bloody seas who can tell? But *summat* ain't right.'

Later that morning, while polishing brass in the wheelhouse, Jack, with his head on his hands and his elbows on the ledge of the wheelhouse window, was watching the waves sweeping over the foredeck; the wind had come around to the starboard beam. Amid the water and spray he saw two oilskinned figures who were with considerable difficulty making their way forward, using the doubtful security of the lifelines rigged on the second day of the storm. Straightening up, the boy turned to see the officer of the watch and the first mate with the chief engineer looking forward, two of them using binoculars. The officer of the watch, the third mate, speaking to the two other officers, enquired, 'How serious is it?'

The chief engineer replied, 'It could be a problem. Just wait and see.'

The boy's curiosity was aroused as the two figures on the foredeck opened the booby hatch, which gave access to No 1 hold. Then he sidled up to the helmsman as the chap fought with the wheel, and asked, 'What's up? Who's that on the foredeck?'

Amid his struggles on the wheel the man replied, 'That's the Old Man and Chippy. They think we might have a leak, a plate sprung, or something damaged when we hit that jetty in Curaçao.'

Jack asked, 'Why the Old Man with the carpenter? Surely he could send the mate rather than risk himself in this weather?'

His question met a whispered reply: 'Gorley, although he's a short arse, would never send anybody to do anything he'd not be prepared to do himself. And Chippy's there because he needs to take bilge soundings and he's a shipwright, so it's his job to know the construction of the ship.'

Jack turned back to the wheelhouse windows to see the two figures emerge from the booby hatch, close it and screw it tight, then go through a door in the for'ard bulkhead leading to the chain locker and forepeak.

By now it appeared that all the senior officers, and a few not so senior, were in the comfort of the gyrating wheelhouse, watching the master and carpenter go out through the door and back into the teeth of the storm. Before the two figures could reach the wheelhouse the bosun came by the internal route to join the throng. Seeing Jack, he promptly sent him, lowly as he was, not through the relative comfort of the internal alleyways, but out into the elements to make his way down from the wheelhouse. As Jack descended to the main deck in the freezing rain and spray he truly realised that rank has its privileges.

In the mess Jack was, for the first time in the voyage, the centre of attention as he told of his ringside seat witnessing the bravery of Captain Gorley and his carpenter. However, when it came to informing the eager listeners of the results of the intrepid master's inspection, he was at a loss to say anything other than 'They think it may be a sprung plate from the knock at the oil jetty.'

' 'Oo thinks?' a would-be sea lawyer enquired. In the absence of a reply, he continued, 'The bleeding ship's cat, or 'oo?'

In a small voice Jack replied, 'The QM.'

'A bleeding lot 'e would know,' was the conclusion of the assembled men, voiced by the Queen's Council Able Seaman, common at law and everything else.

Later it was circulated that although there was a slight ingress of water in the lower forepeak, the situation was under control and the pumps were easily dealing with the situation. While the storm extended Jack's misery, not everything was a challenge for him. 'Within the next 15 to 20 minutes the *Queen Mary* will be on our starboard beam, passing us on her way to France,' said the quartermaster, who had been sent from the bridge to inform each mess of what would become a unique item of maritime folklore for years to come. Wrapped up in oilskins, Jack and his chum made their way to the moonlit starboard side of the boat deck, and sure enough as their vessel rose on the top of a sea, a glow could be seen in the distance across the moonbeam-illuminated tips of the heaving ocean, bringing some welcome light to the wild North Atlantic night. In no time at all, within a half mile was the second-largest merchant vessel in the world. What a sight! Light towered upon light, except for the navigating area, where all that could be seen in the darkness was the red glow of the port-hand navigating light. As the mighty bulk of the liner came abeam of the corkscrewing *Port Lincoln* a signal lamp on the liner's bridge came to life, sending, 'WNIE, *Queen Mary*, New York to Cherbourg AA AA,' meaning, 'What ship?' Jack was not in the position to read the reply from the *Port Lincoln*, but then from RMS *Queen Mary*, as she overhauled *Port Lincoln*, came the message, 'Godspeed'.

By now the *Queen Mary* was well ahead, and in the gloom caused by the spray – and probably against the rules of the road – she briefly illuminated her three mighty funnels. What a truly memorable and inspiring sight, particularly in the appalling wind and seas. By the time the *Port Lincoln* could have illuminated her single weather-swept funnel, with the same company colour marking, the Queen Mary would have been so far ahead that the gesture would have had little significance. When Jack and the rest of the spectators returned below, the excitement of the mid-ocean meeting had dispelled both the cold and the discomfort, for a time at least.

The atrocious weather prevailed until the vessel reached the approaches to the English Channel, though, while on their arrival at the Brixham pilot station the seas had moderated, even the green hills of Devon were obscured by heavy cloud. However, while slightly subdued in comparison to those aboard the *Port Brisbane*, the 'Channels' crept into the character of many men, as pay-off day was but two and a bit days away.

'I want to see you two in my cabin at 16:00 hrs,' said the mate to Jack and his chum. The last time such an order had been addressed to them was when the mate of the *Port Brisbane* had told them that they were not required on her next voyage. But this time: 'I've been pleased with your work and your conduct during the voyage. I'm offering you both another voyage in this ship, and promotion to junior ordinary seaman.' The boys eagerly accepted the offer, especially as they were well over the qualifying period from boy to ordinary seaman.

Jack's last-ever two days of peggying was the only time that he found the task a pleasure. It was still a matter of anger for him that he had been trained at no small cost in all aspects of seamanship and more, yet until this point he had been employed as nothing more than a servant, and to some – but thankfully not all – culturally challenged individuals. And then off home the boy went to regale – and possibly bore beyond words – his friends and family about his odyssey.

Second voyage

All too soon Jack's leave was over and he returned to his vessel, now no longer the lowest form of deck life but a full-time sailor, though not yet a watchkeeper. On joining the *Port Lincoln* in the London docks, Jack met up with his shipboard chum from the past two voyages, and they moved from the boys' cabin to one for ordinary seamen. That move, seemingly so minor, meant so much to the boys. They could, and would, lord it over the new boys doing the peggying.

They unconsciously adopted the swagger known as the North Atlantic roll, the preserve of the long-established sailor, until they were taken to task for their impudence by several able seamen, who presumed that the boys were mimicking them. It was generally accepted in the sailors' mess that these two upstarts were taking the piss, and the result was that the boys had quite a rough time for a week or so. That was principally caused by their ignorance of deck duties, and this state of affairs was not alleviated, as would normally be the case, by a quiet word here and there from the senior rates. Equally, when the boys asked the men for advice it was not forthcoming, meaning that they had to expose their ignorance to the bosun – not the most auspicious start to their early career as junior ordinary seamen. However, on the bright side, there were many new sailors replacing those who had left after the last voyage, and these younger chaps were rather a different breed; in most cases, they were articulate, smart and at ease in any company, and they helped the boys acclimatise to the new disciplines and challenges of life on deck.

The vessel was by now fully loaded with the usual exports for the voyage from the United Kingdom for South Africa and Australia via the Canary Isles as a bunkering stop. The voyage to South Africa was similar to the earlier voyage, except that the vessel had a new master to replace the distinguished and courageous Captain Gorley, and a new first mate. Also, on arrival at Las Palmas it would appear that either the Spanish Navy did not want any worn-out mooring ropes, or the new mate was not inclined to sell any old ropes or – more likely – the Port Line marine superintendent expressly forbade such practice (in all probability ignoring the fact that in his time as a mate himself he may well have sold old rope …).

In South Africa this time, however, it was not to be Cape Town but Durban. When they docked there, they were met by the usual South African maritime scene, including Ellerman's distinctive City Line boats, British India Line passenger and cargo ships, Clan Line cargo vessels and the lavender hulls of Union Castle liners.

To Jack, the most interesting maritime relics were the coal-fired steam tugs of the South African Railways fleet. Interesting the tugs may have been, but in the case of the *Port Lincoln*, the bosun made his feelings about coal smoke only too clear when his vessel was wreathed in coal smoke whose smuts besmirched her still-wet white paint. The tug master, not the usual casual-to-scruffily-dressed individual, was immaculate in full uniform with four gold bands on his epaulettes, and, sporting a pure white goatee beard with the air of the commander of a warship, did not take too kindly to being called a 'Dirty Yarpie bastard driving a stinking puffer.' But his affected Britannia-trained manner quickly descended below his gold bands and superior air as he replied to the bosun, likening him to a Scottish moron with less intelligence than a dockyard rat. While the crewmen watching this interchange disliked inhaling the smoke of worst-quality South African coal, the spirited exchanges between bosun and the tug master more than made up for it.

When Jack went ashore with his chum and several of the newer senior rates, he found the atmosphere in Durban totally different to that of Cape Town; he enjoyed his brief stay in this city. He also noted the different approach to the native labour in the hold, discharging the cargo and loading some for Australia. Whereas in Cape Town the brutality of the white overseers had been quite despicable, in Durban the same strict discipline existed between the rulers and the ruled, but there appeared to be far less brutality involved. In fact, despite much shouting by the overseer, he saw no instances of the physical brutality in Cape Town.

After two days the *Port Lincoln* sailed for Adelaide. The voyage through the Southern Ocean, although rough at times, was nothing in comparison to how the vessel had suffered on the previous voyage. A fortnight later she was rounding Kangaroo Island, the graveyard of so many sailing vessels during the 19th century and the early years of the 20th, and then it was a short run to Port Adelaide. On this occasion, and after the non-reception Jack had experienced from his relatives on the previous voyage, he kept his word and did not step ashore.

After a week of intermittent cargo handling – due to the usual disputes with the labour unions – the *Port Lincoln* left Adelaide for Melbourne; to Jack this was a much more civilised place than Adelaide, despite the shooting on the waterfront last time round. During this part of the voyage he made a friend of a more senior sailor, Alan, and as it turned out this friendship was to last a lifetime.

On a typically Australian day of hot sunshine, the *Port Lincoln* headed through Port Phillip Bay en route to Melbourne. As she met a tug at Port Melbourne to take up her upriver, to starboard came into view the white liners of the giant Peninsular & Oriental Line. After the vessel was moored Alan and Jack headed uptown and made for a fine Dutch restaurant. Whilst Alan ordered a dish representing the locality with a dash of European cuisine, Jack – to the great amusement of his chum – ordered a non-menu item, a mixed grill, typically English. So much for assimilating the local culture; in Jack's case there was never much chance of that happening!

After a pleasant stay in Melbourne, without encountering the gang culture of five months ago, they left the city, heading down the river, past the coal hulks, out into the bay and on towards Sydney Heads. When the vessel arrived at the Sydney pilot station, she was told that the tug crews were all on strike, so the master was given the choice of remaining at anchor until the dispute was resolved or attempting to take the vessel alongside without tugs, bearing in mind the risk of losing control of the vessel during the manoeuvre. The master who, like Captain Gorley, was never one to shirk what others might have thought was a risk, decided to take the vessel alongside, noting that the weather was fair with no wind, and minimal current. After all, he had a very competent deck crew and engineers who would respond to the more than usual requirements for engine regulation during the final approach. If the mighty Queens could berth in New York without tugs, then so could the *Port Lincoln* at sunny Sydney's Pyrmont jetties.

Under normal tug-assisted berthing the vessel sends ashore a head rope and the for'ard back spring before the lines from the stern are landed. However, on this occasion the stern ropes would be landed first in order to check the forward momentum of the vessel once she had reached her berth. The exercise was quite an experience for Jack, and probably for many others. This was the real seamanship that he had craved since his training establishment days. The mooring line was taken from astern along the outside of the vessel with the eye attached to a heaving line at the break of the fo'c'sle, the other end of the vessel. God help the poor wretch who had the job of throwing the heaving line ashore should he miss the chap ready to catch it. As a presumed precaution against any common sailor making a balls-up of the operation, the throwing would be taken over by the bosun.

Port Lincoln under Sydney Bridge

Under the Harbour Bridge went the *Port Lincoln*, past Walsh Bay, with a turn to port into Darling Harbour and then straight on to Pyrmont. The knuckle of the jetty seemed to be approaching quite fast, but from astern it appeared that the master, with the help of the pilot, had lined the vessel up nicely to avoid the buff-hulled Orient Line liner berthed adjacent to *Port Lincoln*'s place, subject to the deck crew and the engineers doing their job properly. As the end of the jetty came into view, so the head rope's heaving line went ashore, and within seconds so did the for'ard back spring's, to pull the vessel alongside – providing it did not part, as such wire springs were prone to do. A line from the stern went ashore and paid out, with the No 5 hatch winch running at full speed to take in the slack as the vessel went ahead. Shortly all the lines were ashore and the vessel was alongside without a bump. In fact, it was a much better mooring exercise than often achieved with tugs. Opinions of the exercise were as one in the sailors' mess room, concluding that the Old Man had given a good two-fingered salute to these bloody Aussie bastards pretending to be tug men.

This visit to Sydney was to be more of a shipbound affair, rather than being memorable for the trips ashore.

The patron of the training establishment that Jack had attended was Marina, Duchess of Kent, and her daughter, Princess Alexandra, was a couple of years older than Jack. After a brief meeting with him at the Mansion House in London, she was almost the favourite female figure in his adolescent, hormone-driven life. The result of this unrequited passion was that he carried a photograph of this lady with him on his vessels, and since his first visit to New Zealand that picture had been exhibited in a frame made of that country's native timbers. His desk was also adorned with a photograph of Mary, a neighbour of his age and a very special friend from early schooldays, who he had grown up with. These two ladies, the rolling of the vessel permitting, graced his desk until arrival at Sydney.

Returning to his cabin late in the afternoon, Jack had the feeling that all was not quite right. But as befitted his young mind, he ignored the sense of disquiet and after a shower lay on his bunk waiting for Alan to appear and announce where and when they were going ashore. After a lengthy passage of time and no call from his chum, Jack made his way to Alan's cabin – only to find it locked, with no Alan anywhere to be seen. Jack made several enquiries into the whereabouts of his chum, and was eventually told that he had been seen on deck in a very jovial mood carrying what looked like a photograph. Jack looked around the deck and, finding no sign of Alan, returned to his cabin and, fully dressed in his going ashore gear, stretched out on his bunk again.

Glancing around his cabin, his eyes alighted on his desk and – horror of horrors – whilst the photograph of Mary still graced its position, the photograph of Alexandra was missing. Jack leaped up, not quite believing his eyes; but sure enough the treasured photograph was missing. Then the light from the porthole dimmed as, with much laughter, his chum's head, surrounded by polished brass, enquired, 'Lost something?' As his head withdrew it was replaced by his hand clutching the immeasurably valuable – to Jack if no one else – photograph. 'Finders keepers, eh?' his chum enquired as his hand and the photograph disappeared from view.

The language used by Jack towards his chum was not befitting the breeding of a young gentleman as he shot through the cabin doorway towards the deck, where a chase began between the two friends. From the main deck to the boat deck, up the companionway to the bridge wing, upwards to the monkey island (the wooden structure above the wheelhouse, which held the magnetic compass and the direction finder), across it and down the starboard side went the chase. It extended to the foredeck, back to the boat deck and then down aft and along the starboard alleyway. Here Jack lost sight of Alan, but he continued searching the entire exposed decks, lockers, booby hatches and even the coils of mooring lines. However, to the frustration of the boy there was no sign of the photograph or the thief. Jack lot's was not helped when many of the sailors joined in the fun; they misdirected the boy all over the ship, shouting, 'There he is, over there,' accompanied by raucous laughter. The boy followed every red herring planted until exhausted he staggered into the mess room. There, with other sailors, sat Alan calmly enjoying a plate of the cook's cold collation, as if nothing had occurred.

From Jack's lips another torrent of unseemly language was directed towards his laughing chum – amongst which was a very angry demand to know the whereabouts of his photograph.

'What photograph?' his chum asked with an enquiring lift of the eyebrow.

'You know bloody *well* what photograph,' Jack shouted, getting even wilder as the minutes passed.

'I should make sure that Mary's still there before you accuse anyone of stealing Alexandra,' advised his chum.

Jack shot out of the mess room with the derisive laughter of the sailors ringing in his ears as he headed for his cabin, almost certain that Mary too had gone missing. He entered his cabin, flinging back the door with an almighty crash, and there on his desk was not only the photograph of the beloved Mary but also that of the almost equally – on reflection, perhaps not quite almost equally – beloved Princess Alexandra.

The sheer effort of expressing his temper made Jack quite exhausted and although he desperately wanted a cup of tea his courage deserted him on the thought of returning to the mess room, and facing the laughter of the sailors. It was more than he could cope with, so in total exhaustion he collapsed onto his bunk.

This particular voyage to Sydney taught the juvenile Jack an important lesson relating to character. He eventually realised that he was taking life too seriously, particularly on this occasion where he inadvertently gave the crew an evening's free entertainment all for the sake of a bit of fun by his friend. In the process, he had made himself look very immature indeed.

With his mental equilibrium restored, Jack enjoyed several trips ashore with Alan including a memorable trip to Taronga Park Zoo. It was memorable not for the place itself – although that was quite spectacular – but for their journey home. Two-thirds of the way across Sydney Harbour Bridge the tram came to a halt with much flashing of electrical earthing and the extinguishing of all lights and motive power. Having been told to remain in the vehicle, as it was very dangerous to alight because of live power lines, Jack and Alan – in the centuries-old best tradition of British merchant mariners – ignored the advice. To their mind, in order not to wait to be fried, they promptly legged it across the blacked-out tramway to the station on the city side of the bridge and without further ado made their way back to their vessel at Pyrmont. While Alan was a model of British rectitude, Jack, as was his wont, coloured the incident with a little exaggeration here and there as he held the occupants of the mess room captivated by the story of their narrow escape – from at the very least death by fire, electrocution or falling into Port Jackson – in their quest to return to the vessel. It is doubtful if he was totally believed by his colleagues, but the yarn entertained them for an hour on an otherwise boring Sunday evening.

With the last of her outward cargo discharged the *Port Lincoln* sailed from Sydney with the aid of tugs. The tugmen had to endure the derisory comments of the sailors relating to their recent strike because the ship had berthed without the aid of any 'bloody colonial tugs' followed by 'no bleeding use turning up now – any dick, even you lot, could undock a boat.' The one-way conversation was brought to a halt by the second mate with an admonishment to the after gang: 'You've had your fun – now shut up before I get annoyed.'

With that, the vessel was cleared away for sea, heading past Fort Denison to Sydney Heads and away to Brisbane, to commence loading more beef in all its guises.

At this time Jack still had his girlfriend, Sheila, at home. By pure coincidence in the name association, Sheila had for many years been a resident of Australia and as was usual with his girlfriends – before, at the time and afterwards – Jack was besotted by her. Yet, however besotted he might have been by Sheila, she did not warrant a photograph on his desk beside Mary and Alexandra. When the *Port Lincoln* had completed loading her frozen cargo along the Brisbane River, she headed out through Morton Bay, turning to port and heading through the bottom end of the Great Barrier Reef towards Townsville – the beginning of tropical Queensland, and the final port that mirrored Jack's previous voyage. So, mindful of the limitations of his wardrobe, and in an effort to impress Sheila on his return home, he was determined to spend his shore pay, recently earned by cleaning a hold at Brisbane, on a new, and fashionable, jacket and trousers. With Alan, the boy went ashore and under the covered verandas of main street Townsville, persuaded by his friend that the jacket and trousers looked perfect, he bought the items and thought he was the cock of the walk with his newfound sartorial elegance. But unfortunately on his eventual return home this opinion was not shared by Sheila; she was last seen in the centre of Bristol walking away from him for ever with words that included, 'If you think I'm going out with you looking like *that* ...'

The *Port Lincoln* made her way up through the Great Barrier Reef, en route to Wyndham on the north coast of Western Australia. The vessel appeared to be moving more slowly than usual, but this may well have been an illusion due to the calm sea and perfect weather as she negotiated the various headlands and islands – most with tropical vegetation and the almost obligatory white sandy beach. At one point Jack was astounded to be able to look through the water for several fathoms with all the beautiful sea life clearly visible. These Great Barrier Reef trips never lost their attraction for the boy and over the years, probably by coincidence, they were always in perfect weather. The pilot was dropped off at Thursday Island, and the vessel then rounded Cape York, the northern tip of Queensland, and headed across the Arafura Sea towards Wyndham.

The bells rang for the deck crew to go to their harbour stations. Jack rolled out of his bunk and joined his colleagues in looking over the handrails into a very wide and muddy-watered estuary with almost barren land either side of the vessel. If anything the air temperature was even higher than in Queensland.

The mate had been constructing a model of a galleon during the voyage, and the progress of the build was regularly inspected through his cabin window. Allegedly, as the vessel approached Wyndham the galleon set sail in the river because its maker had decided that something was not quite perfect. Whether or not this tale was true Jack could not determine, but what was true was that a look through the mate's window did not show the model for the rest of the voyage.

The *Port Lincoln* tied up to the single curving jetty, with the settlement of Wyndham in plain view. Between the vessel and habitation was a salt plain with a long semicircular road/railway leading to what might be called the main drag, but the meat-processing works, the reason for the settlement at Wyndham, dominated everything.

In the mid-afternoon Jack and several of his chums were allowed ashore, as when the beef loading had finished for the day they would then have to go back to work, sealing and covering the holds; at this port the stevedores did not cover up, as they did in most ports. As the route across the salt plain was a shorter route than the roadway, the men headed directly for the wooden buildings making up the settlement. As they neared their goal a policeman with a rifle approached them and warned, 'A word of advice for you Poms, don't walk across this way after dark. The whole flat's full of crocs, snakes etc.' When asked what he was after with his rifle the policeman told the men, with a typical expressionless Australian face, 'Pommie seamen and wild beasts. Not much difference between 'em.' Although the consensus amongst the deck crew was that this might have been a wind-up – Australians being Australians – they decided not to take any chances with the local wildlife or mouthy, cocky cops.

The first shop that they came across was the – almost obligatory in Australia and New Zealand – Chinese greengrocery shop; ever-industrious Chinese traders could be found throughout both countries. On the opposite side of the road were the bat-winged doors of a pub, and a little further on was a surgery staffed by a nurse, and then the police station. From Jack's point of view this was sweltering Wyndham in what appeared to be a godforsaken part of Western Australia, existing solely due to the meat works. By law Jack was not able to consume alcohol, so his shoregoing life was limited, involving the likelihood of snake bite and attacks by alligators or crocs, and the certainty of massed attacks at sunrise and sundown by every stinging midge the Almighty had created. Apart from the beautiful cockatoos, nothing about the place was attractive.

Jack learned that all the meat workers and associated tradesmen were shipped up from Perth for the slaughtering season, and when they returned all that remained in Wyndham were the policemen, the nursing sisters and the Chinese traders. He was told that the cattle were rounded up right through the Northern Territory from the Queensland border and across the north of Western Australia to the meat works at Wyndham. A round-up could take two years, the same drovers riding from the start to the finish at Wyndham, to eventually load the carcasses onto whichever ship was in port at the time. This was Wild West film scenes come to life, without the six-guns, the buffaloes and the baddies, but in an authentic Australian setting.

The *Port Lincoln* left Wyndham full of foodstuffs for London, heading across the Indian Ocean for Aden to refuel. At that time Aden was a British protectorate, its only claim to fame being that in the 19th century it had been a coaling port created after the opening of the Suez Canal; as the fuel changed from Welsh coal to fuel oil, Aden prospered as part of the route to the rest of the mighty British Empire, and India in particular.

As Jack leaned over the rail in the sweltering heat, Aden's impressive rocks came into sight, and his mind turned to the tune of 'The Barren Rocks of Aden': to him that was exactly what the scene represented. As the vessel was tied up to the buoys, the pontoon with the fuel hose came alongside, and it was connected to the vessel. Within minutes Arab traders were swarming aboard from their bumboats, selling everything from, 'best quality Swiss made watches, sah – for you special price, you're my friend' to the trader with his hand in his voluminous dirty clothes with an all too obvious attempt at playing the conspirator as he whispered, 'For you, Sahib, I have feelthy pictures at very good price – look, they're very, very good.' Out of curiosity Jack looked at the slim volume of 'feelthy pictures' and saw – judging by their hairstyles, stockings and shoes – women from the late Victorian period, some of them printed upside down, and some top halves of bodies were not attached to the lower halves. As he flicked through the pages, trying to match tops to bottoms, the Arab – swiftly glancing back and forward – leaned even closer, and demanded, 'You see the pictures, now you pay,' and held out his hand.

'I don't want this rubbish,' retorted Jack, 'I saw better from Health and Efficiency behind the bike shed at school.'

Jack put the book back in the trader's hand, at which he said with some feeling, 'You English *bastard*,' then turned away and, of all the people to choose, tried to sell his pictures to the bosun. With the minimum of fuss Bose pushed him down the gangway, where the poor Arab lost his footing and had, along with his pictures, an involuntary wash.

Under a huge Arabian moon the *Port Lincoln* left dry, dusty Aden, heading up the Red Sea for Suez and the next stage of her voyage home. The canal had started construction in 1859, and ten years later it opened, expediting the passage of steam-powered vessels, in particular French and British vessels servicing their empires in the East. Having transited the Panama Canal on his past two voyages, this transit of the earlier great canal was to be a new experience for Jack. Here there were only live donkeys and no mechanical mules; he noted that there was no attempt to employ the Panama's bread for the mules ruse. The Suez Canal being simply a water-filled trench through the desert, linking two seas, Jack could not compare it with the highly-engineered Panama Canal and its lush vegetation.

Before entering the canal the vessel was briefly anchored while a barge arrived with a large searchlight inside a metal box, which was fitted over the prow and plugged into the vessel's electrical system. During night transits of the canal the light would illuminate the vessel ahead, allowing the pilot to keep a safe distance between vessels.

This transit took place only 16 months after the ill-fated invasion of Suez by the French and British when General Abdul Nasser, leader of Egypt, had unilaterally decided to take over the ownership of the canal from the Anglo-French Suez Canal Company. The Suez Canal Company and its governments saw that take-over as an act likely to have severe consequences for the free movement of international trade, as the canal would be now under Egyptian political control and subject to the whims and pressures of a single person – Colonel Nasser.

The invasion of the Canal Zone in 1956 had begun well; even though the Egyptians had blocked the waterway, within hours British troops had taken control of Suez and were preparing to meet up with French troops further down the canal. However, neither country had told the USA of their plans. This offended the Americans and they warned of severe sanctions against France and Britain unless they immediately left the Canal Zone. This both countries did – and it marked the end of Great Britain as a world power. The result of this humiliation was that the Russians aided the Egyptians to restore the use of the canal, and never again did French or British pilots navigate vessels along it. So now the *Port Lincoln*, perhaps for the first time, had a Russian or Eastern European pilot to take her along the canal past Ismailia, and past the towering Canal Defence Force monument to the men and women of the Commonwealth and Empire who had given their lives in protecting the Suez Canal during the First World War.

When the vessel arrived at Suez, she anchored in order for the searchlight to be removed. On the canal bank an imposing statue of Ferdinand de Lesseps, the chief engineer and creator of the canal, had been erected, and Jack looked for it, but in vain. It had probably been destroyed, but it may have been lying alongside the plinth, as Jack, looking through a pair of Japanese binoculars purchased from a bumboat at Aden, could see something that might have been the rest of the monument.

After taking on fresh water, the *Port Lincoln* entered the Mediterranean and shaped a course for Gibraltar. The weather was fair, so much painting and sprucing up took place at that time, in case the weather became inclement when they emerged into the Atlantic, as was often the case. The passage through the Gibraltar Straits occurred at night so the sight of the imposing rock was denied to Jack and several others who were experiencing their first Mediterranean cruise. In the open Atlantic the inclement weather did not arrive, and the vessel turned onto a course to pick up the Ushant light, turn into the English Channel and head for home. With the Channel now under the keel, the 'Channels' took over the crew and all was happiness, with a distinct 'hail fellow well met' sentiment between even the most implacable of enemies. When the *Port Lincoln* docked, Jack noted that the paint on the starboard side of her funnel was intact (unlike the bare rusty steel created on the previous voyage by the savage North Atlantic Ocean), and that on this occasion the vessel did not look so sad.

With a fond farewell to Alan, Jack headed to Leadenhall Street and an interview with the boss. In the train home, Jack, with much satisfaction, thought of his interview and the promotion to senior ordinary seaman followed by his appointment to the *Port Auckland*, which was at Cardiff for dry-docking. In the meantime he looked forward to his home and the quiet of the Somerset countryside.

4

TSMV *Port Auckland*

First voyage

'Cardiff Central, Cardiff Central,' the railway announcer declared before telling the passengers that this was the disembarking point for Cardiff and a series of unpronounceable destinations in Wales via branch lines. Jack collected his luggage; now ranked senior ordinary seaman, he could just afford a taxi from the city to the dock via Bute Street, a street notorious in times past and still a place not to venture alone after dark.

The boy's great-aunt had worked in the Bute Street surgery in the late 19th and early 20th centuries. She had spent her days and often nights patching up seamen and others with stab wounds, battered heads and broken limbs, usually the result of drunken fighting. Rarely were police involved, and even more rarely was the street policed. It would appear that the favourite medicines given to the unfortunates in her surgery, no matter what their injury or disease, were iodine, spirit of salts and syrup of figs. The syrup of figs in particular was administered in overdose amounts; her opinion was that open bowels cured most ills, and if the men were sitting on a lavatory they were not inclined to seek a fight.

In joining the *Port Auckland*, Jack was not going to an unknown vessel, as he had been well acquainted with her in Lyttelton during the incident of the sailors on the wrong vessel. As for the geography of the vessel, she was in almost every respect a sister to his first vessel, *Port Brisbane*. In no time at all the taxi delivered him to the Mountstuart dry dock and his new home for five months. Walking up the brow – a right-angled gangway – Jack could see tangled cables and rubber pipes crisscrossing the formerly white teak alleyway decks as dockyard mateys appeared to inhabit every square inch of the vessel.

On reaching the deck Jack left his bags under the care of the watchman – not, perhaps, the safest place to leave bags – and went up to the first mate's cabin. There

Port Auckland. Painting by Robert Blackwell.

he presented himself, plus his letter from Leadenhall Street and his discharge book. This mate did not appear to overly concern himself with shipboard deck department matters, simply saying to Jack, 'There's little for you to do until the mateys have finished. Go to the bosun and get your cabin key. He'll tell you what there is to do, if anything.' As Jack turned to leave the cabin the mate, without looking up from his desk, said, 'Welcome aboard.'

Never before had the boy been welcomed aboard by the chief deck officer on any of his vessels – it was all rather a surprise. He was still thinking about it as he found the bosun in the petty officers' mess room. His new boss, equally laid back in relation to Jack's duties, gave Jack his cabin key and told him, 'Just be around every now and then. We've nothing to do as we have a shore gang doing the work. Why they sent you here this early God only knows.' Taking his leave of the mess room, Jack collected his belongings from the watchman and sorted them out in his cabin. Looking through his cabin porthole he found he was looking directly at a wartime motor torpedo boat sitting on blocks, apparently being restored. The boy's mind went into overdrive as he looked at the inspiring lines of the craft. What tales could that distinctively shaped hull tell of derring-do in the English Channel? The high-speed chase, the fervour of action and the glory of victory was grist to the mill in his adolescent mind. That he had a vivid imagination was accepted by him as part of his character, and he quite revelled in that satisfying, but time-, effort- and opportunity-wasting state of mind.

Owing to the work going on, Jack was for the time being denied the pleasure of exploring his new vessel, but nonetheless he went wandering amongst the dockyard mateys as they stripped every bit of cargo-handling running gear for inspection by the various surveyors. As he looked around, Jack considered the measurements of the *Port Auckland* compared to *Port Brisbane* and marvelled that the designers had produced two vessels with size and gross registered tonnage so close; the *Port Auckland* was just 3 grt bigger than the *Port Brisbane*, while *Port Brisbane* was two inches longer than her near-sister. To Jack's eyes the vessel, even in her present dishevelled state, was in very good condition, with her teak decks at Nos 3, 4 and 5 hatchways carefully covered in tarpaulins to prevent grease from the running gear marking their pristine surfaces.

For the next six weeks Jack went across the Bristol Channel to his Somerset home for weekend leave, which would often end up as a long weekend. However, deck work was beginning to build as the crew began to follow the dockyard workers when they completed the reassembly of the various cargo-handling equipment. While, in general terms, the Mountstuart workmen did a competent job for the survey, much still needed to be done to bring the equipment and the ancillary items up to Port Line standard. By the time the dry dock was flooded and the *Port Auckland* took to her natural element again, all the shackle pins were seized with wire and the canvas covers for the blocks and topping lift drums of the jumbo derrick had been scrubbed and restrung. When the workmen had retreated, the decks were cleared and scrubbed with a mixture of caustic soda and a pink liquid cleaner using Bass brooms under long-handled metal-capped instruments known as bears.

As the time to leave Cardiff approached the running crew began, in dribs and drabs, to join the vessel to take her to London, where the deep-sea crew would join her. The tide was right for the *Port Auckland* to leave Cardiff at night and head down the Bristol Channel. As she passed the darkened Somerset coast the twinkling lights of habitation reminded Jack of home, but when the Lundy lighthouse sent out its warning beams of light any nostalgia for home dissipated; jobs still needed to be done, night-time or not.

As the No 8 berth, King George V Dock, hove into view, the quay wall and pontoon appeared to be covered with every rank and rating from the Port Line dock office. As the gangway was lowered, a mass of jobsworths, slackers and hangers-on boarded the vessel. The shore gang promptly took over the pristine crew recreation room, to spend the next few hours reading their *Daily Heralds* and *Daily Mirrors* while rolling their ticklers and fumigating every nook and cranny with the acrid smoke – so thick that the men on the far side of the room were nigh on invisible from the doorway. Until the running crew were paid off, the shore gang simply sat and drank tar masquerading as tea, smoking a large proportion of the content of the W.D. & H.O. Wills warehouse;

some of them read their papers whilst those not given to such academic pursuits looked at the pictures and grunted.

Until the deep-sea deck crew had signed on, the shore gang were supposed to do the work of the deck department with their own bosun and charge hands. If at any time during the period between 8 a.m. and 5 p.m. more than 50 per cent of these men ever left the crew recreation room, it was only on a Friday, to collect their weekly wage. To Jack, these men were the idlest individuals he had encountered anywhere in the world. The only conclusion he could achieve in the question of why Port Line would employ such wasters was that wheels within wheels ensured that those idle shore gangs could justify a reason for the employment of those further up the greasy pole of management.

For the first time with Port Line, Jack saw a ship only part-loaded for her voyage to New Zealand; in 1958, outward trade with that country was beginning to fall away. Soon the new deep-sea deck crew was signed on, and so began the two-year professional association between Jack and Boatswain Murdo. Murdo was a giant of a man who brooked no dissent from anyone – rather more by reason of his size than any deep logical argument as to why someone should or should not do something. Murdo was not a man for idle chatter or, other than when in his cups, social fraternisation. His sentences were very short and to the point, and his features never betrayed any emotion. When things were not going right for him, caused by someone else's failure or omission, he would put his emotionless face about a foot above that of the miscreant and simply stare. When the unfortunate blinked, Murdo would nod, unclench his fists and without further ado leave the scene. No one was left in any doubt that should they be the recipient of the 'Murdo stare' they were in trouble; and Bose had a long memory. At their first meeting Jack was rather intimidated by the sheer bulk of his new bosun and his typically abrupt Isle of Lewis interpretation of English. Like so many of his colleagues from those islands, Murdo was much more at home speaking Gaelic. Other than his language, his other identifying mark with his heritage was the home-made white cloth cap so beloved by the men from the Hebrides and the Shetlands.

The *Port Auckland* went out through the King George V locks stern-first into the Thames before being turned by the tugs to point her bow downstream and begin her voyage to the antipodes. Jack, not yet qualified for watchkeeping duties, spent sailing day clearing away the detritus of London docks, dockworkers and the Port Line shore gang.

One of a multitude of benefits for Jack from no longer being a peggy was that he did not have any responsibility for clearing up the crew's recreation room after the sailing-day evacuation of that room by the shore gang. As a peggy, Jack had appreciated the help of the shore gang mess-men in making his load a little lighter by looking after the sailors' mess room as well as their own accommodation – but when it was time for the shore gang to leave the vessel the mess-men were the first down the gangway, leaving clutter and filth behind them for the deck peggies to clear up.

After a week of the ship ploughing a steady watery furrow towards Curaçao, Jack came across his new master, Captain Claude R. Townshend. Accommodation inspections were carried out alternately by the mate and the master, and Jack was in the crew accommodation as Captain Townshend, accompanied by Murdo, was conducting the inspection; as Jack walked through the cross-alleyway the master and the bosun appeared at the other end of it. Standing behind the master, Murdo indicated that Jack should move, and pretty quickly at that. Jack promptly about-turned and shot up the starboard accommodation ladder. The sight he had beheld was a severe-looking master, yet a picture of uniformed sartorial elegance, carrying a large torch in his white-gloved hand. With just one exception, all the masters that Jack served under were by any standards immaculately turned out: the one exception was a character with a most engaging disposition and of a more corpulent dimension than many masters. But Claude Townshend was in a class of his own. To Jack he was a walking advertisement for Gieves & Hawkes, uniform tailors to kings, princes, admirals of the fleet and Port Line masters, along with some of the mates.

The refuelling at Curaçao went with perfect timing as usual, and the vessel left for the Panama Canal. On arrival at Colon, Jack was yet again very impressed by the pilot launches, the handling of the craft and the deep-throated roar of the Chrysler engines as they sped away, having deposited their passenger at the foot of the gangway.

It was on this occasion that Jack was able to watch Captain Townshend for a long period of time without the captain necessarily noting his presence. Captain Townshend was, as always, immaculately turned out in tropical dress uniform: white shoes, long white trousers, single-breasted high button-up single-collared dress jacket with shoulder epaulettes, and braided uniform cap. In contrast, as Jack remembered from his first trip through the canal, the American pilots were dressed in what could be described as stereotype American garb: wide-brimmed stetson, bootlace tie and footwear nearly identical to cowboy boots.

On most Port Line vessels smoking was not allowed on the bridge or in the wheelhouse, but when the *Port Brisbane* had gone through the canal, Captain Bailey had appeared not to object when the pilot smoked several cigars during the transit. On the *Port Auckland*, however, it was a very different regime. On this vessel there was no leeway from Captain Townshend; rules were rules and everyone would obey those rules. The master's displeasure at any infringement of his rules was something to be avoided at all costs. Jack was spellbound as the pilot came up the companionway to the starboard bridge wing with a huge cigar clenched in his teeth. The captain was just inside the wheelhouse door with his hands clasped behind his back looking towards the bow. The pilot strode up behind him, gave him a hearty slap on the back with the seemingly customary greeting of 'Hi-ya, Cap' followed by a huge lungful of smoke exhaled around his head. Jack watched as Captain Townshend's neck, brimming over the back of his choker collar, turned red and then almost purple.

Port Wyndham

With apparently great difficulty he gave navigational command to the pilot with the very stiff-sounding words: 'She is twin-screw and handles well, Pilot.' There was no 'Good morning' and no small talk, simply an example of the British attitude to some foreigner not versed in the niceties of the hoped-for courteous British deference to their host. Jack came to the conclusion that if he had been close enough to his master he would surely have seen steam coming from his ears. During Jack's subsequent voyages with Captain Townshend through Panama, the master's dress, attitude and bearing never changed – and when he retired, the Panama Canal Authority gave him an honorary canal pilot licence in recognition of his long and distinguished association with the canal.

After leaving Panama the *Port Auckland* began her fortnight-long transit of the Pacific Ocean. This turned out to be a quiet, truly pacific, sojourn with only the odd turtle, albatross, porpoise and whale to break the monotony. The night-times were so very different, with the almost magical sky of the southern hemisphere – to Jack a continuing fascinating beauty beyond compare.

When the passengers began to quibble about various minor matters, it was a sign that the voyage was coming to an end. The derricks were rerigged and the mooring lines lifted from below decks. Chippy opened the brakes on the windlass and walked the anchors out a few links of the anchor cable to ensure all was well should they be needed on arrival at Auckland. The canvas hood was taken off the ship's bell and the gangway was broken out, to be checked over before being returned to its bed. With her house flag aloft on the starboard outer halyard, the *Port Auckland* was ready to return the courtesy dip from the homeward-bound *Port Wyndham*.

The *Port Auckland* turned into Hauraki Gulf, then glided past Rangitoto and onto her berth at Auckland. For Jack, looking at the city from his docking station at the vessel's stern, it was as if he was coming home, even though it was almost two years since he had last visited the city. Amongst the cargo of the *Port Auckland* for discharge were domestic wares, machinery and motor cars, together with some of the steel which would be used in the creation of the 'coat hanger' bridge that was eventually to link the north shore to the city of Auckland. When Jack ventured ashore it was as if he had never been away. The Seamen's Mission, Padre Brown and the dances were just as before, and Queen Street felt as familiar as Bristol. He spent the next fortnight at the Civic cinema, at the Mission dances and at the numerous milk bars, very much enjoying the company of the local girls and – like most of his colleagues – social life with the local. Life was good, and sometimes Murdo would even half-smile as his compatriots from the other vessels in port came to visit him with the obligatory bottle of Scottish mist to be swiftly emptied, the next one already open.

The *Port Auckland* did the usual run of the ports for the discharge of her outward cargo – Wellington, Lyttelton and Port Chalmers – before her crew cleaned the holds and lockers ready for the foodstuffs for Britain. Hopefully, if there was a shortage of dockworkers there would be some shore pay to supplement the generally poor wages of the British merchant seamen. Once the discharging was completed at Port Chalmers the first of the lamb carcasses arrived, with barrels of tallow and bales of wool.

From Port Chalmers the vessel made her way up the coast to Timaru, the capital of South Canterbury at the southern end of the Canterbury Bight, there to load more lamb, tallow and mutton. The Timaru of the time was an exposed harbour with a part-enclosing breakwater in Caroline Bay, and although the normal mooring ropes were used fore and aft, the vessel was secured at both ends by a large multi-entwined mooring line with a Stenhouse clip, connecting her to the quay wall. In the event of a Southerly buster the crew could quickly free her by releasing the Stenhouse with a sledgehammer, then put to sea to ride out the storm safely. In the days of sail one of these weather systems in May 1882 caused two sailing vessels, the *Ben Venue* and the *City of Perth*, to be overwhelmed by the sea at Timaru. The *Ben Venue* was wrecked and broken up, while the *City of Perth* was refloated and repaired to emerge with a New Zealand name, *Turakina*, to trade under the ownership of the New Zealand Shipping Company.

At Timaru the larger overseas vessels, mostly home boats, used the berths along the curve of the breakwater while the smaller, local vessels of the Union Steamship Company and the Holm Line would berth at the smaller jetty between the breakwater berths and the golden sands of Caroline Bay. The arrival of the *Port Auckland* had coincided with the Timaru carnival weekend, so those golden sands were dense with swimmers, strollers and sunbathers under a near-perfect sky. As soon as their duties

Caroline Bay, Timaru

allowed, Jack and his chum Ginger were down the gangway and heading for the beach. There were so many shapely young women about, without any obvious male escorts, that the two sailors thought they were in paradise. The only difficulty appeared to be just where they should start charming the Kiwi girls. Eventually amongst the bikini-clad bodies they saw a couple of girls of about their own age and promptly made a beeline for them. Fortunately, the girls did not rebuff them and a pleasant afternoon was had by all. Within the hour Ginger made his mind up that he would team up with the fair-haired girl, leaving Jack with the dark-haired one, which suited him well.

As they got into animated conversation with the girls a startlingly attractive girl passed them, with quite a few chaps following her. The dark-haired girl, in a decidedly disparaging tone of voice, said to Jack, 'That's Miss Caroline Bee.' Jack thought for a moment about the tone of voice before asking why she appeared not to be too keen on this Miss Bee. The prompt rejoinder was, yet again, 'She's Miss Caroline Bee – and doesn't she *know* it!' With that, the fair-haired girl told the boys in a hushed voice, but with some relish, that Miss Caroline Bee was not a 'nice girl', and described her night-time apparel as the definition of what was a 'bad girl'. The thought shot through Jack's mind that girls will be girls – particularly when the girl under discussion is very attractive. At the end of a very convivial afternoon, with the Miss Bee episode being the exception, the boys and girls parted, with an agreement to meet in a milk bar in Stafford Street, the town's main road.

In the evening Jack dressed ready to go ashore, but no Ginger appeared. After a hunt, he found him, who said that he did not fancy the 'blonde bit' and would be staying aboard. At the milk bar Jack found his girl waiting for him without her friend, who had apparently decided that she didn't fancy Ginger either. So Jack, after a quite wonderful time of doing nothing but talking, invited the dark-haired girl to the vessel on the following day, a Sunday, when she was open to the public, as was the custom in New Zealand. But the girl declined the invitation in case her association with Jack and being aboard his vessel might cause her to be labelled a 'boaty', a disparaging term for girls of low moral standing who mixed with sailors.

After much thought about Caroline Bee, it suddenly dawned on Jack that she was in fact the Timaru carnival queen, Miss Caroline Bay. The Kiwi pronunciation of the letter A translated into E, and this was not her name but her title. No wonder the girls rubbished her – jealousy and all that. This was the first of several mistakes by Jack in understanding the female mind, and in this case pronunciation! However, despite her misgivings about being seen about town with a sailor, the girl Jack had met continued to meet up with him during the rest of the *Port Auckland*'s stay as the vessel continued to load lamb tallow and wool. After ten days at Timaru it was time to sail to Lyttelton – and for Jack, to kiss goodbye to his newfound girlfriend: heartache all around!

At harbour stations as the ship put to sea, the lovelorn Jack stood watching the disappearing Timaru. He was the subject of much teasing about his love life by the men aft, and even the second mate joined in the mirth, much to Jack's annoyance. Within hours the *Port Auckland* had rounded the Banks Peninsula and was headed for Lyttelton. As the vessel drew alongside her berth, stern to the town, again Jack was subjected to taunts by his colleagues relating to his friend in Timaru. The taunts were mostly, 'Can't see her waving,' while another threw in his sixpennyworth with, 'Nah, she's gone back to her Kiwi boyfriend by now.'

With the vessel tied up the ribbing stopped, and the deck crowd set about topping the derricks ready for cargo loading to commence as soon as the lamb carcasses arrived. In the meantime, there was a queue of lorries carrying bales of wool on the jetty, waiting for the labour to load them. Social life for Jack at Lyttelton was very different to that he had enjoyed at Timaru; at best a trip to the rather tatty cinema, or a rush for the six o'clock swill at the nearest pub. However, all was not lost as each evening he rang his girlfriend in Timaru, which lightened his mood. The only downside to his phone calls was the almost nightly chant from his colleagues of, 'We know what you're doing,' and many other comments as they passed the phone booth on their way ashore for their swill in the pub backroom – here the landlord would, if challenged, claim to the police that this was a private party and produce a sheet of paper claiming that it was Joe Bloggs's birthday and these were his friends. It was quite apparent that the police knew it was all hogwash, but they had to inspect licensed premises, and such visits, although a total waste of time, demonstrated the fact that the law was being applied, even if less than half-heartedly.

The time came for the *Port Auckland* to leave Lyttelton. On this visit there had been no repeat of the alcohol-induced fiasco involving the deck crews of *Port Brisbane* and *Port Auckland*, and there was no ambition to climb the volcanic hills around the port. But Jack, probably thanks to his nightly phone calls, had enjoyed visiting a port that he knew very little about. The last consignment of chilled lamb arrived, continuing a trade that had started with frozen lamb in the 1880s, and with it loaded, the hatches closed and the derricks back in their crutches, the vessel left Lyttelton at 17:00 hrs and headed for the Cook Strait, and on to New Plymouth, on the west coast of North Island.

At 20:00 hrs the *Port Auckland* was under full power and travelling at a good 16 knots when the navigation lights of a fast-moving vessel appeared astern. Within a short time the *Port Auckland* was swiftly overhauled by the inter-island ferry vessel *Hinemoa*, en route from Lyttelton to Wellington and probably travelling in excess of 19 knots. To Jack this was not quite as exciting as when the *Queen Mary* had overhauled the *Port Lincoln* in the North Atlantic, but nonetheless the bright lights from the *Hinemoa* as she drew abeam were a spectacular sight. Westwards through the Cook Strait – on this occasion, calm – followed by crossing the South Taranaki Bight, the vessel then went around a headland probably created by lava of Mount Egmont thousands of years ago, and into Port Taranaki and the city of New Plymouth, capital of Taranaki province.

Although the sea entrance to Auckland is a spectacular sight, the view of Mount Egmont as the *Port Auckland* approached New Plymouth is outstanding. The mountain is an exact copy of the Japanese Mount Fuji and naturally dominates all around it. New Plymouth, as its name suggests, is named after the Devon city from where most of its settlers had originated. Much of the land was purchased by the Plymouth Land Company, and was settled from 1840. At New Plymouth the *Port Auckland* began to load dairy products, with the first part of 2,000 tons of boxed butter going into the lower holds. On the homeward voyage this would add to the vessel's stability in all weathers and provide superior steering qualities – as long as the engineers managed to keep both screws at the same revolutions; not always an easy task.

Unlike the South Island cargo, which was mostly associated with the sheep industry, Taranaki was predominately a province producing cattle-based cargo. The butter was followed by chilled and boxed beefsteaks, milk powder and bagged casein. With the loading going smoothly in fair weather, Jack took himself ashore, and for the first time in his life saw black sand on a beach. This was a phenomenon caused by the volcanic ash of many thousands of years ago. Although he enjoyed his time on the beach he never really took to the colour, but along with the sight of Mount Egmont the black beaches were a lasting memory of New Plymouth for him.

Jack found that in several respects New Plymouth was very similar to Timaru, Devon Street being in many ways the same as Stafford Street. Although both places were titled 'city' as they were the capitals of a province or sub-province, in reality they were more like towns. The local Seamen's Mission in New Plymouth was run by a most pleasant couple, the Missioner having been an RAF pilot during the last war. Jack spent many a happy hour in the Mission listening to his unassuming first-hand stories of life in the air during the darkest days of the war. These times counterbalanced the equally harrowing first-hand stories of wartime life at sea. Although still young enough

THIS PLAQUE COMMEMORATES THE SAILING OF
THE SIX PLYMOUTH COMPANY VESSELS
CARRYING SETTLERS FROM CORNWALL, DEVON AND DORSET
TO ESTABLISH THE SETTLEMENT OF NEW PLYMOUTH
IN THE COLONY OF NEW ZEALAND.

WILLIAM BRYAN	BARQUE 312 TONS	SAILED 19 NOVEMBER 1840
AMELIA THOMPSON	BARQUE 477 TONS	SAILED 25 MARCH 1841
ORIENTAL	BARQUE 506 TONS	SAILED 2 JUNE 1841
TIMANDRA	BARQUE 382 TONS	SAILED 2 NOVEMBER 1841
BLENHEIM	BARQUE 374 TONS	SAILED 2 JULY 1842
ESSEX	BARQUE 329 TONS	SAILED 3 SEPTEMBER 1842

UNVEILED BY THE LORD MAYOR OF PLYMOUTH
COUNCILLOR GORDON DRAPER
AND HIS WORSHIP THE MAYOR OF NEW PLYMOUTH
D.L.LEAN, J.P. ESQ.
ON THIS 25TH DAY OF JULY 1988

Plymouth plaque

to yearn for the imagined excitement of the derring-do of wartime life, Jack well understood the anguish, fear and horror of wartime active service – particularly in the Merchant Navy – and was thankful that he was eight years too late to have participated.

The *Port Auckland* left New Plymouth bound for Wellington to continue her loading schedule – and during the ten-day stop at Wellington the weather was completely dry, much to everyone's delight. So on this particular visit the hatch tents – canvas hatchway covers hauled up in the middle by a cargo runner and secured on the outside of the hatch coaming – did not see the light of day.

In Port Nicholson at the same time as the *Port Auckland* was the dainty 7,179-ton *Port Montreal*, built in 1954. This attractive and well-proportioned vessel had been, as her name would suggest, built for a rather different trading route to the majority of the vessels of Port Line. In conjunction with the New Zealand Shipping Company, and Ellerman Bucknell Steamship Co. Line, Port Line had taken over the Australasian service of the Canadian National Steamships in 1936. This service, from Montreal to Australia and New Zealand, had its title abbreviated to MANZ Line, and in time the three companies built vessels specifically designed for those trade routes. In the case of Port Line, the vessels built for trading with the MANZ Line were smaller single-screw vessels with Canadian names. The crews, from the master down, were expected to remain with the vessels for a full two years of service, the maximum time allowed under the MOT Articles of Engagement. The only time that anyone could be paid off before two years was if the vessel had to return to a United Kingdom port for repair, survey or trading. When Jack was told of the length of time to be served aboard a MANZ Line vessel he decided that service aboard those vessels on that trade was not for him – six months on one vessel without leave was enough, he felt.

From Wellington, the *Port Auckland* made for Auckland, the final loading port for this voyage. The return to Auckland was not quite like the previous visits made by Jack. It was raining, and raining heavily. This unseasonable weather meant that the final loading was disrupted, and the hatch tents were now a vital part of the cargo-handling operation, much to the annoyance of the deck crowd. Ashore, it was much the same as before – but wet. Jack did his usual Auckland things, but now added nightly phone calls to Timaru from the annex at the Queen Street Post Office. No parties any more – he was in love.

Eventually the downpours ceased, to be replaced with a very overcast sky. But it was dry at least, so the milk powder and casein could be loaded. Within nine days of loading the vessel was down to her marks, and with passengers and a doctor aboard she left the Hauraki Gulf and headed for the north-about route towards Panama.

The passage across the Pacific was quite uneventful, with only the regular lifeboat drill to break the monotony. The early days were occupied with the sailors stripping the cargo-handling gear and storing it for use when the vessel arrived in the English Channel. The mooring lines were stored for the trans-Pacific voyage until they were required at Panama. Within days of sailing, up went the canvas awnings and up went the canvas swimming pool – as at the same time out came the sugi mugi wads followed by the paint and brushes. Strange as it might appear to those not versed in the ways of the sea, even leaving from New Zealand it was quite a relief to the vessel's complement to get to sea and settle down to the routine of the voyage. In those days the Port Line vessels, apart from where the paint was the mast colour, were painted both outward and homeward bound; on some voyages this included the funnel as well as the bulkheads and bridge foreparts. This maintenance included chipping away the rust and painting various parts, including the fore and quarter decks, which were steel.

On arrival at the Balboa end of the Panama Canal, another rather brash pilot boarded the *Port Auckland* and yet again Captain Townshend – looking the archetype model of the British sea captain who commanded the sea and all in it, on it and around it – acted his part to perfection. With the pilot came the long-awaited mail from home; addressed to the individual aboard the vessel c/o Port Line Ltd at 88 Leadenhall St, London EC3, and forwarded to the ship's agent in Panama for delivery to the crew.

Once the vessel had entered the first of the locks, Jack collected his mail: a letter from his mother and one from his sister. Both letters, as usual, brought the welcome minutiae of their village life. However, something of greater interest to Jack was in his mother's letter. Much to his surprise, she recounted the details of a visit to the *Port Launceston* and the partaking of afternoon tea. Apparently she had received a letter from Leadenhall Street inviting her to inspect Port Line's new ship on her maiden trip to Avonmouth; Mother was, amongst her many roles, the president of the Women's Institute. In reply to invitation, Mother had accepted but asked if she could take a party from the Wraxall Women's Institute with her to the *Port Launceston*. By return of post a manager stated that the company would be delighted to welcome the party, but to avoid any risk they would be received on a non-cargo-working afternoon. Later, Mother had a letter from Cunard Line, the vessel's agents in Bristol, to tell her that subject to her agreement the visit to the *Port Launceston* would be on a given date at 2 p.m. at O shed, Royal Edward dock, Avonmouth.

On the appointed date and time Mother and her charges boarded the vessel, to be met by the master, who made them very welcome. He then handed the party over to the unfortunate fourth mate – the lowest form of deck officer life – and two apprentices, who took them all over the vessel, including the accommodation and the bridge, but with the exception of the engine room and holds. They were then taken back to the passengers' lounge, which in all probability was the dining saloon, for their afternoon tea, before they took their leave of the vessel. It appeared that the invitation was probably the result of Mother's original concern that any company named Port Line would be an organisation similar to those of her early years, namely Runciman, Reardon Smith, and the Nailsea Shipping Co – all of them shipping companies operating tramp ships regularly towed by her uncle's tugs. After the visit Mother wrote to the crew manager and the chairman to thank them for suggesting the tour of their, 'very fine and impressive ship', and commended the officer and apprentices who conducted the tour and, 'their courtesy to my group'.

After the transit to Colon, the *Port Auckland* refuelled at Curaçao then travelled through the Windward Islands and into the Atlantic Ocean heading for the English Channel, en route for Hull, to discharge wool for the Yorkshire mills. Within a day of passing the Azores, down came the awnings and down came the swimming pool, and the sailors began holystoning the teak decks with the lamp-trimmer's concoction of Teepol, caustic soda and his secret ingredient, plus copious amounts of sand. Unlike his first trip aboard the *Port Brisbane*, Jack was no longer on his knees with a small stone going around the deck ventilators; he was now at the end of a 5-foot pole, pushing the heavy stone backwards and forwards in line with his colleagues. Murdo, meanwhile, commanded the salt-water hose, washing off the teak decks after a delay for the caustic soda to take effect. It was hard work, and there were no overweight sailors to be found on the *Port Auckland*.

The usual 'Channels' occurred as in darkness the *Port Auckland* approached the pilot station at Brixham to embark the Channel pilot. A new experience for Jack was bypassing the Thames estuary to continue the voyage to Hull. On docking there, the first mate came to Jack and invited him back for the next voyage of the *Port Auckland*. But Jack explained that he could not rejoin the vessel because the time was up for him to take his examination for a Certificate of Competency as an efficient deck hand, EDH.

For the EDH exam, the candidates were required to demonstrate their ability to perform the tasks of a deck department rating: tying bends and hitches, splicing ropes and wires, rigging and using cargo-handling derricks, mooring a vessel, understanding the glossary of maritime terms, boxing the compass in quarter points, understanding helm orders and other watchkeeping duties. Jack had to produce his steering certificate from Captain Bailey of the *Port Brisbane*, and his eyesight certificate. The reason for the eyesight test was the need to competently perform lookout duties, mainly identifying the lights of other vessels at night, together with those of marker buoys and fixed lights ashore used for navigation.

Jack took his examination at the Mercantile Marine office at Prince Street, Bristol. On getting his certificate, No. 50342, Jack telephoned the clerk in Mr Lofthouse's office to see if he could do run jobs – short intra-continental trips – as relief crew until the *Port Auckland* returned. This was agreed, and he was sent to the *Port Pirie* at King George V Dock.

5

TSMV *Port Pirie*

In the middle of May Jack found himself on the pontoon looking up at his next vessel, the *Port Pirie*. Amid the cacophony of sound and the seeming mayhem of dock work in discharging the last of her cargo, he saw before him a solid-looking, no-nonsense vessel of square contoured accommodation with a lower hull shape not unlike that of the *Port Brisbane* and *Port Auckland*. The ship, of 10,535 tons with twin screws, had been built in 1947 by Swan, Hunter & Wigham Richardson Ltd at Wallsend-on Tyne, and named after Port Pirie in South Australia – which, like Port Lincoln, had been a famous wheat-loading port for the last of the sailing ships. Her career, like that of so many of her fleet sisters, was mundane, with no noticeable incidents to challenge her reputation as a valuable and capacious vessel serving her owners well.

On boarding her, Jack walked into a former colleague from the *Port Lincoln*. After the initial greetings, the conversation got around to the *Port Pirie*. Jack's colleague announced, 'I ain't staying 'ere to sign on. She's going to Antwerp to dry dock and 'ave her big survey. What in the *'ell* are you goin' to do in Antwerp for a month? And Lofty's goin' to be bosun. I ain't goin' to put up with 'e. 'E punches first and asks after – but 'e do pick yer up after, like.'

Jack digested these words and enquired how many trips his former colleague had served with Lofty.

The sailor replied, 'Oh, I ain't served with un, but 'is reputation I knows all about.'

Jack left him and went in search of the first mate. On finding him he presented his discharge book, which the mate studied closely, noting that Jack had been with Port Line since initial training. He suggested that now he was qualified Jack should take out a company contract. Such a contract gave the sailor or officer the guarantee of employment, and in return the company could send the person to whichever ship they chose for up to a two-year voyage. Jack simply said, 'Yes Sir.' He was then told to find the bosun and get his cabin key. He found the bosun, who turned out to be another former colleague – lamp-trimmer on Jack's home trade voyage aboard the *Port Lyttelton*.

After a few days of 'working by' the vessel under the doubtful management of the shore bosun, it was time for Jack to sign the Articles of Agreement for a home

TSMV *Port Pirie*

trade voyage anywhere from Norway to Spain. At this signing-on ceremony the almost inevitable pronunciation disagreement recurred between him and the crew manager. At the same meeting he was introduced to his new bosun and also to the master of *Port Pirie*, Captain L.J. Skailes. Perhaps, though, the word 'introduced' is not quite the right word for what turned out to be a menacing stare by Bosun Lofty and no more than a passing glance from Captain Skailes.

By 11:00 hrs that signing-on day, Bosun Lofty brought his men together and told them the make-up of the ten men, from boys to able seamen, for whom he was responsible. What his pugilistic abilities might be Jack was unsure, but the intended management of his men was decisive and absolute; he was to be obeyed with no questioning of his opinions, decisions and results by anyone. In the event, 'anyone' meant his superiors as well; Lofty was Lofty, and Heaven help anyone who forgot that fact.

With the litter of cargo handling cleared away from the decks of the vessel, and the derricks lowered and secured, the *Port Pirie* began her short voyage to Antwerp. By a stroke of luck, Jack was on the 12 to 4 watch, which began as the vessel left the locks and headed down the Thames. This was his first experience of proper watchkeeping, and his first two hours of watchkeeping duty was as lookout on the monkey island. From there it was possible to keep a good lookout from right ahead to two points abaft the beam. It was the duty of the lookout to report, via a voice pipe to the wheelhouse, all lights as they appeared. The dilemma for Jack was what exactly should he report – all the lights he could see? He began by doing just that; every one of the myriad lights which appeared he reported. But by the end of his first hour he was fed up with reporting lights and unilaterally decided to only report selected lights for the rest of his duty on the monkey island. No one came to rebuke him, and he decided that in the wheelhouse they were probably relieved that there was no longer the stream of reports from the lookout telling them what they could already see. The rest of his first watch was spent on standby on the bridge wing, as the quartermaster was on the wheel while under the river pilot. Being on the bridge wing was the best part of the watch, and it made the fiasco of his first hour as lookout but a distant memory.

After dropping the Thames pilot, the vessel was under the guidance of a Port Line North Sea pilot and, with only slightly fewer lights to contend with than in the river. But unlike in the Thames, where most of the vessels were travelling starboard to starboard, in the southern North Sea vessels were travelling in every direction – the navigator's nightmare, a maritime Piccadilly Circus. The following day the usual watchkeeping duties occupied Jack, with a brief spell on deck washing down some paintwork and having a lifeboat muster. At the Scheldt estuary the pilot came aboard to take the vessel to Antwerp. Jack was expecting the scenery to be as in illustrations of the Low Countries, but as they travelled up the river he saw that the surrounding country was not dissimilar to that of almost any river in Britain: flat and green with what appeared to be low hills in the distance.

On docking in Antwerp the vessel was taken over by the Belgian equivalent of dockyard mateys, and other than clearing up after docking there was little to do. Up to this point, the relationship between Lofty and his deck crew appeared to be quite convivial, with Lofty sharing a joke with his men. The image of a rough, tough bosun as portrayed by the chap Jack had met when he first boarded the vessel appeared not to be quite true. Certainly in the few days the men had been with Lofty, he had left them in no doubt who was in charge, and no one challenged his authority. To Jack, Lofty was polite and, unlike some other bosuns he had sailed with, was no bully.

It was summertime, and on the Continent it was hot. Lofty decided, in all probability with the mate's approval, to split his men into two groups, one group working in the mornings and the other in the afternoons, on a daily rotational basis. This generosity was totally unexpected, and the talk of the mess room was Lofty: under the circumstances, it was appropriate that he should be the toast of the mess room.

In the hot dry weather Jack and his watchmate made their way ashore, green countryside greeting them. Most of the Belgians spoke good English, and were only too pleased to direct Jack and his chum to the city, which was nearby – unlike some docks, where the nearest civilisation was a route-march away. When they arrived in Antwerp they were surprised to see trams running everywhere along cobbled main streets. In Bristol, the war had destroyed most of the cobbled streets and they had been replaced with tarmac, but the cobbles remained in Antwerp, which had probably suffered as much damage as Bristol in the war, or perhaps more. What appeared to be the main thoroughfare had a true continental fair all down the middle with many hundreds of people enjoying themselves. To Jack's eyes, this fine display of amusements made the fairs of England look pretty puny, and certainly very shabby by comparison with the Antwerp display.

On their return to the *Port Pirie* the story of the fair dominated the mess-room conversation, with a little exaggeration here and there for effect, Jack and his chum persuaded their colleagues to go to the fair that evening. The visit was a huge success, with what might be described as 'hairy-arsed ABs' squealing like adolescents as they tumbled around in the various death-defying rides; all this without a single alcoholic drink inside them. To Jack the whole experience was simply wonderful. He spent quite a bit of money on a rifle range – with real rifles, not the air rifles used in Britain. His large expenditure was in the hope of shooting a perfect bulls-eye and triggering a camera which took a photograph of the successful gunner. Jack had been brought up with guns in the countryside and thought himself a good shot; in his eleventh year at the local flower-show fair he had hit several bulls-eyes to win a box camera. However, at Antwerp his ego was severely tested when after nine or so shots at the target he failed to get his photo taken. Further humiliation followed when several girls, none older than about 14, had several photos taken. It was Jack's good fortune that no one from the *Port Pirie* was with him to witness his humiliation. When he did join up with the other men they were overjoyed to tell him of their wonderful adventures, and when they enquired what Jack had been up to, his exaggerated enthusiasm for the rides at the other end of the fair was a fine display of bravado cloaking his dismal failure as a shot.

On the Saturday Jack and some of the men walked into an area of tall trees between the docks and the city. To their surprise, inside the trees was what appeared to be a large lake with sandy beaches around it. The place was crowded, with everyone having a good time swimming and sunbathing. To the delight of Jack and the men, some very brief bikinis were on display: dozens of women, both young and more mature, were exposing lots of reasonably attractive flesh to the elements. The men from the *Port Pirie* soon made themselves comfortable in their underpants. No one appeared to bother about the substitute bathing trunks and, unlike the beaches at home, when people changed no one put a towel around themselves – they simply stripped off and put on their bikini or bathing trunks. Pleasingly, there was no false modesty here. Anyone putting a towel around them in the 'hop, skip and jump' associated with seaside changing in Britain would have drawn attention and probably laughter.

During the vessel's stay at Antwerp there were many visits to the lake, and it was on one such visit that the men decided to patronise a nearby café and bar. One of the men working there, speaking with a British accent, enquired which vessel Jack and his chums were from. When he was told the *Port Pirie*, he laughed and said that he had been with Port Line until, on a visit to Antwerp, he had fallen in love with a local girl and eventually married her. With her parents, the young couple had taken over the catering establishment. From then on there was a certain affinity between the crew of the vessel and the lakeside café.

The regular trips to town, particularly in the evenings, were always rounded off by a visit to the chip van en route back to the vessel. Jack thought the chips the most delicious he had ever tasted, and ate more than was good for him. From the chip van it was necessary to cross some lock gates over a waterway into Antwerp. Towards the end of the *Port Pirie*'s stay at Antwerp, Jack was crossing these gates when he glanced into the lock to find himself looking down at a craft well known to him: the Bristol Steam Navigation Company's *Hero* on her regular trade with the continent. Her berth in Bristol was at M shed, and when carrying wine on her service from Portugal she berthed at the quay head. This was the only Bristol vessel that Jack had seen from his home city in any of his travels.

With the survey work completed, the *Port Pirie* was taken from her berth to the brand-new graving dock. She was to be the first vessel to enter the dock, so she would test its facilities in preparation for the dock being formally opened by the King of the Belgians. It was a sunny Sunday afternoon and Jack was by the gangway when the master and his lady came into the alleyway and began the descent of the gangway. At that moment one of the several goose-necked ventilators situated along the scupper began to make what might be termed deep-throated bowel sounds, and promptly disgorged black fuel oil over the adjacent deck, down the vessel's side. The oil was believed to splash on the lady's white dress, and probably onto the master too. Perhaps worst of all, the fuel oil floating on the surface of the water produced a black tidemark around the pristine concrete and stonework of the new graving dock. The quartermaster on gangway duty rushed to the nearby ship's telephone to call the engine room while other sailors ran to the engine room to stop the pump. But the oil continued to flow from the ventilator, and a greasy junior engineer with a rather vacant expression appeared at the accommodation doorway with the sailors still shouting at him.

It was difficult to believe that even a junior engineer, when told of the incident by both the sailors and the quartermaster on the telephone, could be so mentally impaired as to waste time coming on deck to see his handiwork rather than turning off the pump. But now, with the realisation that he was solely responsible for the mess, the man swiftly returned to the bowels of the vessel and turned off the flow. Jack heard Lofty's bellow as he saw the desecration of his deck at the same time as the master made his way up the oil-spattered gangway. It was Jack's policy, under such fraught circumstances, to accord with the concept of discretion being the better part of valour, so he promptly removed himself to the isolation of his cabin – thankful that his half of the sailors' grouping was off duty. He never found out quite what happened to the engineer who had been pumping oil into a tank which was already full, leaving the graving dock with a black tidemark before the imminent arrival of the king. However, the mess room was full of so-called facts, together with much conjecture and untrammelled joy at the probable fate of the engineer.

The *Port Pirie* left her problems behind, as within 12 hours she sailed for London. There ended Jack's association with the vessel after a very enjoyable time at Antwerp – thanks to the kindness of Lofty, a gentleman amongst bosuns.

6

MV *Port Townsville*

Back in London, Jack met Alan, his chum from the *Port Lincoln*, to catch up, and in the course of the conversation Jack mentioned that he wanted to return to the *Port Auckland* if possible, but was unsure just where in the world she might be. Alan suggested that they might call in at the Port Line dock office and find out. They were met there by the dock office crew manager, who told them that she was en route to New Zealand.

'However' – he appeared to delight in the use of the word, as a near-smile crossed his otherwise rather dour countenance – 'it's fortunate that you've come here today. I need both of you for the *Port Townsville*.'

Alan explained that he had other plans. To the complete surprise of the friends the crew manager addressed Alan by name. As Alan had only twice worked for the company before the manager's memory was remarkable, if not infallible. However, he

MV *Port Townsville*

could not help himself having a dig at Jack for 'deigning to visit the humble dock office instead of going to Leadenhall Street for a vessel'. In order to enjoy a voyage again with his friend, Alan agreed to one voyage with Port Line before going to pastures new, and much bigger vessels. While Jack had a plain rail warrant to Newcastle upon Tyne, the crew manager gave Alan a warrant for a cosy overnight sleeper to the same destination.

At Hebburn, Jack joined *Port Townsville*, berthed on the outboard side of the new-build *Royston Grange*, which was fitting out after launching from a yard of R. & W. Hawthorn Leslie & Co. Ltd. Amongst the hustle and bustle of work and the smell of molten pitch aboard the *Royston Grange*, Jack stood and took in the sight of his new vessel. This 8,681-ton, 15.5-knot vessel was a single-screw, five-hatch vessel built by Swan, Hunter & Wigham Richardson on the Tyne in 1951. She was the first Port Line vessel to have an extended bridge deck containing a No 3 hatchway, with two deck cargo cranes on the after end of the hatch, instead of derricks. To Jack, the first impression was of a small handy vessel, especially when compared to the *Port Auckland*, *Port Brisbane* and *Port Pirie*.

He made his way to the first mate's cabin only to find that the man was ashore, so he presented his discharge book to the bosun. The first thing Jack noticed about his new bosun was his hands; they were as smooth and manicured as those of a clerk, a most unusual sight in any deck sailor. The bosun took his time studying the discharge book, then looking up said, 'It took you a long time to make EDH.'

Jack replied, 'I took the exam as soon as I could. The delay was caused by my voyages being longer than the minimum time for each rank.' This particular bosun clearly did not like being contradicted or shown to be wrong; he dismissed Jack with a long stare and, in a strong Geordie accent, an abrupt 'Be on deck at seven in the morning.'

Jack left the cabin, walked along the alleyway, and then retraced his steps to the bosun's cabin. 'I forgot to collect a cabin key,' he said.

The bosun replied, 'Not very bright are you?' and delved into his desk drawer before throwing a key at Jack. On catching it, Jack deliberately lengthened his 'Thank you,' then made his way to his cabin. In his time with Port Line Jack had served with some indifferent bosuns and some good ones, in particular, Murdo and Lofty. But this specimen of humanity occupying the bosun's cabin was, he concluded within ten minutes, the worst he had encountered by far.

However, all clouds have a silver lining – and for Jack that was his own single-berth cabin. Luxury indeed! Having collected his bedding he settled down in the peace and quiet of his quarters.

At dinner time he made his way to the mess room and found a few of his colleagues for the voyage ahead. They had joined that day or the previous day, so no one knew much about the vessel. Those who had been working were only engaged in minor jobs, as nothing of substance could be achieved until the dockyard workers had left. In the mess Jack discovered that the bosun was commonly known as Geordie by virtue of –

judging by his accent – his birthplace. According to the assembled men Geordie was a force to be reckoned with and one not to be upset in any way. Jack thought, 'It's too late for me; this voyage, despite Alan sailing with me, is not going to be a bed of roses.'

The following day Alan arrived and Jack also met up with his new first mate. For the most part, mates are competent, courteous and usually smart of dress; Port Line would expect nothing less. But this mate was not very courteous and rather indifferent to sartorial appearance. But to give credit where it's due, he was a very competent mate who, despite his rank, could and would do everything that he expected his crew to do.

Geordie decided that the first job he would give Jack was the unenviable task of frapping the purchase and the topping lift of the jumbo derrick. This derrick is used for heavy lifts, in the *Port Townsville* 60 tons. When the derrick was rigged in its stowed position against the front of the mast it would have both the topping lift and the purchase held in situ with multi-strands of wire heavily greased. When the derrick was required some time after being rigged, rather than it being de-rigged, the topping lift and the purchase wires would be frapped – that is, bound in canvas or burlap and secured with heaving-line-sized rope. This was a filthy job, requiring the person on the job to rig a bosun's chair from the head of the derrick, then lower himself, with his legs clamped around the greasy wires, to wrap the covering around the purchase and the topping lift span, then tie the rope off every 2 feet down to deck level. By the end of the day, with his clothing covered in grease, Jack got to the deck to be met by his new first mate, who, with a very red complexion and a distinct Scottish accent, began their association with the words, 'You have more bloody grease on your rig than was on the fall … what sort of seaman are you?'

Jack was none too pleased to have his competence questioned, and his Somerset-born truculence came to the fore as he examined his ruined denim trousers, socks and shirt. He replied, 'How else can you do the job?' leaving a long rather insolent pause before adding, 'Sir.'

Without a word Mr Mate went over to the unused roll of burlap, fiddled under his jacket and produced a deck knife, then cut off several lengths of the material and wrapped it around his shoes and up his leg, then repeated the exercise over his other leg and up his trunk until he resembled an Egyptian mummy with a cap. The whole exercise took about six minutes, and Jack decided within the first minute that he had lost the argument. Mr Mate stood in front of Jack and said not a word. The silence, despite the almost overwhelming noise from various engineering activities in the vicinity, was profound until the mate finally posed the question and its answer in one word, 'Simple?'

'Yes, Sir,' came the reply with not the slightest tone of insolence.

Decluttering himself from the burlap, the mate said to Jack, 'Get yourself out of that lot.' Then, indicating Jack's filthy clothes, he continued, 'If Bose sees you like that

Jack with a sugi wad atop the wheelhouse

you're in for a well-deserved bollocking. And take your shoes off before you walk anywhere. Remember, son, I'm watching you.'

Whether the mate told Geordie about the incident Jack never knew, but he put on clean clothes and cleaned up the gear he had used, and when the bosun came around to inspect the job not a word was said: no complaints, no praise. Jack had been taught valuable lessons that afternoon. Firstly, to think about the work before embarking on the task: if he had thought to protect his clothes in the first place, the fracas with the first mate would not have happened.

Secondly, Jack realised that unkempt though the mate may have looked after wrapping burlap around himself, he was no patsy cutout of a Navy officer. He was a very competent working officer. Whether or not he would ever achieve command with Port Line was a matter of conjecture, but he was a first-class seaman by any standard.

At the weekend Alan and Jack went to South Shields. There they dined in an exotic restaurant and while Alan and others with them had a curry with all the trimmings, Jack, to their amusement, ordered not some foreign delicacy, but a British mixed grill. Alan was used to Jack, wherever he was in the world, ordering mixed grill. This phenomenon, Alan told the others, he had first noticed back in *Port Lincoln* days, in the Dutch restaurant in Melbourne.

Jack was determined to buy himself a new camera to record his adventures at sea; his original camera, won at a fair many years before and sold to his brother to take away on his honeymoon, was long gone. With the men trooping after him, Jack went into a camera shop and bought himself a Zeiss Ikon, which accompanied him on all his future voyages. The first shot was taken on the following Monday morning as Jack sugied the top of the wheelhouse.

The pattern of work continued with, amongst other things, Jack learning just how Bosun Geordie had such clean, well-manicured hands: he would not deign to involve his hands in any manual tasks, and if there was the slightest risk of getting them dirty, a pair of gloves was always to hand. The other peculiarity Jack noted was that as the bosun walked his arms and hands were held well away from his body, with the fingers constantly flicking each other as if to remove some sticky substance between them – a strange habit.

Occasionally Alan and Jack would go ashore in the evening. Going ashore in the daylight was fine, but returning in the dark was quite a hazard as their route took them across the unfinished deck of the *Royston Grange*. At that stage of the fitting out her metal deck had a series of studs welded onto it, ready for wooden planking. Jack spent his time trying, and mostly failing, to negotiate these studs and in the process taking large chunks out of his shoes. This was his lasting memory of the *Royston Grange*, built for Houlder Line to service its refrigerated cargo trade with South America. Her sister vessel was the *Hardwicke Grange*, and a fine pair of vessels they were. The *Royston Grange* was later tragically lost with all hands.

Eventually the *Port Townsville* was ready for sea and the various duties were allocated. At harbour stations Jack was in charge of the for'ard back spring mooring wire, assisted by an ordinary seaman and a deck boy. The watchkeeping rota ensured that Alan and Jack were not on watch together; there was little reason to wonder why that might have been.

The vessel sailed for London to commence loading for South Africa and Australia. Within a fortnight all was battened down and the vessel, under the command of Captain J.S. Moate, put to sea, her first destination Las Palmas for bunkers. The weather was clement and the deck work of the vessel was carried out without interruption. The sugimugi wads were out in force before the paint brushes took over. Although the decks were of pitch pine, as opposed to the teak of the *Port Brisbane* and *Port Auckland*, the need for overall maintenance was similar, but while the teak required no dressing oil, the pine required oiling with a little red lead mixed in for a warm colour.

Las Palmas came and went, and the next stop was Durban. As the tropics approached, the usual canvas swimming pool and awnings were erected, and tropical kit was broken out. For Jack, with the exception of constant sniping by Geordie and the more vocal criticism from Mr First Mate, life was not too bad. One of the mysteries of the vessel was, as far as the deck crew were concerned, the almost unseen master. Rumour had it that he was not in the best of health, and that may have been the reason for this particular first mate being aboard: to stiffen the command structure.

While it was common for the first officers in the larger vessels to be on the bridge for harbour stations, it was not the usual practice in the case of the smaller vessels of the fleet. However, with the *Port Townsville* Mr Mate gave the impression that he was the commander of the vessel, and was always on the bridge for harbour stations. Such conduct and the unseen Captain Moate fuelled the rumours. Whenever Jack was in the wheelhouse, he never caught sight of the master – nor did he come across him with the inspections of the accommodation.

The *Port Townsville*'s arrival at Durban did not involve any heated verbal exchange between tug master and bosun as on the *Port Lincoln*; the tugs, although probably coal-fired, kept their smoke to themselves. Life ashore for Alan and Jack was visits to the cinema with a bit of sightseeing during daylight hours. The docks, as before, held vessels from Clan Line, Ellerman Lines, Bullard King and the inevitable Union Castle vessels, with a few British tramp vessels adding to the interesting make-up of British-registered vessels – never to be seen together again during Jack's career.

The voyage through the Southern Ocean was without abnormal seas and in general terms it was a comfortable trip to Melbourne. As on their voyage aboard the *Port Lincoln*, Alan and Jack visited the Dutch restaurant on several occasions, but for Jack the best part of the stay was when they went to the Melbourne racecourse, to a motor show. There, amongst the shiny vehicles on show, was a sight to lift his heart, a Bristol 405 – a very expensive aluminium-bodied supercar, a product of part of the Bristol Aeroplane Company.

Apart from the fact that to Jack it was a vehicle of impeccable pedigree, it brought back memories of his old school. Among the governors of his alma mater was Lady Verdon-Smith, lady wife of Sir Reginald Verdon-Smith, a nephew of the founder of the Bristol Aeroplane Company and the chairman of the company. As the aircraft company owned the Bristol car company, Sir Reginald naturally owned one of the vehicles, a Bristol 303. At the school speech day, a treat for senior prize-winners was the opportunity of a short drive in Sir Reginald's Bristol. To the surprise of all concerned, in his final year at school Jack was for the first time the recipient of a senior prize, and duly went for a ride with Sir Reginald – an experience never forgotten.

Melbourne was done and dusted, and the *Port Townsville* headed for Sydney, where the foundations of the Sydney Opera House were taking shape. Two matters dominated the stay as far as Jack was concerned. One evening the crew decided to have a party, and the local nurses' home, as was the custom, would provide some girls to lift the hearts (and sometimes some other bits) of the poor downtrodden sailors. But the officers had arranged a cocktail party, and unknown to either of the organisers, the starting time for both occasions was identical.

Jack was given the task of welcoming the nurses to the vessel. At five minutes before the appointed time he made his way along the alleyway to the top of the gangway and leaned on the bulwark surveying the quay wall, looking for his partygoers. On the for'ard side of the gangway and over the bulwark leaned the mate, also looking along the quay wall.

'Why are you loitering here?' was the question from the mate as he looked towards Jack.

'I'm waiting for some nurses, Sir,' was the reply.

'Why?' was response.

Jack told him that the sailors were having a party.

With that, a rather large party of females appeared to be walking purposefully towards the vessel. Jack thought, 'We can't handle all these women,' just as Mr Mate straightened up and, indicating the approaching women, said to Jack, 'Don't think all of those are yours. Some are for cocktails.'

Jack, not too sure how to reply, took the plunge, and enquired, 'How would I know which ladies are for each of the parties, Sir?'

The mate looked at Jack as if the lad was simple and said, 'Very easy son; ours, for the officers wear gloves; they're the ladies. Yours are simply women – but there again, when they're undressed, I suppose they're all much the same.'

By now a junior officer had joined his boss at the gangway and he escorted the officers' ladies up to the luxurious officers' quarters, while Jack took their noticeably younger 'women' along to the vessel's recreation room, where the doubtful entertainment began with jiving to the sounds of Elvis and others at their finest. The chucking-out time for visitors was 23:00 hrs, and by then many temporary associations had been cemented – just until sailing-day dawned. However, despite his charm and belief that all women would swoon at the very sight of him, Jack found that the female he had set his eyes with nefarious intentions in mind was unresponsive to his advances. Eventually, in the seclusion of his cabin – with more than necessary leg displayed to get Jack's hormones working overtime – she announced, 'My girlfriend wouldn't like me to go any further – sorry!'

Jack, ever conscious of the courtesies that his background and social position should display, said nothing as she got dressed again, and after at least an hour's small talk he escorted her with her chums to the gangway. Presumably one of those was her girlfriend – but which one could it be? Amongst the rest of the sailors someone must have experienced the same dilemma as Jack – but which one? Despite this being his fifth deep-sea voyage it would appear that Jack was in some matters as naïve as a first-tripper. As the men trooped back to the recreation room to finish off the beers, Jack asked the assembled throng, 'Who's been short-changed by the lesbo?' and recounted his recent experience. The derision from his colleagues was quite deafening, and on occasion the topic was brought to light during the rest of the voyage. Jack never discovered who the other disappointed sailor was. Whoever he was, he certainly was smarter – by a mile – than Jack.

'Who did this?' enquired the very irate first mate as he pointed to the bulkhead of the crew alleyway leading to their cabins. He continued, 'I want all of them on deck now.' Bosun Geordie, with a Cheshire cat expression and unable to disguise his glee – not that he would want to – went into the sailors' accommodation and mustered everyone outside the alleyway door. When the eight ABs, two ordinary seamen, two deck boys and four quartermasters were lined up, the officer pointed his shaking finger inside the doorway and demanded that whoever was responsible must step forward.

Alan stepped forward and declared, 'It was me. For an accommodation bulkhead, it's filthy and needs sugi-ing.' He offered no word such as 'Sir' – with no deference to rank expressed or implied.

'Oh, it's *you* again, is it?' said the mate, and dismissed everyone else. As the men made their way to their various duties they, without exception, looked inside the doorway and there the grime-stained accommodation bulkhead carried the legend: 'Please clean me.'

The general consensus was along the lines of 'about bloody time' amongst the men who lived down that alleyway. On the deck outside the doorway, as the officer read the riot act, Bosun Geordie held his – very rarely seen – smile, and with ever more flicking of his immaculate fingers he obviously savoured every minute of Alan's discomfort. Little did Geordie realise that Alan was not in the least discomfited by either him or by Mr First Mate. The officer then went to Alan's cabin. This was without a doubt in the hope that he would find something unkempt or in need of cleaning. But Alan's cabin was, as always, immaculate, and in sheer frustration at not finding anything out of order, the mate expressed his bile through the almost Messianic gleam in his eyes as they fell on the water carafe holder by the bunk. It was minus one of its two glasses. With commendable restraint in not laughing, Alan – in his usual laid-back style – patiently explained that as the cabin only accommodated one person only one glass had been issued. Determined to have the last word, the mate ordered the bosun to ensure that Alan washed all the offending words and the grime off the bulkhead: 'Now.'

Geordie needed no second bidding and ordered Alan to do so. Again he was frustrated when Alan responded, 'Not before time, Bosun; the pleasure's all mine.'

The disputes with Mr Mate continued at the destination: Newcastle, New South Wales. The vessel arrived in the port at 10 a.m. on a Sunday morning. The Articles of Agreement – the document that controlled the activities and conduct of a vessel's crew and the obligations and responsibilities of the ship owner – contained the terms of employment. Amongst these terms were the hours of duty and the conditions of that duty relating to working time at a weekend. Both Alan and Jack had completed their duty watch before they were called to harbour stations, so unless the vessel was in danger, then the rest of that day – in this case, Sunday – was their own.

Mr Mate decided that he wanted the apron – the upper, white-painted, part of the bow – sugi'd and painted, paying overtime for the men to do the job. But as overtime was voluntary, both Jack and Alan declined. Bosun Geordie promptly reported this refusal to his boss, who then appeared in the accommodation to find the two miscreants. With a contorted face like a very red – bordering on purple – balloon, he found Jack and Alan in the mess room having a light libation. He threatened them with almost every kind of punishment he could think of for disobedience and refusal to obey a lawful order. Both men independently thought it best not to interrupt the discourse until the officer eventually ran out of steam and supported himself on the table, trying to get his breath back.

Eventually, when his eyeballs had returned to their sockets, and the vein running down his temple no longer looked like quite such a tree branch on his forehead, Alan took a long deep breath and quietly informed Mr Mate that overtime was not compulsory unless the vessel was in peril; they had both done their watches prior to the vessel arriving at Newcastle, and as it was a Sunday in port, then anyone, unless on duty, was entitled to the day off. The officer looked at Jack and, almost word for word, repeated what he had said to Alan. As Jack locked the eyes with the mate, the officer's face began to colour up again, along with the emergence of the bulging eyes and the thick vein on the forehead.

'Are you going to obey an order?' the officer enquired of Jack.

Jack replied – but with, unlike Alan, a couple of 'Sirs' thrown in – 'As I understand the situation, Sir, you can invite me to do overtime, but unless there is a danger to the vessel you cannot order me to do overtime once my hours of duty are completed. Sir.'

The first mate continued to stare at Jack without saying a word. At that moment someone opened the door at the far end of the accommodation alleyway and sunlight streamed down the alleyway; a shadow appeared, cast by someone by the open mess-room door. Not for the first time the object skulking – believing that he was out of sight – was Bosun Geordie, listening, and no doubt enjoying the roasting being handed out by the irate officer.

Still the officer's wordless stare continued, until Jack broke the impasse by suggesting that the matter should be taken up with Captain Moate. The name broke the spell and no further threats were made. The mate turned and left the mess room with the parting words, 'There will be no further overtime for you two this voyage.' And then looking at Jack he continued, 'Who in the hell are you to understand the situation? You're a sailor, and a poor example at that – a nobody.'

Jack and Alan remained aboard for lunch, then made their way ashore to the Newcastle of the southern hemisphere. Like the city it was named after, Newcastle was a major coal-exporting port and was busy with an assortment of tramp vessels either loading or waiting to load bulk cargoes destined for Japan, North America and Europe. Newcastle has a very pleasant beach, which on that Sunday afternoon was well populated. Jack had his swimming trunks with him and was soon in the sea and enjoying every moment. But in this long and perfect beach, just under the tideline, is a football-sized rock, and with little effort on his part, Jack managed to land hard on this lump. This decided him to abandon his swimming, nurse his damaged knee and relax on the beach. No sooner had he settled down than he espied a group of young ladies dressed in what could only be described as bits of cloth barely covering what was necessary. As they then disported themselves in the water, Jack – just like a dog after a bone and with no concern about his alleged most recent serious injury – was back in the water, doing his best to get as near the girls as he could.

After a brief time he had isolated one girl from the pack and he gave her what, at his age, he mistakenly believed was the benefit of his undoubted charm, wit and magnificently toned body. The girls emerged from the sea and sprawled on the beach; in the presence of such beauty Jack was in paradise. The girl turned out to be a nurse in the hospital overlooking the beach, where she would be on duty from 6 p.m. that day. The making of a date was uppermost in Jack's mind as he prepared to kiss and say goodbye. The beauty was eager to further their relationship the following evening on the beach with one condition: that Jack would donate blood on the Monday at 4 p.m. He had never done that before, but with the chance of furthering his romantic vision, he cheerfully agreed, and their parting was like a scene straight out of *Gone with the Wind*.

The following day, Jack turned to at 7 a.m. to prepare the vessel for cargo handling. The bosun kept his distance from both Alan and Jack. Breakfast came and went, and the sailors got on with whatever duties were required of them. Jack realised that he still had one hour's work to do after his 4 p.m. blood session. Without the slightest embarrassment he approached the bosun and told him that he needed to be at the hospital at 4 p.m. as the local hospital needed his blood.

'See the mate,' was the instruction from Geordie.

Jack thought about the likely reception from the first mate as he made his way to the office. It was pointless knocking on its thick teak weather doors as no one would hear and the damage to the knuckles could be painful. So Jack coughed loudly and put his head through the door – to be closely confronted by the face of the mate about to exit the office. This sudden appearance startled Jack and, judging by the officer's quick back-step, him as well.

'Yes?' came the question from the mate in a surprisingly moderate tone of voice when he faced his antagonist of the previous day. Jack regained his composure and asked if he could have an hour off.

'Why?' asked the mate, still with an unsettling conciliatory tone to his voice.

'I've been asked to donate blood at the hospital at 16:00 hrs, Sir,' Jack told him.

'Tell the bosun I've agreed. When you return, or before we sail, I want to see a record that you did donate blood. Understood?'

With the permission still ringing in his ears, Jack told the bosun that he had the mate's permission and would need to be off the vessel by 15:30 hrs. Plainly Geordie did not believe that permission had been granted for time off, particularly after the Sunday fracas, and shot into the mate's office only to exit the office door with a noticeably dejected look.

A quick wash and change of clothes, and Jack was ashore, heading to the hospital. He donated his blood, not exactly thinking of it being for a good cause, but in lustful anticipation of the evening with the – by now – love of his life. In the evening, with extra foo-foo powder about him, he headed ashore to find and collect his female payment-in-kind for his generous bloodletting gesture that afternoon. But neither his payment-in-kind, nor sight nor sound of his 'new true love' was found. A very dejected and totally humiliated Jack returned to the *Port Townsville* thinking how he could conceal being hoodwinked by the nurse into giving blood without his just reward. He need not have worried, though, as no one asked except Alan, and his lips were sealed. However, the fact that Jack did not go ashore in Newcastle for the rest of the vessel's stay did raise some speculation in the mess that all was not well with his romantic life – but in the end, with the benefit of a day to get over his lost love, Jack decided that all is fair in love and war. Onward to his next conquest was the most positive thought he could muster at Newcastle that November day.

As the *Port Townsville* was manoeuvring to moor at Hamilton Wharf on the Brisbane River, the first mate found his voice and directed his bile towards Jack, who was yet again in charge of the for'ard back spring mooring line, with his two assistants to straighten out the kinks in the wire. As the vessel approached the wharf in the fast-flowing current Mr First Mate appeared to be in command, as from the deck there appeared to be no sight of Captain Moate. Leaning over the port bridge wing with the pilot, the officer shouted to the bow party, 'Get that head rope ashore.' But in throwing the heaving line to the hobblers ashore the sailor made a mess of it and the monkey's fist on the end of the line plopped into the river until pulled inboard, made up and thrown again. During this hiatus in getting the head-line ashore, the mate was clearly heard on deck as he ranted and raved about the quality of his seamen who were, 'totally unable to throw a bloody heaving line one foot without buggering it up.'

The second try was successful; the line was heaved ashore and the eye placed over the bollard. As that was completed the hobblers made their way aft until adjacent to Jack and his spring party. From the irate mate came the very clear order to 'get that spring ashore'. Jack took the coiled line in his left hand and with a mighty throw sent the monkey's fist hurtling towards the hobblers. It fell short and, like the other heaving line from the foredeck, dropped limply into the river. While Jack was quickly pulling in and making up the line again, the formerly reasonably irate mate became incandescent with rage. Judging by the language he used, this seemed to be firstly because the line had fallen short and secondly because it was Jack who had failed so miserably. The language directed at Jack was interrupted by the need to order half astern, and as the engine-room telegraph in the wheelhouse rang its instruction to the engine-room control flat, the stream of vitriol from the bridge continued to rain down on the for'ard back spring group. With the second throw, owing much to strength of arm and some undoubted help from the Almighty, the line reached the hobblers, and the eye was secured around a bollard roughly abreast of where the gangway would be placed.

'Hold that spring!' came the order to Jack from the bridge wing. Almost immediately came the next decision from on high: 'Slack the spring', closely followed by 'Hold the spring' again. As the vessel was pulled alongside the berth by the geometric position of the wire, yet another broadside came from the mate, 'Don't part that spring.' As the forward motion of the vessel was checked by the spring wire it became bar-taut, so Jack allowed a foot or two of slack on the wire: 'Don't ease that spring until I tell you – *do you understand*?' One minute the mate did not want the wire to be parted and in order to prevent that happening Jack had allowed a very slight slacking, only to be told 30 seconds later not to slacken it!

Eventually the *Port Townsville* was properly moored at Hamilton Wharf – and on his way to the mess room, who should Jack meet up with? None other than the still puce-faced first mate: 'Where do you think you're going?'

Jack replied, 'To the mess, Sir, for breakfast.'

Mr Mate informed him that he was going to No 2 hatch, there to be taught how to throw a heaving line properly. As they walked towards the hatch, Jack had the stomach-turning vision of the gloating bosun telling him how to throw. On arrival at their destination Jack saw that there was no one else there.

'Get yourself a line and come here,' instructed the mate in a calm tone, unlike the demented screeching of half an hour before. Jack armed himself with a nearby heaving line, and seeing the mate take off his uniform jacket realised that it was he, the mate, who would provide the instruction. Other than two complaints from the assembled stevedores who were about to start work, concerning the monkey's fists falling amongst them, the instruction on the technical making-up of the heaving line and the despatch of the same ashore was instructive and yet again demonstrated the qualities of Mr Mate as a first-class seaman. The only difficulty was that he took several attempts at analysing Jack's arm motion before belatedly realising that he was left-handed. Satisfied that Jack should now be able to send a heaving line ashore at the first attempt the mate turned on his heel, collected his jacket and walked away from Jack. He then hesitated, turned around and said, 'You've made me late for breakfast – but what else can I expect from a cack-handed object such as you?'

Jack thought it politic to stay silent, even though his own breakfast would be cold, or taken away altogether. As he followed the mate along the alleyway, dodging the swarm of stevedores streaming aboard, the thought came to him that he had moored the *Port Townsville* six times before without any complaint from above. He accepted that the first mate had to calm himself down by picking on someone. Since Newcastle, it had been him or Alan, and this time it was him.

For the next fortnight when moving the vessel from one processing plant to the next, and sometimes back again, Jack was still subject to the wrath of the mate as the *Port Townsville* was moored – sometimes port side to, sometimes starboard side to – up and down the Brisbane river. During these manoeuvres Jack never failed, even once, to get the heaving line ashore at the first attempt, but the mate always found something to rant about concerning the for'ard back spring party not doing something correctly.

When a rumour circulated in the mess rooms that the master had cut off the mate's supply of gin by forbidding one of the apprentice officers to buy the mate a daily bottle, the opinion was that the drying out of Mr Mate was the cause of his recent erratic behaviour. Jack failed to get to the bottom of this allegation, but he did notice that the irascible officer was worse than ever in recent times. Notwithstanding that, he was still, in Jack's eyes, a first-class seaman.

Later, as Alan and Jack were trying to decide how to spend their day off, 'Shall we go upstream?' asked Alan. Upstream turned out to be a river trip to the famous Lone Pine Koala Sanctuary. Ashore they went, and caught the boat to take them upriver, through the remarkable Australian bush until they arrived at a jetty and entered the sanctuary. Although he had seen many pictures of these marsupial bears, a real one had never crossed Jack's path during his two previous trips to Australia. Here in Queensland, he was able to hold a koala: an experience akin to holding a few pounds of wire wool. The impression is that their coat is soft, but the one he held was anything but soft, with some very sharp claws as needed for climbing gum trees to forage for – to the koala – delicious eucalyptus leaves. The sanctuary was exactly that, a place of safety for these threatened animals, which had had to contend with the loss of their habitats by forest fires and with the widespread depredations caused by mankind, including diseases from humans.

The return boat trip back to Hamilton Wharf was just as interesting as the trip upriver, but when the friends returned to their vessel and related their experiences to their colleagues they were met with derision by some sections of the mess room.

'What the bleedin' 'ell did you go there for?' was the first question, closely followed by, 'Bit of a waste of time going to look at animals, wasn't it? There's plenty of pelicans 'ere if you wants to see animals.'

Alan turned and went to his cabin as Jack told his two main antagonists, 'You're right. Why would I pay to look at animals when I work with you two?' He continued, 'By the way, a pelican has webbed feet; work it out for yourself.' As he was about to exit the mess room very smartly after deriding several of the occupants, he realised that they had not even noticed that he had insulted them. Instead of the odd punch, plate of food thrown at him or uproar, he left the mess to the sound of a mimicking voice intoning his words: 'A pelican has webbed feet, work it out,' followed by, 'Bloody smart arse, proper know-all-dick.'

Just before the *Port Townsville* left the berth at Brisbane, several boxes, unloaded from an armoured car, were stored in the vessel's strong room in the fo'c'sle bulkhead, clearly visible from the bridge. Rumour had it that they contained valuables being repatriated to wherever they had come from during the Pacific war.

The *Port Townsville* left Brisbane bound for Port Alma, the port for Rockhampton. On arrival just after daybreak, the deck crew and officers were again attacked by swarms of sandflies, so when the vessel was moored everyone on deck made a mad rush for the safety of the accommodation and scratched themselves over breakfast. With the sun rising after breakfast, the men were able to get the vessel ready for loading. At this port, the sailors had to open the hatches and remove the insulating plug hatches on the refrigerated cargo hatches. It was an unenviable task, particularly at on completion of loading each day, when these plugs had to be replaced.

Port Alma was just a jetty in the middle of a swamp, and both the cargo and the dockworkers were brought to the vessel by train from Rockhampton. The only recreation

Jack and Alan enjoyed was the nightly 'barbie' on the jetty, where the fare ranged from the very best beefsteak to crayfish, cooked over 45-gallon drums. The officers and crew joined in without anyone pulling rank, and everyone had the opportunity to be the chef. So during the vessel's relatively short stay at Port Alma, Port Line must have saved quite a bit of money on food. The proof of the quality of the café on the jetty was that no effort was made by the ship's cooks to take on the duties of chef.

From Port Alma the vessel made her way to her namesake town of Townsville, but there was little social life there. Jack wouldn't let Alan persuade him to buy a girlfriend-losing jacket and trousers again, and decided that his life in Townsville would be just the occasional wander around town; he viewed it as a true Queensland semitropical frontier experience, and enjoyed the ambience of the town and the area.

However, the next port – Cairns in the far north of Queensland – was even better than Townsville, in that Jack felt he really *was* on the edge of the jungle. The attractiveness of the area was enhanced by the flora and fauna of the town, with its raised sidewalks and permanent awnings, mixing into the surroundings. As in New Zealand, Jack found that it was the friendly local population which made the whole North Queensland experience so memorable.

From Cairns, the *Port Townsville* made her way through the Great Barrier Reef. It was decided that the strong room should be painted out, so the boxes were dumped alongside No 2 hatch coaming and the painting began. After two days they were returned to the strong room before being taken out again, to be discharged, along with the Barrier Reef pilot, to a vessel from Thursday Island. Jack wondered what would happen to the mate and his career should the valuables have suddenly found themselves in a warm watery grave on a dark night. He shook his head, mused for a moment and smiled to himself as the thought crossed his mind …

The vessel crossed the Arafura and Timor seas before entering the mighty Indian Ocean, setting a course for Aden, for bunkering. En route a message was received from the owners that on the advice of the British government the vessel should make for Djibouti instead; at Aden there was an insurrection. From the mess-room scuttlebutt it emerged that none of the sailors had berthed at Djibouti before and the general opinion was that it might be more welcoming than Aden – although the delight was tempered by the fact that the area was administered by France, which was not the favourite nation to get involved with, according to the sages of the mess.

The *Port Townsville* arrived at Djibouti in the late afternoon, and it looked much the same as any other bunkering port in the tropics. After dinner Alan and Jack went ashore and were fascinated to pass the houses of French colonials and watch them eating, for everyone passing to see, with their many Somali servants in attendance. On arrival in the town centre they found a great many beggars with distorted limbs, many of them able to speak English and all of them vying to tell of their distress, and their dozens of relatives and countless children who depended on the meagre income from 'nice Englishmens'.

When surveying the many bars and drinking dens, Alan and Jack came across several men from their vessel who, despite the short time between going ashore and meeting the two, already knew the ins and outs of every premises selling alcohol. When the sailors congregated to swap ideas for the evening's entertainment – ranging from whoring to drinking themselves under whatever table was at hand – a circle of beggars formed around them, literally barging into them on their home-made trolleys. The sailors broke free with much shouting, swearing and substantial kicks; it was remarkable to see most of the distorted limbs straightening out and speeding the beggars out of range of the fists and feet of the enraged men of the *Port Townsville*.

Alan and Jack, still looking for a suitable watering hole, moved on, only to see ahead of them a catering boy from *Port Townsville*. This particular boy exhibited decidedly effeminate tendencies, and towards the end of the voyage around the Australian coast the friends attempted to warn the boy of the many pitfalls associated with the path that he appeared to be taking. In order to show him a more positive heterosexual life they took him under their wing when ashore, and to their satisfaction the boy did begin to take a more positive view of women, and turned away from his rather unsavoury association with older men. The lad had assured Alan and Jack that he intended to remain aboard the vessel while she was in Djibouti, so under the impression that the boy was safely aboard the vessel, they found it a surprise to see him ashore, surrounded by Arabs. The friends soon rescued him and gave him a severe lecture on the dangers to which he was exposing himself. With the boy in tow, they continued their reconnoitre. Their second surprise of the evening came when they saw Captain Moate and the chief engineer in full tropical uniform, drinking at a table by the very dusty road; apart from their surprise at seeing the master ashore, the fact that they saw the master at *all* was remarkable. Eventually they found a bar free of beggars, settled down to a drink or three, and watched the world go by. A convivial evening ashore was had by all, but it was noticeable that their protégé was somewhat the worse for wear, so they returned to the vessel and put him to bed. On the long trek back to the port at 10:30 p.m. they saw that the French colonials who had been enjoying their repast at 6 p.m. were still eating, with their servants still in attendance.

The jetty was a long one because the water was so shallow, but eventually they reached the gangway and went aboard. As Jack stepped off the gangway, his foot came into contact with something soft which let out a yelp. After recovering from his fright, Jack found the prone body of one of the ABs. After much huffing and puffing the fellow was hauled to his feet; he was very wet and very drunk. It turned out that the fool had swum, in the shark-filled waters, from the beach to the end of the jetty, then climbed onto the jetty and up the gangway, only to collapse drunk and exhausted at the top. When he was able to talk his only concern was that he had left his very expensive pair of shoes on the beach. Alan and Jack left him in the less than capable hands of the duty quartermaster and put the catering boy to bed. Then they went back to the gangway to help their colleague to his cabin, but there was no sign of him. They found the quartermaster, who told them that the sailor, still concerned about his shoes, had jumped over the side to swim ashore and rescue his footwear. The man made it to the beach, collected his shoes and was spotted by some of his colleagues who brought – or perhaps dragged – him back to their vessel.

Jack and Alan made their way to the mess room for some of the cook's cold collation to soak up some of the spirits. No sooner had they settled down to their midnight repast than they were summoned to the after end of the starboard alleyway, where they found the catering boy sitting stark naked under a torrent of salt water from the fire hydrant on the deckhead. Although the boy now appeared to be reasonably sober, he was in a fighting mood, his Glaswegian voice heard near and far. However, a good slapping soon dissipated his temper, and for the second time the friends locked him in his cabin. In the morning the boy told the chums that he wanted to pursue his former lifestyle as a rent boy, which he had led since he was 12 years of age, allegedly getting ten shillings a time. The chums realised that their intrusion, albeit well-intentioned, into the boy's way of life was doomed, and probably had been from the start, and that the boy being amongst 70 men made their task impossible. With that realisation their Good Samaritan impersonation was at an end – for good.

From French Somaliland the *Port Townsville* made her way through Suez to the Mediterranean. She left Port Said in the evening – and the following morning she was twisting, turning and plunging in the most ferocious storm Jack had encountered in this normally clement sea. As the vessel had left Suez she had entered the eastern limit of a severe meteorological depression, spreading from the Azores to the Barents Sea, and probably because of the relatively shallow waters of the Mediterranean, the storm's effects seemed to Jack as bad as any he had experienced in the Roaring Forties. While the swells might not have been as mountainous as those of the Southern Ocean, the waves were vicious in the extreme. The movement of the vessel was so severe that whenever Jack was on the wheel he found Captain Moate in the wheelhouse, day and night, sitting in the lashed-down pilot's chair.

On the final hour of the 04:00–08:00 hrs watch Jack took over the wheel. Apart from the sea state and the incessant severe motion of the vessel, the visibility was very much restricted by spume from the waves and the murky overcast sky. Looking around the wheelhouse, he noticed that the pilot's chair did not contain Captain Moate. Turning to the officer of the watch, the relieving third mate, he enquired as to the whereabouts of the master.

'Gone to freshen up and have breakfast,' was the reply as the mate ran between studying the radar screen and combing the non-existent horizon through the clear view rotating disc in the wheelhouse window.

The *Port Townsville* was really testing Jack's steering capability, and the vessel often found the sailor wanting as he fought to prevent her from yawing too much, in an all

The calm of the Red Sea

but futile attempt to maintain the course. Then the third mate, after one of his brief glances at the radar repeater, dashed to the window, then turned toward Jack and shouted, 'Hard a-starboard!'

Jack spun the wheel to starboard – and in from the chartroom rushed the first mate, who almost screamed, '*Belay that!* Wheel amidships – hold her steady, *very* steady.' The third mate was standing by the engine-room telegraph as the first mate kept repeating, 'Steady, steady, hold your course, for Christ's sake hold her.'

With his eyes fixed on the gyro repeater compass, Jack, in those milliseconds of order and counter-order, had no idea what was happening.

'Steady, boy, steady,' came from the senior officer again, and Jack took the opportunity to look up and see what the electric atmosphere was all about. Both officers were looking to port, so he followed their gaze through the salt-stained port-hand wheelhouse door window, and became transfixed as, like a maritime wraith through the mist and spume and rain, a huge grey bow approached. It appeared to be approaching on a course parallel to that of the *Port Townsville*, seemingly only a few yards away, and heading for the port-hand bridge wing. Through the spume Jack could read the vessel's name: *Esso Bristol*. In that fraction of a second he knew fear, but it was the first mate's menacing Scottish voice which dissipated the fear again as he commanded, 'Nothing to port.' Fortunately for Jack, the mate had given the order without turning around to see his helmsman gazing not at the compass but out of the window.

In rapid succession, Jack operated the wheel, looked at the compass and glanced at the large grey hull as it slid past just a few feet away. At that moment the third mate rang on the engine-room telegraph, presumably to stop engines. The first mate turned quickly from the window, grabbed the handle of the telegraph and moved it back, with the double ring, to Full Ahead. 'I want all the power I can get,' he said to his subordinate as the telephone rang from the engine room, probably to enquire, 'What's going on?' That question went unanswered. The stern of the *Esso Bristol* went past the wheelhouse, and both officers' bodies almost deflated, whilst Jack, still seized with stomach-churning anxiety, continued to fight a losing battle with the Mediterranean. His tension manifested itself through the pain in his upper jaw; his teeth had been clamped together by sheer terror during those few brief minutes. Both officers looked at each other as Captain Moate, probably hearing the engine-room telegraph ringing, burst into the wheelhouse from the chartroom. Speaking to no one in particular, the first mate, with a stare that defied any argument, said, 'They didn't even *see* us – bloody tankers.' It crossed Jack's mind that in truth, the bridge staff of the *Port Townsville* had never seen the tanker approaching, either – so much for radar. The master and his chief officer disappeared into the chartroom as the second officer arrived to take over for the rest of the 04:00–08:00 hrs watch. He and his junior went into a huddle over the radar screen, talking about the likely conversation between the master and first mate in the chartroom.

After being relieved at the wheel Jack went to the mess room ready to recount his heroic action which had saved the vessel and in turn, their lives. When he had quite run out of breath after sharing his dramatic story, he looked around him and – not for the first time – he found that no one had taken a bit of notice. His moment of glory had failed miserably. No one had noticed anything to be breathless about; a few had heard the engine-room telegraph ringing, but had thought nothing of it … what crisis? The interest of the men in the mess room was summed up by 'Aw, shuddup.'

There was no cessation of the storm as the *Port Townsville* continued her passage towards Gibraltar and while she was battered, she was better off than several other vessels – mostly small but one large – that were sunk, with loss of life. Out in the Atlantic Ocean the weather was little better, but the wind and sea, now on the beam, made the vessel roll ever more dramatically. Past Cape St Vincent, up through Biscay, past Cape Finisterre, across the mouth of the English Channel, and onward through St George's Channel the gale continued, eventually blowing the *Port Townsville* towards the Mersey.

'Chief wants you now,' the bosun said to Jack, with a look of a triumph. The vessel was one day from berthing at Liverpool, and this was the time when the first mate would inform each deck rating whether or not they would be required on the next voyage, or even sacked, with a DR – Decline to Report – stamp in their discharge book. Presumably Geordie believed that this meeting would be Jack's nemesis. Both Alan and Jack had prepared themselves to find a DR in their books. For Jack, that would mean the end of his career with Port Line. During the voyage neither Jack nor Alan had got on with the mate, and their undisguised contempt for the bosun was widely known aboard the vessel. As Jack knocked on the door he had resigned himself to the worst.

'Enter,' came a voice from the depths of the cabin. In he went to be met, surprisingly, by a calm and collected officer. In a most conciliatory tone he related all the faults he had found in Jack. Then, after a long pause, he continued, but now talking about the few things he was satisfied with about his sailor. Jack did not know what to make of the discourse and the mild tone in which it was delivered. His ears took over from his mind as his first mate then declared, 'I do not intend to sack you. But in the most simple of terms and on the presumption that you will remain with Port Line, I do *not* want you on my vessel in future, or in any crew of mine. Understood?'

Jack looked at his officer for longer than was perhaps polite before saying, 'Yes, Sir,' whilst thinking, 'Not a chance in hell that I would sail with you again.'

'I know exactly what you're thinking, and that suits both of us, son.' These were the final, sage-like, words ringing in his ears. Jack left the cabin thinking, 'You've not quite mastered my thoughts yet, Mr Mate. Even more important for me is the fact that I won't sail with your totally useless bosun again.'

Alan and Jack had much the same lecture from the mate, but both men were still a little apprehensive about the likely entry in their discharge books. Fine seaman that the mate most certainly was, it was not advisable for either sailor to presume too much, even if he had spoken in a more conciliatory tone of voice than usual.

After the *Port Townsville* had berthed the pay-off commenced, and when Jack and Alan were given their discharge books they both found they had 'Very Good' for conduct and 'Very Good' for ability; the first mate, no doubt mindful of the difficulties the pair had inflicted on him, had been generous nonetheless. They left the vessel with no small relief, because they were seeing the back of a very unhappy experience, yet with a good –– in fact very good – discharge. Wonders would never cease! A taxi dash to Lime Street railway station saw Jack en route to Crewe, Bristol Temple Meads and home, whereas Alan, as was his wont, took a more leisurely departure of the *Port Townsville*. At the gangway he bade Jack a fond farewell with a shake of hands that ended their final voyage together; Alan moved to the mighty P&O Line with a berth aboard the veteran liner *Canton*, whereas Jack remained with his beloved Port Line despite this less than enjoyable voyage.

7

TSMV *Port Auckland* revisited

Second voyage

Jack had yearned for a Christmas at home. Since leaving Dover his Christmas holidays had been spent aboard one vessel or another, none of them particularly memorable. Now, having paid off from the *Port Townsville* during December, he had achieved his wish, and was at the family home on West Hill in Wraxall for what he saw as a great occasion.

As usual in southern Britain there was a total absence of Christmas card weather. It was wet and chilly as Jack made his way to the midnight communion service at his parish church of All Saints, Wraxall. When he arrived home at 1:30 a.m., his mother was still in her chair reading. 'Happy Christmas, Mother,' he said, 'I thought you'd be in bed by now.'

Mother, without looking up from her book, replied, with little enthusiasm in her voice, 'Happy Christmas, son.'

The atmosphere on Christmas morning was not much better, and lunch was little different from lunch on a normal day. The afternoon was spent in front of the fire, Mother with her head in her book, as appeared to be the usual pattern of life at home. In the evening Jack hoped to find solace at his watering hole, the Failand Inn – but he found it closed. That was the last straw, and he hoped that for all future Christmas celebrations he would be back at sea.

Since Jack had gone to sea his mother had taken the Lloyd's List shipping newspaper, enabling her to follow his voyages. On leave Jack would immerse himself in the paper, looking out for a likely vessel to join. Now he carefully studied every page for an entry relating to the *Port Auckland* and her whereabouts. He found that she was in Auckland, heading for Britain shortly.

When his leave expired, head office contacted him with instructions to join the *Port Chalmers* at Liverpool, and bring her around to London via Hull. As if by magic Jack succumbed to an illness which precluded him from taking up his duties aboard that ship, and 88 Leadenhall St, London EC3 wished him a speedy recovery, with instructions to let them know once he became available. Over a period of two months Jack saw a couple of doctors, including the Shipping Federation doctor, who declared that he was not fit for sea duties. The *Port Auckland* arrived in Britain to discharge her cargo and Jack began to feel much better. In March he persuaded the federation doctor to declare him fit.

A telephone call to the firm resulted in a letter and a railway pass to join the *Port Auckland*, yet again at Cardiff. The long wait and manipulation of circumstances paid off when Jack took another journey to the dock. As on his previous visit, it was a scene with several 'London Greek' general cargo tramping vessels, all laid up for the want of cargoes. At one time they would have been busy carrying best Welsh anthracite coal to all parts of the world before returning with grain for the silos at Cardiff or Avonmouth, or bulk ores for the steel works in Northumberland or South Wales. But those trades were being taken over by specially designed tramping bulk cargo vessels of companies such as Buries Markes, Runciman, Ropner and Reardon Smith.

On joining the *Port Auckland* Jack discovered that she was in the Mountstuart dry dock for her bottom to be cleaned and painted, before proceeding to New Zealand via Curaçao and Panama. With the exception of the master, Captain Townshend, the bosun, 'Big' Murdo and the bosun's mate/lamp-trimmer, it was an entirely new deck crew that Jack joined after the gap of two years. Murdo acknowledged Jack's presence in his dour way with, 'When did I last sail with you?' When Jack told him, Murdo nodded; seemingly this reply satisfied him, and all was then right with his world.

The first mate, on studying Jack's discharge book, said, 'I see you've sailed on this vessel before with Captain Townshend. Was the bosun here at that time?' After a reply in the affirmative, the mate told him, 'You know the standards set, and what the captain and the bosun expect of you. I will expect nothing less.'

From this brief interview, Jack had the impression that the voyage with this first mate was going to be very different from his experience aboard the *Port Townsville*. As he walked away from the mate's office, he had the comforting feeling that he was aboard 'his' vessel, and was working with Port Line as he knew it; it was in contentment that he settled into his cabin.

With the passengers and doctor aboard, the *Port Auckland* sailed for Curaçao. From there she went to Panama, where yet again Captain Claude Townshend was the epitome, in both dress and aura, of a British officer and the master of one of the finest vessels in the huge British Merchant Navy. This time, however, Jack was nowhere near the bridge for the transit of the canal and did not witness the conduct of his master when confronted with the all-American pilot. However, when talking to the apprentices during a smoke-ho he found that little had changed in Captain Townshend's attitude and the condescending way he handed over control of his vessel. The Panama Canal is the one place in the world where the pilot actually takes control of the vessel. Everywhere else, a sea pilot is aboard as an adviser to the vessel's master, who remains responsible for the control and safety of their vessel.

The voyage across the Pacific was quite unremarkable; Jack was involved in the usual watchkeeping duties, and during daylight the vessel was steered by the Iron Mike, enabling the helmsman to carry out other duties on the deck: painting, or refurbishing and re-rigging the cargo-handling equipment. The Iron Mike was an early self-steering gear; unlike a human helmsman who would proactively turn the wheel to counteract any veering off course, Iron Mike responded reactively to deviations, creating a zig-zag wake. This was not appreciated by some of the watchkeepers, and nothing delighted them more than the Mike developing a 'headache' and going on sick leave, a not uncommon occurrence. They could then return to the serene comfort of the wheelhouse, well away from the noisy and arduous duties on deck.

One of the highlights of this 14-day passage was the film evening. A canvas screen would be hoisted between the after Samson posts of No 4 hatch, and current films would be shown to the passengers, officers and off-duty sailors, who would be seated according to rank on the various levels of decks from the boat deck down. Whatever the film, with the gentle rolling of the vessel under the Southern Cross it was considered by those of a romantic nature to be not only pleasurable but also a quite magical experience.

Unlike the outward passengers of the *Port Brisbane* on Jack's first voyage, the passengers on this voyage were all elderly and retired; a faceless bunch as far as the crew were concerned. The only contact they had with the geriatrics was during boat drill when, to the unbridled joy of the passengers – this exercise was clearly better sport than their almost continuous games of deck golf – they had to don lifejackets and watch the lifeboats being swung out on their davits.

Jack's return to Auckland was a matter of coming home. Even under an overcast sky and rain, he felt that Auckland was its usual welcoming self. As before his social life was dictated by Padre Brown and his Mission, the Civic cinema and the telephone at the Queen Street post office. Whilst he had been in contact with his girlfriend in Timaru since he had met her during his first voyage aboard the *Port Auckland*, his voyages to Australia had stretched their bonds of friendship to the extreme. Now that he was back in New Zealand he was hoping that his vessel would, during her loading programme, visit Timaru and bring them back together again.

Because of the *Port Auckland's* relatively small amount of outward cargo, her loading ports were announced only shortly after their arrival at Auckland – and Timaru was not to be a port of loading. The telephone line between Auckland and Timaru grew red hot; the angst created by further separation took its toll on Jack, not the most passive of people at any time. In order to have at least some time with his girlfriend he decided to ask for leave now instead of in Britain. He told her of his idea and asked if she was happy with it. She was, but proposed a variation; her mother was going to see her brother, who lived in Wellington, and if Jack could meet her there she could go too.

Jack asked the first mate if he could take a week out of his leave entitlement once the vessel was in Wellington.

The officer told Jack, 'It's the bosun who decides if he can run the deck department without you. He'll tell me whether he can, and then I'll either refuse or grant your request. Off you go,' with a rapid dismissive gesture. Jack perceived that his request was the least of the mate's concerns.

The bosun, as to be expected when faced with a question almost asking for a cutting reply, told him that he could have the next three months off as far as he was concerned. Overlooking the dismissive opinion, Jack dashed up to the deck office to tell the mate that the bosun had said he could manage without him. The first mate looked at him for quite a while before saying, 'I bet he did, and probably a bit more as well. When do you want leave?'

Jack said he wanted to start his leave when the vessel would be in Wellington. His heart sank as the mate told him that the *Port Auckland* would first be going to Napier, the major port of the Hawke's Bay area on the east coast of North Island. Jack could have the same dates off, but he would have to travel independently between Napier and Wellington. That evening saw yet another phone call to Timaru as Jack explained the situation, but he was relieved that the dates were confirmed and his leave in New Zealand was assured.

After a week at Auckland the vessel sailed for Napier. On arrival the harbour looked little different to that at Timaru, with a high bluff overlooking the docks. But unlike at most of the ports, the vessel was moored at Napier without any fenders. Jack asked the bosun why such a mooring system, with the multi-stranded shore-secured lines, was used rather than the vessel's own lines. Murdo told Jack that the shore lines were designed to allow the vessel to slip them swiftly in an emergency due to weather or an earthquake, just like those used at Timaru. Murdo continued to explain that all bosuns of meat boats hated having Napier as their final port because, unlike Timaru where fenders were used, mooring at Napier damaged the paintwork; all the paint on the hull between Nos 2 and 5 hatches would be scraped off on the quay wall, exposing bare steel for the ravages of rust to take hold on the hull during the long voyage home, making the otherwise immaculately-painted vessel look like a Greek tramping craft.

Napier itself was a delightful town. It had been virtually destroyed by an earthquake in 1931, and the new Napier was built with 20th-century planning for services, motor vehicles and shopping streets. At the first opportunity Jack made his way into town to work out how he could travel to Wellington at the lowest price. Having decided that he would go by coach via Palmerston North, he returned to the *Port Auckland* along Marine Parade. The walk along the sea front was attractive; like Timaru, Napier had its sound shell for concerts on the parade, and a little further on stood a distinctive statue, Pania of the Reef.

Pania, according to Maori legend, hearing the siren song of her lover from the

Pania, painting by Michael J.D. Brown

sea, swam out from the beach, only to be turned into the reef which runs along part of the seafront. The only fault with the outstanding sculpture that Jack so admired was that Pania looked, despite her headdress and grass skirt, distinctly European rather than Maori: nit-picking criticism perhaps – but a beautiful creation nonetheless.

Prompt phone calls resulted in Jack boarding his coach. For a sailor more used to the coastal view of New Zealand, this trip through the hinterland was a real eye-opener. He had already decided that New Zealand was a beautiful country, and on this journey through the centre of North Island he found it reminded him in places of Somerset in the summer; the hills and pastures were akin to those he had known in England. Jack was in his element.

On his arrival at Wellington he reported to the Port Line marine superintendent, who suggested that Jack should stay in the Edinburgh Hotel, in the interests of economy. Whilst 'economy' may not have been the correct word to describe the hotel, it was rather spartan in comparison to similar hotels in Britain. The room was no better than a room at the Mission in Commercial Road, London. The evening meal was awful by any standard; tough beef, undercooked potatoes and boiled cabbage appeared to be the staple fare.

However, Jack cheered up early on the following morning: by 7 a.m. he was waiting at the inter-Island ferry jetty for the arrival of the *Maori* from Lyttelton with his lady love and her mother.

When a few days later he began to run short of money, a trip to the head office gained him an interview with a very understanding superintendent's clerk, and he was given funds to cover the rest of his hectic social life in Wellington.

Then it was time for very sad goodbyes, as the *Hinemoa* departed, taking Jack's girlfriend and her mother back to Lyttelton. Meanwhile, the *Port Auckland* arrived, and Jack went back to work with plenty of stories for the mess room and a thank you to the first mate and Murdo for his leave. While the mate enquired if had enjoyed himself on his period of leave, Murdo only let a brief grin cross his face as he told Jack to help the lamp-trimmer with some wire splicing.

Jack remembered his less than cheerful associations with Wellington, its weather and its Customs and Excise officials. But this time, following his pleasant stay there, he was sincere in bidding a fond farewell to the city as the *Port Auckland* sailed for Port Chalmers. She stayed at that port for almost three weeks, loading the usual lamb carcasses, casein, milk powder and general cargo. To complete her loading the vessel sailed for a fortnight's stay in Lyttelton, where she loaded Canterbury lamb carcasses, mutton, tallow and baled wool.

The *Port Auckland* sailed from Lyttelton for Dunkirk via Panama and Curaçao. The homeward voyage was as uneventful as the outward, and by the time they reached the English Channel the 'Channels' were being experienced by just about everyone – even though the 24-hour visit to Dunkirk put pay-off back by a day. Dunkirk in those days still carried the scars of war and, from his fractured French, Jack had the distinct impression that the locals, despite what the British and Americans had done to save them twice in one century, disliked the British even more than the Germans; for Jack, the 24-hour stay to discharge wool was 24 hours too long.

On sailing from Dunkirk in daylight Jack was on the wheel while the vessel was in a restricted area of navigation but not under a pilot. Captain Townshend was on the bridge conning the vessel along a buoyed channel. On the bridge there were also an apprentice, the first mate and the officer of the watch. All was going well with the master, through his chief mate (or as Claude would have it, 'chief officer') giving helm orders to Jack using compass degrees. In response, Jack would move the wheel until the vessel's head was just about to point to the direction the master had told him, then he would use a few degrees of opposite helm in order to stop the swing of the vessel's head, thus ending up on the course required. These manoeuvres, without any specific course being given to Jack, were going along quite nicely when, via the first mate, the master gave the order Starboard 15. Jack put the wheel over until he had the required 15 degrees of rudder movement to turn the vessel to starboard. He watched as the vessel's head swung to starboard, awaiting the counter-order to meet her and stop the turn. As the vessel's head was swinging the mate, in the wheelhouse, was watching the head swinging and the gyro compass alongside Jack at the same time. Captain Townshend on the port-hand bridge wing was studying something through his binoculars. The mate swiftly left the wheelhouse and went towards the master. He did not reach him before Jack, looking through the starboard door of the wheelhouse, saw in the corner of his eye a tall shape resembling the mast and rigging of a yacht. At the same time the officer of the watch was also staring out of the starboard wheelhouse window as the sound of a very large collision went through the vessel. 'Hard a-port. Stop engines,' called the master as he, with the mate in tow, raced through the wheelhouse onto the starboard bridge wing. 'Meet her and give me your course,' called the master directly to Jack – who noted that this time he did not give orders through the mate.

As the vessel head stopped swinging Jack told the officer of the watch the vessel

A 'Brief Encounter' moment aboard the inter-island ferry *Hinemoa*

heading in compass degrees and concentrated on keeping the vessel on that course. The absence of engine power made his task very difficult, especially as the current now had hold of the vessel.

'Get the carpenter to sound the bilges,' ordered the master, as both he and his senior officer returned to the wheelhouse. By now the chief engineer and radio officer were also assembled there and much discussion was going on, but out of Jack's earshot. The master was looking in his direction as the mate came over and gave him a course to steer while an apprentice rang the engine-room telegraphs to Half Ahead. The only other words Jack heard were the master ordering the first mate to tell the radio officer to inform the harbour authorities about the incident, and that a buoy was damaged.

By this time Jack was getting distinctly sweaty. The first mate went and stood by him, no doubt watching the course he was steering, as the Chippy came into the wheelhouse and told the officer that the bilges were all sound. This welcome information was passed on to Captain Townshend.

Jack, still rather concerned that there had been no mention of salvaging the yacht or saving life, plucked up courage to enquire from the now hovering mate, 'What's happened?'

'Hit the landfall buoy, you swung her too far,' he replied.

While Jack was digesting that information the quartermaster arrived to relieve him at the wheel. Jack told him the course, then went to the officer of the watch and gave him the course as well. The mate told him to go to the master and give him the course.

Jack turned to the first mate and rather bravely said, 'It wasn't my fault, the Old Man didn't tell me when to stop her swinging.'

The mate replied, 'I know it wasn't your fault. The Old Man was probably distracted by whatever he was looking at – but go on out, tell him the course and apologise.'

Jack gave much thought to the bit about apologising, then thought again before defending himself with, 'But I only followed the helm order, it's not my mistake.'

'I've just *told* you that I know it's not your fault,' the mate said, then indicating to where the master was standing, he continued, 'He too knows it wasn't your fault, but you will go to him, apologise, give him the course and skedaddle down the ladder, okay?'

Needing no second bidding, Jack with some trepidation went to Captain Townshend and did precisely as he'd been told in double quick time. Then, going off watch, he went to the mess room for a cup of tea and to tell anyone who would listen about how he was the loser for the Old Man's mistake. Just as he got into full flow AB Walsh appeared at the mess-room door, pointed at Jack and brusquely announced, 'Mate wants to see you now.'

This stomach-churning demand did little for Jack's confidence; the looming realisation of the sack ran through his head on approaching the mate's door. 'You wanted to see me, Sir?' he squeaked as he saw his officer at his desk.

'Are you sailing with us next voyage?' enquired the mate.

Although Jack attempted to speak, nothing came out for a second or two ...

'Well, yes or no?' asked the mate impatiently, 'I have many others to see before we pick up the pilot.'

'Yes please, Sir,' replied Jack, regaining his composure. 'But what about just now, Sir?'

'I've spoken to the master about your future, and he told me that he wants you back here. That's the end of that.'

Jack heard nothing more about the landfall buoy incident. As he made his way back to the mess room to finish his tea, he thought, 'I wonder what the entry in the log book is relating to the collision with the buoy?'

On pay-off day, Jack carefully studied the sheet which detailed his income and leave entitlement plus the deductions: subs during the voyage, income tax, national insurance and his (very reluctant) payment to the National Union of Seamen. When studying his leave entitlement he could see no reference to the time off that he'd had in Wellington, but the sub he had taken there had been deducted. The question was, should he ignore the matter, or should he bring the discrepancy to the notice of the purser/chief steward, or should he ask the first mate about it? Jack settled for the purser, who told him that no one had told him to deduct the leave. Jack then went to the mate, who was very busy. He told Jack that he had brought up the matter of the leave in New Zealand with the master, who had said the leave in New Zealand was to be ignored – so ignore it and be grateful. Jack was indeed very grateful and kept his mouth tightly shut about the kindness of the master.

Most of the sailors from the islands were returning for the next voyage. Of the others, some had not been invited to return, and others had politely refused the opportunity to sail aboard the *Port Auckland* again; a couple or so did not get on with Murdo and were moving elsewhere within the fleet.

Third voyage

After four weeks of leave a rail warrant arrived from Leadenhall Street for Jack to return to his vessel for another voyage to New Zealand.

As Jack went into the first mate's cabin to announce his return to *Port Auckland* he was met by a scene which took him back to his training establishment and his former naval officers; standing there was the sartorial epitome of a naval officer even to the point of his Gieves & Hawkes cap being carefully placed on his desk with the peak facing whoever sat at it. It must have been of some disappointment to the wearer of the cap that its peak did not display gold oak leaves.

'Yes?' was uttered through regulation raised jaw and tight lips – as *Boys' Own* magazines and films liked to depict naval officers – by a man whose finely chiselled features included a slightly cleft square chin on a perfectly proportioned body.

Recovering from his shock that the man was not his former first mate, and his surprise to see in his place this superb living advertisement for a career in the higher echelons of the Royal Navy, Jack said, 'I'm reporting back for duty, Sir.'

'Who are you?' enquired the first mate.

Jack explained who he was, and the officer said, still through an almost clenched jaw, 'If you were here last voyage, you know the vessel, and you will find out what I expect of you in due course. Are you a reservist?'

'No, Sir,' Jack replied, and handed the mate his discharge book.

As the officer took the book Jack noted the well-manicured hand and the

Jack checking that all is well on the foredeck

perfect length of the shirt cuff. The mate looked at the discharge book and in his clipped tones said, 'I see that you were trained privately to naval standards and discipline. Good.' He then told Jack to find the bosun and collect the key to his cabin.

This had been his introduction to a very distinctive first mate. Most of the previous first mates he had served with were men from a slightly different mould, the notable exception being the chief mate of the *Port Townsville*, excellent seaman that he was. Well dressed, well spoken and with an air of authority they may have been – but this officer was cut from a different cloth. Jack decided that for the deck crowd this voyage was probably going to have a very different type of professional relationship for everyone concerned.

Jack found Big Murdo, and as he was given the keys to his cabin he commented to Murdo about the new first mate and his naval mannerisms. Murdo's only comment was, 'I've sailed with him before when he was third mate.' Almost as monosyllabic as ever. Jack was then told to be on deck at 7:00 prompt the next morning.

At lunchtime Jack made his way to the mess room and found a couple of his colleagues from the previous voyage, together with a few new faces. The conversation in the mess, not aided by any input from Jack, got around to the new mate and his demeanour. 'I sailed with 'im when 'e were a' apprentice,' said a rather diminutive older man. He continued, 'E weren't able to get in the Navy so came 'ere instead.'

'He's Naval Reserve,' the words came from the AB sitting in the corner of the mess room. 'He's all right. He's been second, then first mate with me. He sometimes gives the impression of being full of his own piss and importance, but he's okay. He never bothered me.'

Within days the *Port Auckland* left King George V Dock bound for New Zealand again, and, for Jack, hopefully the reignition of his association with his girl from Timaru. The outward voyage was a matter of a watchkeeping routine, with nothing that had not happened before. Murdo was his usual very competent but dour self; the first mate was entirely as expected by Jack. The sailors were a good and efficient bunch, and the passengers were much the same as passengers past, just different faces. Whilst on his watch, one pleasure for Jack was to chin-wag with the fourth mate; they had served together when the mate was an apprentice, and they had laboured long and hard over *Monroe's Nautical Tables*, Jack making particularly heavy weather of it.

On arriving at the Panama Canal the *Port Auckland* went alongside to take on water, and the crew was given some shore leave. With three other sailors, Jack went ashore and enjoyed a couple of hours in a bar open to the tropical night sky and the usual myriad of flying insects. It was obvious that a couple of his colleagues were on the lookout for any presentable local whores to relieve their sexual tensions. However, none came up to the standard of looks, figure and likely cleanliness that the still-sober sailors would spend their $20 on – if they'd had sufficient time for the alcohol to permeate their brain cells, they would not have been quite so particular. The group decided that it would be safer to take a taxi back to their vessel rather than walk and find themselves on the wrong side of local rogues or unspecified wild animals. The taxi swung away from the bar and immediately, as far as the sailors could see, entered a jungle with large pools of what appeared to be green stagnant water. As the taxi slowed to turn a corner, the headlights of the vehicle caught a particular pool, allowing Jack and the other three to see two of the whores they had seen earlier parading in front of the bar, here squatting over the pool with one hand holding up their bit of material known loosely as a skirt and the other hand apparently washing out their genitals. The expletives resounded around the body of the cab as it continued its journey to the quayside.

The sight was enough to put an end, once and for all, to any sexually inspired thoughts by the virile young sailors. Observations such as 'Did you see that?', 'Christ Almighty!', 'Bloody 'ell!', and more detailed analysis of the situation from those with a more academic view concerning the world, its women and its ills continued as they ascended the gangway and went into the mess room. With the shore leave time about to expire, other sailors, greasers, engineers and passengers were flocking aboard the vessel. In the sailors' mess Jack and his companions were still sitting there when the rest of the men who had gone ashore returned. They were promptly informed of that which had been observed from the taxi, down to the smallest detail. and none of the scene – sometimes very slightly exaggerated – was excluded. As the yarn unfolded it was noticeable that some sailors, three of them in particular, had fallen very quiet and they took no part in the often very ribald mess-room banter.

In the morning as the *Port Auckland* was in the Gatun Lock, three sailors were seen outside the doctor's surgery looking very sorry for themselves. Jack to his shame – but enjoyable shame – joined in the laughter as a sailor passing the three remarked loudly, 'On the pox doctor's parade, lads?' Once the laughter had subsided Jack was tempted to quote, or misquote, the Old Testament proverb 'As ye shall sow, so shall ye reap', but thought it might just be too near the knuckle for his relationships in the mess room.

In no time at all, the *Port Auckland* was about to join the Pacific Ocean from the Miraflores Locks. On the bridge, Captain Townshend did not have any sartorial competition from the first mate's Royal Naval Reserve membership. Mr Mate was a picture of pure white, but other than the non-rake of his cap and the clipped tones from his mouth, he was no different from most other Port Line senior deck officers in their tropical socks, shorts and shoes.

Landfall in New Zealand was again made at Auckland, where Jack discovered that one of the loading ports for the vessel would be Timaru. Throughout the outbound voyage, the first mate sometimes acknowledged Jack's presence, but generally chose to ignore not only him but just about every other sailor as well. By the same measure, Jack had no particular reason to take umbrage or acknowledge the presence of his senior officer. However, it was with much trepidation that he approached the officer to ask if whilst the vessel was in Timaru he could take some of his leave. Unlike the first mate on the previous voyage, there was no referring Jack to the bosun for his opinion whether or not he should be granted leave; without hesitation the officer told him that he could take the leave once the vessel docked – and that Jack must be back aboard before she sailed.

The usual run of discharging ports came and went. New Zealand was as wonderful for Jack as it had been in the previous three voyages. In Jack's opinion a friendlier nation could not be found on the planet. Wherever the *Port Auckland* was berthed, the nightly telephone call to Timaru took precedence over everything else in his social calendar.

While at Wellington during the discharge phase of the voyage, Jack saw another officer wandering around with four gold rings on his sleeves. There were no purple inserts between the bands, so he was not a chief engineer; he had to be a master. An enquiry of an apprentice gleaned the information that the officer was in fact a Port Line master and would sail with the vessel during the coastwise voyage. By the time Jack went to the mess room with what he thought was exclusive red-hot news, the sailors in the mess were already in conversation about the arrival of this master mariner aboard the vessel. Although Jack had never seen this captain before, several of his colleagues knew him and had many tales relating to his past. But it all came down to the fact that no one on the lower deck knew why he was here aboard their vessel, which already had a master, the renowned Captain Townshend, and a very efficient first mate. The first rumour was that the other captain was aboard in order that the first mate could go on leave, a not uncommon situation, as several officers and a few masters had their homes and family in New Zealand. But the best answer that the sailors could reach between them was that he was acting as a sort of staff captain, a position normally reserved for large liners and the like.

Unlike both the master and the first mate, this master integrated well with the sailors. He would often engage the men of the deck department in conversation relating to their work, their pleasures, and their service with Port Line. Neither Jack nor his colleagues had the impudence or the nerve to ask him the reason for his being aboard. While none of the sailors would be comfortable asking the first mate the reason for this captain being aboard, they did ask the rest of the deck officers, with totally negative results other than, 'He's having a change from driving a desk in the marine super's office in Wellington.'

The rumour mill was in full flow with contributions from many 'experts' who had known this master on other vessels. One recounted a yarn about when the master had been in command of another Port Line vessel and, outward bound in the Thames, had limited visibility. The vessel was under the guidance of a Thames pilot, when off of the Isle of Grain, a petroleum refining site, a tanker was seen at the last minute to be crossing the bow. Allegedly the pilot yelled for the engines to be put at Full Astern, and to drop both anchors. Again allegedly, this order was countermanded by the master within seconds, as he used the megaphone to yell at those men for'ard, 'Clear the foc'sle head!' at the same time ringing the engine room telegraphs not to Full Astern as the pilot had ordered, but to Dead Slow Ahead. At that point only the first mate, the carpenter and one AB were on the deck, and like lightning they slid down the ladders from the foredeck as, with a mighty rending of steel, the Port Liner cut into the tanker, which turned out to be a Russian-registered vessel.

Yet again allegedly, the reason for the master's countermanding of the pilot's order was that the engines could not have been put astern in the seconds available, and to have dropped both anchors under the prevailing currents would have swung the Port Liner broadside into the tanker. This would have probably caused even greater damage, particularly to his vessel, with an increased risk of fire engulfing both vessels if the tanker's cargo had ignited. The damage to the Port Line vessel was not as extensive as it might have been, but regrettably the same could not be said for the tanker. However, no one was killed or injured, probably – if the tale was true – due to the quick thinking of the master, who was now aboard *Port Auckland*. While Jack took this information in, he was not convinced that it was all true, particularly as the yarn-teller had not even been at sea at the time of the incident – but it made a good story.

Jack occasionally talked to this master and once observed him at a reception for shippers in the saloon. Here Jack noted that while everyone else had a dainty glassful of whatever, this officer rolled his own cigarettes and carried a pint mug. The next meeting of the two was in the wheelhouse at 21:00 hrs; *Port Auckland* was voyaging from Wellington to Port Chalmers. When off the Banks Peninsula, the Akaroa light illuminated the wheelhouse as Jack steered the vessel. The calm of the wheelhouse was slightly interrupted by the arrival of the staff captain. He walked towards Jack and looked at the compass repeater. At that moment the officer of the watch was taking a bearing of the light, from the repeater compass on the starboard bridge wing. The additional master had gone back into the chartroom, and as he emerged he almost collided with the officer heading in there to plot the bearing. They both went into the chartroom and Jack was again at peace with the world, as the *Port Auckland* almost steered herself, thanks to the engineers achieving much the same revolutions on the twin screws. Both officers soon came back the wheelhouse, a flame illuminating the additional master's face as he lit his cigarette.

'Take her in a bit,' he commanded. 'You'll end up in Antarctica on this course.'

The officer of the watch told him that the master had written up the night orders, including the course to be steered.

'Take her in a bit or you'll probably lose the next light. I'll sort out the course,' ordered the additional master.

He then turned to Jack and told him the revised course, and without comment from the officer of the watch Jack complied. The additional master took himself and his roll-up cigarette into the chartroom, then presumably down into his accommodation.

Port Auckland from a painting by Robert Blackwell

Quite who said what was not known to Jack, but within a short time Captain Claude was in the wheelhouse. He went to the bridge wing and spoke to the officer of the watch. Both then went into the chartroom before the officer emerged to tell Jack to resume the course that Captain Townshend had determined originally. Townshend returned to the wheelhouse and pointedly sniffed at the lingering odour of cigarette smoke, then walked from one bridge wing to the other, leaving the port-hand wheelhouse door open – no doubt to dissipate the odour – before returning to his cabin. As mentioned earlier, Claude, along with all other masters Jack had sailed with, did not allow anyone – except the Panama Canal pilots – to smoke on the bridge wings or in the wheelhouse, and in the case of Captain Townshend this concession was granted with noticeable ill grace.

Jack, although quite satisfied with his association with Captain Townshend and the first mate, did find the more cheerful character of this additional master a refreshing change from the rather distant approach of Claude Townshend and the sometimes rather disdainful attitude of the mate towards the men and some of the officers.

Port Chalmers was its usual rather sleepy self, with a mixture of weather to delay the loading, and there the additional master left the vessel. He was probably just as pleased to leave the very formally run *Port Auckland* as Captain Townshend and the first mate must have been to see the back of him.

When the *Port Auckland* arrived at Timaru, Jack was ashore with his bags as soon as the gangway was down. He was off to stay with the family of his girlfriend in Cain Street and enjoy a full seven days ashore. During that week he attended an interview to become a New Zealand policeman, and his success meant that when he returned to New Zealand he would change his occupation radically.

The week in Timaru went by all too quickly, and he rejoined the vessel, which continued her loading at Lyttelton, New Plymouth and Wellington before returning for topping up at Auckland. The voyage home via Panama was as uneventful as the outward journey, but this time no sailors appeared to be too keen to go ashore! In the event, the vessel did not go alongside, and the temptation of a shore run was removed by the dictates of circumstance.

As the *Port Auckland* approached the English Channel, the first mate offered Jack the opportunity to rejoin the vessel for her next voyage. With some regret he declined the offer, explaining that he had been offered a job as a policeman in New Zealand. Much to Jack's surprise, the mate told him that the company needed men like him and if he remained with Port Line he was assured of advancement in the company. Jack thanked him for his consideration, but said that his mind was made up – he was going to live in New Zealand.

Mindful of the fact that in the two years that he had sailed with Captain Claude Townshend, the master had spoken to him only once – and that was when the vessel had struck the buoy off Dunkirk – Jack was very surprised when on the boat deck that day he came out of his accommodation and said, 'I understand that you will not be joining us for the next voyage.'

Not for the first time, Jack was almost dumbfounded, and after hesitation replied, 'Yes, Sir.'

The master continued, 'I regret the fact that you are leaving us. Should you decide to change your mind you will always be welcome to serve in any vessel under my command.'

As Jack left the vessel he passed his first mate who cast a thin-lipped smile in his direction, and Jack realised that this was the one and only time that he had seen the mate almost smile in nearly five months. He might well have smiled during the voyage, but not in front of Jack. With that invitation ringing in his ears from a captain who in two years had only spoken to him on that one occasion, Jack made his way home to begin planning his new life in New Zealand.

His first challenge was to convince his mother that his future lay in that country, a challenge that – unsurprisingly – Jack failed. On her maternal side, all of his mother's family were either living in Australia or New Zealand, but her resolve to keep her youngest child anchored in Britain, even though she saw him only every six months or so, was of the paramount importance in any argument. Apart from the difficulty in handling his mother and her prejudice against his plans, finding a way to work his passage to New Zealand was consuming the time allowed for him to take up his job there. Eventually he found that the company Simon-Lobnitz, builder of dredgers and similar craft, had a dredger sailing to New Zealand and needed a running crew. Jack applied, and was offered a place on the delivery voyage. At that time all seemed to be going well.

However, the dredger's sailing date kept being put back. Eventually a letter was received from the New Zealand police telling Jack that as he had been unable to proceed with his training the offer was withdrawn. Worse, on receiving the news, his girlfriend in Timaru decided to end their relationship, as she could not envisage a happy future with Jack remaining at sea, even for a short time. The failure of Interflora to deliver a bouquet to her for her birthday did not help Jack's cause, especially when he queried why she had not written a 'Thank you' note. Thus came the heartbreaking end to a most meaningful romantic relationship.

To his mother's delight, and eating a large helping of humble pie, Jack put through a phone call to Leadenhall Street and was greeted by a clerk saying, 'Oh, I thought we'd lost you, according to the chief officer of the *Port Auckland*. When I see the boss I'll let you know where you're going.'

Time went by and Jack heard nothing, thinking to himself, 'They're doing this deliberately, to show who's boss.' But eventually a letter arrived with a railway warrant for Falmouth and instructions to join the *Port Hobart* at the dry dock there.

Port Auckland on her 12th and final visit to Avonmouth, 27 May 1976. From the collection of Stuart Kirkby.

8

TSMV *Port Hobart*

First voyage

Jack had a most pleasant summertime steam train journey from Bristol to Penzance, then via the single-track line to a Falmouth that was basking in late afternoon Cornish sunshine. As he left the station he looked toward the dry docks of Silley Cox & Co. and then out into Falmouth Bay – a scene of considerable activity, with the vessels of British Tankers, owned by British Petroleum Co., dominating the traffic. Although Jack was not aware of it at the time, Falmouth was the collecting point for these tankers, awaiting either orders or their turn in the dry docks.

In the late afternoon he made his way to the *Port Hobart*, a vessel uniquely designed for the company. He had not previously seen her, and she looked a rather solid craft of pleasing appearance with a forepart and wheelhouse set out from the accommodation between two Samson posts on the after end of No 2 hatch. One of her unique features was the company crest on the forepart of the accommodation below the wheelhouse, whereas all the other vessels of the fleet had the crest in the eyes of the bow.

The design of the *Port Hobart* was from plans that had been drawn up by the Shaw Savill & Albion Line and the Blue Star Line, before the Second World War. In conjunction with the shipbuilder Harland and Wolff at Belfast, a class of vessels was built, known generally as Empire Food Ships, and during the war the Ministry of War Transport continued the design for large, fast vessels capable of countering the U-boats. Even so, several were lost due to enemy action, with many acts of supreme bravery by crews in these vessels. Towards the end of the war the Ministry ordered another two of this design, with twin screws and a cruising speed of 16.5 knots, and the resultant vessels, the *Empire Wessex* and the *Empire Mercia*, were launched towards the end of 1945.

The *Empire Wessex* was bought by Port Line Ltd and renamed *Port Hobart*, and her building was completed in August 1946, at 11,138 tons, and 540 feet long by 70 feet wide. Her near-twin, *Empire Mercia*, was purchased by Blue Star Line for the same trading area as the *Port Hobart*, and renamed *Empire Star*. The two vessels had been created together, and they were sent for scrapping in 1970 and 1971.

On boarding the *Port Hobart*, Jack found the vessel in the usual condition associated with ship-repair yards: oxy-acetylene hoses and cylinders everywhere, with dirt, cotton waste, dustbins, wires and the like in every conceivable place. He went through the usual joining ritual and for the first time had a cabin in the poop housing. While many of that class of vessel had a flush deck aft, the *Empire Star* and the *Port Hobart* had a poop deck for crew accommodation, probably because they were built to carry about 130 passengers amidships in their wartime guise. Another notable difference to any other Port Line vessel was the location of three adjacent Samson posts situated at No 4 hatch, probably because of the proximity of the superstructure to the hatchway, necessitating short cargo derricks.

Over the next fortnight Jack found his way around the vessel and did odd jobs; nothing concrete could be achieved because the Cornish version of the dockyard matey made sure that nothing was completed until the day before sailing. When that day dawned, little went right in either the engine room or on deck. Engine trials began – and ended within seconds, as a very loud noise came from one of the engine's two crankcases. It turned out that when the crankshaft started rotating, several metal dustbins, filled with the detritus of engine overhaul and left in the casing, were being crushed. Quite what occurred next down below Jack did not discover, as he had his own difficulties on deck; when the sailors attempted to lower some of the derricks it quickly became apparent that the dockyard workers who had been overhauling the cargo running gear had put the wrong blocks on the derricks. In some cases the topping lift wires were for different derricks, and in other cases when the derrick was lowered, fathom upon fathom of wire

Port Hobart

lay on deck. In short, total mayhem broke out on deck as eight sailors attempted to work out where various pieces of cargo-handling gear belonged. The following day, with the aid of shore cranes and much swearing, order was restored.

Two days later the *Port Hobart* was ready to set out on her voyage to Australia via Suez. Probably because of her refit, she was not carrying any cargo, so she was a 'light' ship. She had accommodation for 12 passengers, but on this voyage there was only one: Mrs Craig, known affectionately by the deck crowd as Mrs Captain Craig.

For the first and only time during his career with Port Line, Jack was aboard a vessel whose master had taken his wife with him. When finally sailing from Falmouth in the warm summer sun, Jack came across his new master: Captain William Craig. He was avuncular in both appearance and speech. Both the first mate and the bosun were new to Jack. The first mate was a typical Port Line senior officer with few illusions of grandeur; this suited Jack, who did not quite know what to make of the bosun, seemingly a quieter man than many bosuns and on occasion not too sure of himself.

The first day out from Falmouth, Jack, washing down the decks, noticed that against the coamings of each after hatch were stacks of new dunnage timber to line out the empty cargo holds, ready for the refrigerated and general cargo to be loaded in Australia. Nothing of any particular note occurred during the passage to Suez, and other than a stop to lift the Suez Canal light onto the bow, encountering the usual bumboat and 'gilly-gilly' men, it was a straightforward transit.

Once through the canal Jack was summoned to the bridge to be met by Captain Craig, who pointed to the courtesy flag of Egypt at the foretopmast head. Jack followed his gaze, wondering what could be wrong, and seeing nothing amiss except that the flag should have been hauled down by now, as the vessel was no longer in the Canal Zone. Indicating an apprentice standing by No 2 hatch and looking up at the foretopmast, the master said to Jack, 'Be a chum – go up and get the end down. He's only a boy, a silly boy, and too young to go up himself.'

Jack realised that the poor apprentice, when he had successfully hauled the flag down, had undone the lower clip and allowed the breeze to carry the flag, still attached to halyard, onto the hatch. In his panic he had hauled on what he believed to be the downhaul and instead of stopping when he saw the flag rising he had continued to pull. So the Inglefield clip of the halyard had ended up fouling the sheave in the mast button, and the flag was stuck at the masthead. Quickly going to his cabin and picking up his camera then returning to the deck to take a heavy shackle with him, Jack went up to the jammed halyard. With both arms around the topmast he grabbed at the flag and pulled the clip free of the sheave. He then pulled flag and halyard around the mast, disconnected the flag and stuffed it into his shirt while holding the halyard against the rungs of the footholds. His next challenge was to tie the shackle onto the halyard. Not an easy task when doing it blind behind the mast, as that was the only way to hold on with both hands and bend the shackle onto the halyard.

Captain and Mrs Captain Craig on the bridge wing

With great difficulty Jack shouted to the apprentice to pay out the halyard and allow the weight of the shackle to carry the halyard down. It became apparent that the boy simply did not understand what was required of him; he appeared to be too frightened to let go in case he made another mistake. So the duty quartermaster was sent from the wheelhouse to relieve the poor lad, and in no time both parts of the halyard were reunited. Coming down from the topmast onto the mast table, Jack took two photographs, one of Captain and Mrs Craig on the bridge, and the other a stern view of the *Port Hobart*.

When Jack was back on deck he went to the bridge, to be met by Mrs Craig as he produced the flag from his shirt. Mrs Craig, with her husband, was making up the company house flag, and for Jack it was a surprising sight to see a master with his hands on a flag on his own bridge. An apprentice appeared, took the fly of the house flag from the master, and continued to make it up with Mrs Craig. Captain Craig had taken no more than two steps towards the wheelhouse when the only female voice aboard the vessel said, 'Give him a hand with that flag,' and indicated Jack with a nod of her head.

Captain Craig looked at his wife while taking another stride towards the wheelhouse door.

Embarrassed that the master should be involved in such a menial task, Jack told her, 'I can manage, thank you, Ma'am.'

'It'll be easier with two pairs of hands,' said Mrs Craig. 'There's nothing else for him to do now.'

Without another word, Captain Craig took hold of the hoist of the flag and helped Jack make it up ready for the pigeonhole. For the second time aboard the *Port Hobart*, Jack had a first and last experience – the first and only time a master helped him make up a flag.

A few days later Jack's cabinmate told him, 'A little shit came down with this for you,' and handed him a wrapped bottle with, written on it, the words 'Thank you'. On opening it Jack found it was rum. He decided that as an apprentice had delivered it, the bottle must have come from the apprentice who had lost the halyard. But how would an apprentice get hold of rum? A few days later, he saw the purser, and asked him why he had allowed an apprentice to buy spirits.

'He didn't,' the purser replied, 'it was on the Old Man's account, but the apprentice wrote on the wrapping.'

Jack, whilst not looking a gift horse in the mouth, was not at that time an imbiber of rum, and enquired if the steward would kindly replace the rum with brandy – only to be told that ratings were not allowed spirits. Jack was about to point out that … then thought better of it and, perhaps wisely, shut his mouth.

On approaching the coast of Western Australia, it was decided to take down the awnings. Jack and two others were told to take down the starboard awning on the for'ard end of the boat deck, and were happily removing the awning from the spars and the lashings on the outboard awning wire. While his colleagues were folding the canvas, and making it up into a bolt, Jack was standing at the rail studying the empty ocean. He heard a door open from the accommodation, and almost in an instant a voice enquired, 'Enjoying the view?' The voice belonged to Captain Craig and before Jack could gather his wits the master continued, 'The view would be enhanced if idle buggers such as you didn't leave Irish pennants flying.'

Rarely seen ship's name pennant

The silence was golden before Captain Craig launched himself onto the rails; for a split second Jack thought that his master was going over the rail into the ocean, until he held onto the awning post. Once he had regained his balance, Captain Craig fished in the pocket of his tropical shorts and produced a pocket knife. Letting go of the post in order to open it, he was again in a precarious position. Jack was thinking of the expression 'only fools and firemen sit on rails' when a forceful female voice behind him demanded, 'William, get down at once – *now*.' Jack turned to see Mrs Craig wagging her finger in emphasis.

The master gingerly climbed back down to the deck. He said not a word as, with Mrs Craig still laying into him, they disappeared into the accommodation. Jack then cut down the remnants of the awning lines, and never again allowed 'Paddy pennants' to sully the view. He thought deeply about the incident and, other than the remonstration from the master, thought it amusing that he, probably an Ulsterman, would talk of scruffy Irish pennants.

Port Hobart, minus the Irish pennants, continued to Melbourne, where loading commenced – and the bosun deserted. On arrival it was found that some of the cargo dunnage had disappeared, probably in Suez, most likely the reason for the bosun's disappearance. From Melbourne the vessel headed for Tasmania, and eventually ended up in her namesake port.

Someone in authority had decided that the two outboard-side lifeboats should be exercised afloat in the waters of Hobart. With a very junior apprentice – and a junior engineer aboard to look after the sometimes unreliable engine – Jack took to the water with the intention of exercising the No 2 lifeboat, sometimes under sail. Giving little thought to any consequence of his choice of route, he took the lifeboat through the pontoon bridge across the Derwent estuary. So far, so good; a reasonably competent display of sailing was practised, and the decision was then taken to return to the vessel in time for dinner. On turning the boat around, it was discovered that the lifting span of the pontoon bridge was closed to shipping. The No 2 lifeboat was stuck. Much shouting and the waving of arms failed to attract the attention of the bridge operators. With the fierce current running it was difficult to keep control of the boat – but thankfully the engine did not fail, mostly thanks to the engineer's skill in poking and prodding it, with particular attention to the valve push rod controls to keep them active.

After what seemed to be an eternity of abuse from the crew, the span was lifted and with much relief all around the boat found open water. But then, when approaching the *Port Hobart* and expecting to see someone on the winch ready to lift the boat, the boat crew were less than happy to find no one there. Yet again, much shouting emanated from the lifeboat, but to no avail: no one answered. More abuse came from the crew as the lifeboat motored past the bow of the *Port Hobart* to the quay wall, to send someone to alert the vessel to their plight. Eventually the boat was hoisted aboard and the crew dashed to the mess room, hoping that dinner was still being served. Fortunately for Jack in particular, it was. He was never invited again to man the lifeboat – much to his relief, and most certainly to the relief of the sailors. However, the escapade had demonstrated that the lifeboat engine worked, even if Jack's idea of route planning hadn't quite worked.

From Hobart, and a painful experience for Jack as a novice on the city's ice rink, the *Port Hobart* went north on the familiar route via Sydney, Brisbane and Cairns before heading back to Aden for fuel and the eternal haggling with the bumboat men.

Jack was on watch on the monkey island, as the vessel was heading for the Gulf of Aden. In that area it was not unusual for the vessels which had transited the Suez Canal as a convoy to still be in a group as they came down the Red Sea, past Perim Island, past Aden and onward to India or the Persian Gulf.

When Jack took over the lookout at 20:00, he could see many navigation lights, bunched together, on the horizon. He reported them to the watch officer and paid little attention to much else. Suddenly he was conscious of a glowing green mist enveloping the sea and sky ahead, yet the lights ahead, by now little closer, were still visible. As Jack reported this phenomenon he became aware that the sound of the vessel's passage through the water had stopped, as had the sound of the engines. By now the third mate was on the starboard bridge wing looking over the side, and he called Jack down from the monkey island. As they looked down, the sea appeared to be translucent, with fish and sharks clearly visible.

While the officer went back to the wheelhouse and called for the master, Jack remained on the bridge wing, keeping an eye on the group of vessels heading toward them – by now quite close. As Captain Craig arrived in the wheelhouse, the officer was on the phone to the engine room to make sure the vessel was still under way. It was, and had been since leaving Cairns. Turning from the phone the officer hastily told the master of the event. By now several other officers were in the wheelhouse or on the bridge, all looking into the green sea and the creatures therein. Captain Craig told them that the phenomenon had been caused by an undersea earthquake which resulted in the dormant phosphorescence on the sea bed being agitated and giving off that green hue. This glow from the deep gave rise to the illusion of a mist, which is why the lights of approaching vessels could still be seen. Apparently these submarine earthquakes were quite common in the waters around the Persian Gulf. As the master stopped speaking the sounds of the vessel's wash returned as the mist lifted and the first of the approaching vessels passed the *Port Hobart*. Later, during the watch, neither the third mate nor Jack could understand why all external sounds were absent during the incident – something to which Captain Craig's knowledge did not extend either.

After refuelling at Aden, *Port Hobart* transited the Suez Canal into the Mediterranean, then past Gibraltar and on to Britain. Another interesting voyage was completed, with a request that Jack would sail her again, an offer he was pleased to accept.

Second voyage

Jack returned to his Somerset home and by chance, his neighbour John, a third mate with the Prince Line, part of the large Furness Withy shipping group, was also on leave. Over a drink one evening John suggested that they should go somewhere lively for a holiday. Where in Britain was lively enough for two seafaring men in their early twenties? After a search far and wide they settled for a week at the brand-new Butlin's holiday complex at Minehead; not that far away from their homes, but far enough from their parents. The boys had a first-class time, and as was the nature of such places, soon found a pair of single girls. A good time was had by all, with special enjoyment in outsmarting the security men. In many respects it was cruel in the extreme to pit the craftiness and experience of two British merchant seamen against the predictable minds of the so-called security men. The long and short of it was that sometimes the boys deliberately goaded the security staff, and led them on a wild goose chase. This was fun, and most certainly impressed the ladies – just as intended. The staff's discomfort added to the entertainment of the holiday complex rather more than the funny hats, wrestling, dancing and pool games which Butlin's so kindly supplied.

After the most successful leave he had ever had, Jack left Somerset for Liverpool to join the *Port Hobart* for another voyage to Australia. He found himself with a new master, Captain Edward W.R. Young, a first mate he had sailed with on another ship, a new bosun and many new sailors. Jack was sorry that Captain Craig had moved on, and hoped that Captain Young would be as good. Jack had been very lucky with his masters; without exception they had all, even Captain Townshend eventually, shown themselves to be kind and courteous. Above all, they had the respect of Jack and his ilk – perhaps not a view of their masters that would be shared by some of the junior deck officers. As the *Port Hobart* left Liverpool, this

Jack with Jennifer – maiden voyage to Butlin's

voyage was slightly different insofar as this time the vessel was carrying both cargo and passengers.

En route for the Suez Canal, and as the weather became more clement, it became apparent that Captain Young was addicted to deck golf. Soon he had the passengers and his officers playing, one officer telling Jack that he did not like deck golf but as the Old Man was so keen he dare not refuse to play in case that might cloud his end of voyage report. During these first days of the outbound voyage, Jack noted that the first mate, unlike others that he had sailed with, appeared to take little note of what was going on with his deck crew and their work. Very little overtime was offered to the watchkeepers, and in Jack's view the vessel was not quite as spick and span as she might have been. The work of overhauling the running gear appeared to occupy all of the available deck crew's time.

Through Suez the vessel went – no on-deck dunnage sold to the Arabs this time – and then down the Red Sea heading for the Perim Island light before turning gradually to port to head for Aden. As could be expected at any time of the year, it was very hot in those latitudes – in the opinion of the first mate, far too hot for painting. So Mr Mate in his wisdom decided that at Aden the vessel's funnel should be washed down and painted at night-time, using the funnel floodlights. On this occasion, even paying some watchkeepers overtime (1/9d per hour) the mate put his clever – or, to most people, crackpot – idea into practice. When Jack was told of the 'job and finish' task he laughed, believing it was some kind of joke – but it wasn't. At 22:00 hrs local time, the lamp-trimmer appeared with buckets of sugi mugi, eight bosun's chairs, and eight strops and line. These were rigged to the rim of the funnel, and the men set to washing down the metal, still warm. When that task was over, and after a mug of tea, pots of Cunard Red and black paint were issued; the sailors went aloft again and began painting the black top to the funnel. It was obvious, even to the dimmest-brained individual, that the funnel was still too hot for the paint to be applied smoothly. The opinion of the eight men involved with the paintbrushes was noisily communicated to the bosun; he was told to 'let the bloody mate know'.

After a short while, with nothing happening in response, Jack and his chums were informed, 'The mate's having a nap and can't be disturbed.'

The general opinion on the funnel was that someone – that someone being the bosun – had not even attempted to speak to the officer. Onward and downwards the men went, from the black top onto the Cunard Red area. But not surprisingly at 02:00 hrs the metal of the funnel was still quite warm. Still descending, the men went on to the first black line, then resuming with the red paint, then to the next black line and finally on to the red paint again, ending up on the engine-room fiddley. It was now about 04:30 hrs, and the first mate, forsaking his bunk, appeared and inspected the result. He was overheard telling the bosun what an inspired decision it was of his to paint the funnel during the cool of the tropical night.

Dawn broke with the rising of a most beautiful, very large, sun over the stern of the vessel, illuminating an Allen & Black Thistle Line British tramp ship which had been stuck in Aden for months. She had a damaged engine; pity the poor crew marooned in the overwhelming heat of Aden for months, with no sign of a respite. As dawn was breaking, there also commenced the breaking of the mate's heart – with a remarkable manifestation of his frustrated temper. As predicted by the sailors, the funnel, instead of being the pride of the company and a superb example of the sailors' art of painting, looked truly appalling. The black paint was in curtains, and the red paint had more holidays in it than Bournemouth.

From Aden, the *Port Hobart* sailed out into the Indian Ocean for a smooth crossing to Australia. There was some doubt amongst a few of the deck crowd whether the first mate was looking forward to a voyage through benign seas with his funnel in a mess and the overriding thought of all the overtime paid out at Aden – and the need to pay even more overtime to put the matter right before arrival in Australia. However, the officer sought solace from his self-inflicted difficulties by spending many hours sunbathing *sans* clothes atop the monkey island, no doubt planning his next brilliant idea. In the event he must have come to terms with his dilemma and, probably against his principle of watching every penny, he paid out the overtime needed to remove the unsightly curtains of paint and fill in the holidays, to make the funnel more like one expected on a Port boat.

One of the deck officers was, unusually for a comparatively young man, inclined to consume alcohol in quantities likely to impair his competence as an officer of the watch. Whether Captain Young was aware of this character deficit Jack was not too sure, but whenever this particular officer was on watch Captain Young paid more than the usual number of visits to the wheelhouse. As well as his ability to imbibe, this officer fancied himself as the dream of every female he came across. This became apparent when he made overt advances towards the only female passenger under 65. It was noted that these advances were not rebuffed, and from an entertainment point of view, this public half of the love story kept the men happily making jokes for hour upon hour. The other half of the love story kept Captain Young in the dark, or so the officer clearly believed, about what eventually became a carnal event – particularly on the chartroom couch. Like so many deck officers, he tended to think he was deceiving the master when, from the viewpoint of the ratings, who saw both sides of the equation, none of the masters – certainly not the masters Jack sailed with – were deceived by their duplicitous officers.

In the *Port Hobart*'s wheelhouse, the radar screen stack, which was in front of the chartroom door, could have the top viewing section wound up and down to provide a comfortable viewing height for its operators. One evening Jack was at the helm with the imbibing romantic officer as the officer of the watch. For much of the first half-hour of his trick at the wheel, Jack saw very little of his officer – and in fairness to the officer there was nothing for him to make a decision on, as in the middle of the Indian

Ocean there was little, if any, surface life except the vessel itself, ploughing on at a good 16 knots. The serene peace and quiet that Jack was enjoying was suddenly shattered by a figure hurtling through the chartroom door curtain and connecting with the radar stack with a heart-stopping, crunching sound followed by a long-drawn-out grunt. In the gloom Jack made out the figure to be a female by virtue of the long hair illuminated by the chartroom light. He left the wheel and went to her as his officer, appearing at the doorway, asked him to lend a hand. They lifted her up, to find she could not stand unassisted. All the time she was moaning and holding her stomach and chest. The officer put his arm around her and went to the wheelhouse door, telling Jack as he went, 'If the Old Man appears tell him I'm on the monkey island and should be down soon.' Jack returned to the wheel and, most fortunately for the errant officer, the master mysteriously came in from the chartroom seconds after the officer had arrived back in the wheelhouse via the starboard bridge wing.

Towards the end of his watch Jack heard the relieving officer of the watch arrive in the chartroom, ready for the next four hours. As he strained to hear what was being said between the two mates, it transpired that the woman had dashed out of the chartroom because she had believed she had heard the master's footsteps heading for the internal chartroom door, and her violent contact with the radar stack was because she had emerged in a panic from the chartroom into the total darkness of the wheelhouse.

As Jack was relieved at the wheel he went into the chartroom to report the course to his officer. As he turned to leave, the relieving officer, who Jack had known since apprenticeship days, handed him a pair of lacy knickers and a single shoe, and said, 'Throw these over the lee side as you go down – and discretion, please.' As Jack made his way onto the boat deck, he wondering, not for the first time, how such total idiots managed to get their certificates of competency. His watch officer still appeared to believe that the Old Man knew nothing. The fact that Captain Young did not actually catch the mate and the woman on the chartroom couch was probably intentional. No doubt the footsteps which had spooked them had been the master's, and his appearance in the wheelhouse seconds after the officer had reappeared on the bridge appeared to be deliberate. That the Old Man had been through the chartroom and almost certainly seen the underwear and shoe, still did not, apparently, enter the dimwit's befuddled brain or persuade him to mend his ways.

Indeed the lessons were plainly not heeded as within another week, when Jack was on the monkey island towards midnight he saw a figure on the bridge. The officer of the watch came out of the wheelhouse and went over to the person. Very soon that person disappeared down the bridge companionway to the boat deck, and the mate came up onto the island to tell Jack, 'We have a problem. A lady passenger came up here to report that an officer in a state of undress is in her bunk and asleep. No prizes for guessing who it is, and we have to do something about it before the 12:00–04:00 watch comes up here, otherwise, all hell'll break loose and someone will be in the kaki-poo.'

Jack asked his officer, 'What can you do?'

'Go and get him *pronto*,' came the exasperated reply.

Jack was alarmed that this officer, who he had known for years, was willing to leave the bridge; if caught he could have his ticket suspended, and that would be the end of his career with Port Line – and probably with any other premier shipping company as well. Nevertheless, at considerable risk, Jack and his officer rescued his errant colleague from the passenger's cabin, removing some skin from the man's bare backside as they dragged him over the brass-bound weather step of the cabin and away from the distressed passenger. However, as they attempted to get the drunk to his feet, they noticed that the door of the communal bathroom was open, with a pair of eyes peering around the door, watching them …

As the Iron Mike was steering the vessel during the day, Jack did not meet up with his officer of the watch until the following evening. When they were alone, Jack enquired if the passenger, or whoever had been watching them from the washroom, had reported the incident. But nothing further had been heard, nor had there been any thanks from the errant officer. It had been noted, however, that a certain deck officer been noticeably circumspect in sitting down. Nothing further was seen or mentioned about the incident amongst the executive branch, but in the catering department the bedroom stewards' scuttlebutt had it that a steward had found a pair of uniform trousers, a pair of black shoes, a pair of socks and some underpants in the communal passengers' laundry room. Allegedly the same steward had reported to the second steward that he'd had to mop up smears of blood from the deck of the passengers' quad. However, this bit of gossip did not reach Jack's ears until the vessel had docked in Australia and the passengers had disembarked.

For the next fortnight the *Port Hobart* made her way around the Australian coast discharging her cargo, then began the process of loading the cargo for the United Kingdom. As on the previous voyage, the vessel made her way to Hobart, where she was due to load fruit, both canned and fresh. This time, much to Jack's relief, no lifeboats were exercised; there were several people aboard who had witnessed his disgrace on the last visit to this city.

At the end of the quay walls at Hobart was a large factory bearing the legend IXL. This, intended to be read as 'I excel', was the brand name of a well-known jam and preserves company, which supplied 5lb tins of apple and greengage jams, pears etc. When Jack mentioned that he would like a tinned pear or two, a sailor said he would show him how easy it was to get some without spending any money. As the factory girls trooped by the bow of *Port Hobart*, the sailor shouted, 'How are the world's biggest old slag Sheilas today? Bloody 'ell you ain't 'alf ugly!' Jack was stunned by that, and then by the torrent of abuse, with far worse language, from the women on the quay. 'Pommie bastards' was the most moderate of expressions in the tirade.

'Hang on for about ten minutes, and then,' the sailor told Jack, 'get ready to run.' Jack had visions of the women returning with their menfolk to give the British sailors a severe slapping and saw Captain Young on the deck. With the ill-timed appearance of the master all hell broke loose as tins of fruit began to hit the side of the vessel, while others landed on the deck. This barrage was accompanied by threats uttered by female Tasmanian voices about what would happen to any Pommie bastard from the vessel venturing ashore, disembowelling and emasculation the minimum punishment. Jack stood almost surrounded by the bent and battered cans, which the ladies of IXL jams had so kindly donated to the welfare fund for the crew of the *Port Hobart*.

'I'm not too sure what the chief officer will think of the divots in his decks.' Jack knew without looking who the words had come from before turning around to see his master studying the cans and the slightly – very slightly – damaged pinewood. Before Jack could deny all knowledge Captain Young continued, 'I'll get the steward to take these cans to the store room. They can't be returned to the factory, dented as they are.'

The master looked directly into Jack's eyes. Jack struggled to find what to say. He could hardly say that all he'd wanted was a few canned pears. So he simply looked at his master as Captain Young took his handkerchief from his cuff and wiped his nose. Then he indicated the cans, some now leaking juice, and said to Jack, 'I suppose you think it's a new idea to rile these women in order to get these? But it's not – when I was an apprentice we did the same, probably to the mothers of these women you torment.'

Jack found his voice in an attempt to deny that he had said anything, but as he began his defence in a squeaky voice, Captain Young said, 'I saw, young man, that while you may not have been the protagonist, you accompanied him. Don't think of excuses for my benefit. Save them for the chief officer when he sees his deck. He too will know the cause of what you have done to it, and will certainly not be inclined to thank you.' He turned on his heel and, kicking a can aside, walked away. No sooner was the master out of sight than the entire deck crew descended and grabbed as many unpunctured cans as possible before the assistant cook and the second steward appeared, to remove the rest to the stores.

Within half an hour Jack was summoned to the mate's office where his first officer laid into him, no doubt at the instigation of the master, and completed his diatribe with, 'Now shove off and enjoy your ill-gotten gains – but not until you've washed the juice off the deck.'

Jack did as he was told and enjoyed several tins of pears, but he paid a high price; he sat on the lavatory for several days afterwards.

After leaving Hobart, the *Port Hobart* plied her way up the eastern coast of Australia, visiting the usual loading ports of Sydney, Brisbane, Townsville, Rockhampton and Cairns before finally heading for Wyndham, in north Western Australia, the back of beyond. This was the first time Jack had visited Wyndham since the *Port Lincoln's* visit. When the *Port Hobart* was berthed at the curved jetty, nothing appeared to have

changed over the years; as before, the
deck crew had to unseal the holds in the
morning and reseal them in the evening.
The cargo was just the same: sides of beef
from the nearby abattoir.

The first mate announced that the
vessel needed to produce a cricket team,
because a team from Wyndham, made up
of men from the abattoir and associated
service businesses, had challenged the
Port Hobart to a match. Jack was included
in the team. On the appointed day a lorry
appeared alongside the vessel and the team
climbed aboard in the belief that the match
would be held in Wyndham. No such
luck. The men were taken on a long ride

Port Hobart cricket team –
including three future masters

into the bush, through red dust past the stalks of burnt trees and the corrugated iron
huts of Aborigines, before being deposited on a barren plot with myriads of colourful
parakeets swarming overhead. No such luxury as a green pitch there, either: a length of
coconut matting was the wicket. The bowling by Australia was savage in the extreme:
the batting by the United Kingdom was woeful. Wisden would not carry an entry titled
Port Hobart. Jack and his team failed miserably – even the beers afterwards did not
lighten the load of failure on the shoulders of the team – but it was a unique occasion
for him in the burnt, barren land of Western Australia.

When *Port Hobart* eventually sailed from Wyndham she had on board the sword of
a swordfish caught by a sailor. Of all the fish Jack had seen landed on the various vessels
of the fleet, this was by far the most interesting, and it was the centre of attention for
several days.

When the ship was nearing Indonesian waters, Jack was on watch on the monkey
island. The night was quiet and still, the only breeze created by the vessel's passage.
Jack, as usual when on lookout on an empty ocean, tended to daydream or – if no one
was about – would read his textbooks for his second mate's certificate. It was not an
ideal place to study, but this was a more useful manner to occupy his time rather than
watching the ocean and the sky, however remarkable. Having his head down yet again
in *Monroe's Mathematics for Deck Officers*, he looked up and could hardly believe his
eyes. The entire fore end of the vessel had vanished, with just the mast and Samson posts
poking out above the water – which was absolutely flat. The vessel was not pitching or
yawing, there was none of the noise of taking a header in a rising sea. No noise, no
vibration, no sensation of unusual movement. As quickly as it must have arrived, the
water fell away, exposing the fo'c'sle head then No 1 and No 2 hatches. Jack, tucking

his book away, called down the voice pipe to report what he had seen to the man at the helm. The helmsman told him that he had seen it all too, but the duty mate had been in the chartroom and had arrived in the wheelhouse only in time to see the water receding. The officer of the watch came up to the binnacle platform and between them they determined that the water had risen over the bow rather than the vessel pitching into it. The sea was still flat calm, with no swell of any kind. They finally decided that it must have been a tsunami, probably created by an earthquake somewhere in this earthquake-prone region. However, neither mariner could explain why the vessel displayed no indication either by sound or movement that she had been submerged for a few very brief minutes under what must have been hundreds of tons of water. When Jack related the events in the mess room, no one believed him, and the general opinion was that he had been dreaming or pissed – until his yarn was corroborated by his watchmate at the wheel. But then the deck crowd decided, not for the first time, that the two of them were 'lying little sods with bugger all else to do'.

The voyage concluded at Hull. When the wool was being discharged, Jack, summoned to the master's day room, was feeling concerned that he had not been invited by the first mate to return to the *Port Hobart* for the next voyage. And for the master to demand his presence was really serious. Jack decided that he had probably roughed up the master at some time or other – probably with the tins of fruit at Hobart. The summons to see the captain was ominous, to say the least; this had not happened to him before – the only contact that he'd had with a master after the end of a voyage had been the very surprising meeting with Captain Townshend aboard the *Port Auckland*. By the time Jack reached the office door he had concocted very scrambled excuses to present in response to any displeasure the Old Man might, and probably would, throw at him.

Jack tapped lightly on the door, and Captain Young invited him into the cabin not only addressing him by his surname, but amazingly by prefixing it with 'Mister'. Captain Young, even when putting Jack in his place, had always been extremely polite, but this was an experience Jack was never to forget. Captain Young then said to Jack, 'We have a new vessel building at Harland and Wolff in Belfast. She's named *Port Nicholson* and when her fitting out is completed I shall take command of her. I'd like you to come with me to her.'

Jack, despite the 'Mister', was still expecting trouble in some form or another. Now he had this very surprising, and to him unique, offer of a brand-new vessel from his master. Refusal was the last thing on his mind as he stuttered the words, 'Yes, yes, Sir. Thank you, Sir.'

'I'm pleased that you'll be joining her. However, it won't be for several months yet, and I'm afraid that you will have to do home trade runs and 'working by' until she is ready. I'll tell the office of this conversation, and they'll facilitate your being free when *Port Nicholson* is ready. Do have a good leave. Goodbye.'

Jack left the *Port Hobart* on cloud nine – a brand-new vessel and a master who wanted him there! Life was pretty good after all.

9

The interregnum

TSMV *Port Sydney*

'You, *Port Townsville!*'

As Jack took his first step on the brow from the dry-dock wall to the deck of the *Port Sydney*, he looked up, to see a man in an immaculate white shirt, his gold cufflinks glowing through the grime of the Tyneside ship-repair yard. The figure was smoking a cigarette in a long holder and wearing epaulettes with three gold bands. Jack closed his eyes and opened them again, but the image was still there. The sight was a novelty in itself, but the accent gave away the identity of the immaculate figure at the top of the brow.

TSMV *Port Sydney*

Jack replied, 'And you, *Port Townsville*,' thinking to himself, 'I'm off, back to London on the first train.' The figure at the top of the brow was none other than the first mate with whom he had major disagreements aboard the *Port Townsville*. Judging by the man's recognition of Jack, he had not forgotten either, despite the passage of time.

But when Jack reached the deck, he could hardly believe his eyes. Gone were the sunken eyes, red face and purple nose. Before him stood a picture of health, in perfectly creased trousers and well-polished uniform shoes. 'In view of what you said to me when we last spoke aboard the *Port Townsville*, I take it that you don't want me here with you?' Jack enquired.

'Why are you here?'

'Because they decided, Sir, that as you don't have a bosun or any men, I should be here until you get a bosun. But as you said I was not to be on the same vessel as you ever again, I'll go back to London.'

'Now that you're here, you may as well stay. I've heard they're sending two men to me tomorrow. Come to the office and I'll give you some keys.'

His officer gave him the keys not to the bosun's cabin but to that of a quartermaster. He then handed Jack the deck store keys and a couple of others, including that to the forepeak. As his left hand came out with the final set of keys, Jack noted with some surprise a wedding ring on his finger.

'At the moment there's nothing much to do except keep it a bit tidy on deck and make sure that they're re-rigging the cargo gear correctly. The galley's closed – no cooks. You'll have to find food ashore. At lunchtime meet me in the pub.' He indicated its direction through the dock gates.

'Yes Sir.' What else could Jack say?

By the time he had settled into his cabin, there was no time to acquaint himself with the *Port Sydney*. As it was nearing lunchtime he made his way ashore, through the yard gates and up the slope to the typical Tyneside pub. Sure enough, the mate was sitting in the smoke room tucking into a plate of God knows what concoction. He indicated where Jack was to sit, and began a conversation relating to the company, ships and associated matters. Under the circumstances it was a very convivial lunch.

When he went towards the bar for a drink he politely enquired what his newfound friend wanted, expecting the request to be for a gin, and he was flabbergasted to hear that the mate wanted just Indian tonic water. Jack wanted to find out more about the transformation from the mate he had known aboard *Port Townsville* to this model first officer of Port Line Ltd. Having navigated carefully between the protocols of rank and unadorned nosiness, Jack was able to elicit the fact that the mate was now married, and to an Australian – or perhaps, because of his accent, an East Anglian. Jack did not enquire further: the chumminess could, he felt, disappear as easily as it had arrived.

The *Port Sydney* was a 10,166-ton twin-screw vessel delivered to Port Line in 1955 by Swan, Hunter & Wigham Richardson, and a sister vessel to the *Port Melbourne*.

When Jack was a boy aboard *Port Brisbane*, he had been aware that a certain rivalry existed between the proponents of the merits of *Port Brisbane* and *Port Auckland* and those of *Port Sydney* and *Port Melbourne*. Quite why, considering the frequent change of personnel, such emotions were created was a mystery to him. Inter-company rivalry he could understand, and on occasion – particularly in Australasian pubs – he joined in the arguments, but *Port Auckland* and *Port Brisbane* versus *Port Sydney* and *Port Melbourne* he simply couldn't follow.

The next day, when the two seamen arrived aboard the *Port Sydney*, the first mate could find little to occupy their time except to follow Jack around. He decided to keep them busy chipping the paint off No 4 hatch's Samson posts, and just for once there was no hurry to complete the task. With short hours plus prolonged smoke-hos and lunchtimes, the task – including painting with red lead, priming and the final white coat – took the fortnight that Jack remained aboard the vessel, and he decided that this playing bosun was a doddle. But it was soon back to reality when he was despatched to the *Port Napier* under the command of Captain Lavers, for a 12-day home trade, or run job, voyage from Liverpool to London.

TSMV *Port Napier*

The *Port Napier* was an 11,834-ton twin-screw vessel built in 1947 by the Tyneside company of Swan, Hunter & Wigham Richardson Ltd. The vessel was, in design, Port Line's answer to the Empire Class of food ships of Shaw Savill & Albion Co. and Blue Star Line Ltd. The hull shape was from the heritage of the *Port Jackson*, as was, to a

TSMV *Port Napier* (Courtesy D. Western)

MV *Port Townsville* – a seaman's yacht

certain extent, the superstructure. Until the end of the 1940s the same hull form was used by all the Port Line twin-screw vessels, including in the *Port Brisbane* and *Port Auckland,* and all these vessels had much the same cargo capacity to within a few tons. Until the advent of *Port Auckland* and *Port Brisbane,* with the exception of a poop deck in some of them, all the larger vessels of Port Line had the same hold configuration: two for'ard holds, one abaft the bridge and three on the after decks.

The time in Liverpool was nothing of note for Jack. The usual tasks occupied his time: looking after the cargo running gear, washing off the decks before the stevedores came aboard, and checking the lowering of the lifeboats and the gear inside them. As far as his social life was concerned, he met up with his cousin for the first time in 15 years, at the Legs of Man pub alongside Lime Street railway station. She was in Liverpool, studying at the School of Tropical Medicine, and they had a fine time together, changing their views of Liverpool for the better and contributing significantly to the Legs of Man's coffers.

London, and pay-off; Jack spent the next couple of weeks 'working by' the *Port Napier* until she signed on her deep-sea crew. His next appointment was with the *Port Townsville* in Hull. To Jack it seemed rather ironic that he had so recently been reunited with his former antagonist from the *Port Townsville,* and now he was to join the very vessel on which he had experienced such a difficult voyage.

A train took him to Hull and the King George Dock, where the *Port Townsville* was discharging bales of wool. As Jack approached the vessel, the memories flooded back. There was little doubt that the vessel was, in cargo ship terms, a yacht as far as a deck crew were concerned; a sailor would have described her as being 'light' on deck, meaning that her cargo-handling equipment – derricks, running gear etc – was relatively minimal and easily handled.

Jack found that a number of the deep-sea deck crew were still with the vessel for her run job to London. He knew a couple of the men, and they told him of a good voyage with a good mate and bosun, but both of those men had gone on leave. The first mate and the bosun taking the *Port Townsville* to London were not previously known to Jack, but during the brief period he served with them, he found they were infinitely better than the first officer and, above all, the bosun he had served under during his deep-sea voyage on that ship.

On the *Port Townsville's* arrival at London she had a light covering of snow on her decks. As it was Christmastime Jack was offered the opportunity to go home for two days, but after his last Christmas at home he decided to stay until he paid off on New Year's Eve.

What started the exercise Jack did not know and never found out, but when most of the officers and crew left the vessel early on Christmas Eve, he noticed that the dockside cranes, which should have been unmanned, had figures in the cabs, with binoculars seemingly trained on the after decks of the *Port Townsville*. Soon afterwards, a number of Customs and Excise officers boarded the vessel and confined the few remaining crew to the accommodation. The customs men began to search the cabins, then headed for the tonnage hatch, presumably because they had found nothing of interest in the cabins. When a vessel from abroad berthed in the United Kingdom, it was not unusual for a rummage crew of customs officers to descend on a vessel and search high and low for contraband – in Jack's experience, with little or no success. These customs men busied themselves until about midday and, probably because it was Christmas Eve and they wanted to be home early, left as promptly as they had arrived.

That evening, Jack made his way to Plaistow and had a wonderful Christmas Eve in a typical London pub, the piano working overtime. Every popular song from 1900 to 1955 was sung with gusto as only original East End Londoners can – a truly superb evening. With slightly more 'home brewed' in him than usual, Jack was in a happy mood when he went through the King George V Dock gate, even wishing the gate constable a cheery Christmas greeting which – surprisingly – was returned. He boarded the almost deserted vessel. At the top of the gangway he found that the watchman was not quite as amenable to festive cheer as the constable, and Jack was told not too politely to bugger off and get his head down. Christmas Day was mostly spent looking for somewhere open to eat. Finally, Jack and two others found a 'greasy spoon' in North Woolwich which provided them with food – not perhaps Christmas fare but very acceptable nonetheless.

On their return to the *Port Townsville*, Jack and his chums made sure that the dockside crane cabs were empty, and then went to the tonnage hatch, looking for whatever the customs men had been after. They found nothing until, as they were about to ascend the ladder, they saw that one of the beams supporting the deck above was different from the rest; it had no lip on it. Although it was painted silver-grey like the rest of the deckhead, they could see that there was a piece of plywood concealing the

MV *Port Nelson*

Port Nelson in the Thames

space between the beam and the wood, so they pulled the plywood out of the beam. Lo and behold, in a cavity stretching from one side of the vessel to the other were packs of 200 Senior Service cigarettes. Strangely, amongst the cigarettes were numerous boxed Dinky toys. The men concluded that the toys were export cargo, so the cigarettes were probably destined for Australia. Quite how the customs men at London had got word of the stash would never be known to the three men. In view of the interest of HM Customs and Excise they decided to leave the booty, return the plywood cover and pretend that they had found nothing. In the ensuing years Jack often wondered if the vessel would go to the breakers yard with her hoard still aboard. Like so much of maritime lore, it was to be yet another mystery of the sea – Who? Why? When?

On New Year's Eve, Jack left the *Port Townsville* in rather a better mood than the last time he had taken his leave of the vessel, in Liverpool. A Buddhist might have said that the meeting with his old adversary from the *Port Townsville* and his subsequent unexpected joining of the latter vessel was his karma.

His next destination was his home at Wraxall for a couple of weeks' leave. He mostly spent it clearing up the gardens and woodland – not an easy task in wintertime, but a necessary one. His neighbouring chum was at sea with Prince Line, so life for Jack was work and a few visits to the village church – and, to counterbalance the piety, the Royal Oak afterwards. 'Come unto me all ye who are weary and heavily laden, and I will refresh you'; surely George's beers did just that for Jack on a Sunday evening.

Just after his fortnight's leave had expired a phone call from the dock office summoned him back to London. The actual instruction was that he should get to London soon. Jack took the clerk at his word, and as his tasks at home were not quite completed 'soon' became another seven days,. When he presented himself at the dock office that 'soon' translated into the week's extra leave being without any pay. However, the powers that be could not decide what to do with him, so he booked a room on the Sailors' Home in Commercial Road. For about a fortnight he hung around with daily visits to the dock and the office; he was on shore pay, but with no work.

Eventually the *Port Nelson* appeared from New Zealand and Jack was sent to the vessel to 'work by' as part of the shore gang – former seamen who worked as labourers aboard vessels when the crew were on leave. While this was not his choice of occupation, Jack had to make do and tolerate the shore bosun, who was treated with totally unjustified fawning reverence by his charge hands – not the type of person he would take to – and judging by the bosun's reaction to him, this sentiment was reciprocated. Jack was sidelined. He had a cabin aboard the vessel, which was rather better than the Mission, but the tasks required of him were so menial as to be extremely annoying.

The *Port Nelson* was a well-proportioned, handsome single-screw vessel of 8,950 tons, built in 1951 by Harland & Wolff Ltd in Belfast. Her engines were built by Harland & Wolff on licence from Burmeister & Wain, and those, like the *Port Townsville's* Doxfords, could achieve 15.5 knots. The *Port Nelson* was, in most respects, similar to the *Port Townsville* with very much the same dimensions, but she had a more upright wheelhouse and a taller, less angled, funnel top. Although he would not go to sea in her, and his working conditions were appalling, Jack took to the vessel as another example of the eye-catching modern lines of the post-1948 Port Line vessels. In the mess room he heard the shore gang talking amongst themselves about the *Port New Plymouth*, the largest refrigerated cargo ship in the world, berthing ahead of the *Port Nelson* on the afternoon tide.

TSMV *Port New Plymouth*

Jack had been privileged to serve in just the post-war fleet of Port Line. His vessels had ranged from the utilitarian *Port Lincoln* and *Port Lyttelton* to the dignified shape of the *Port Pirie* and, more recently, the *Port Napier* and the very similar *Port Hobart*. These vessels then made way for the ageless design of the *Port Auckland* and *Port Brisbane*. From this quite revolutionary shape came the *Port Townsville* and *Port Nelson* – all graceful vessels, distinguished by their outline all over the maritime world. At that time, however, Jack was not so conscious of the attractiveness of the Port Line vessels until he looked up from the starboard bridge wing of the *Port Nelson* to watch a vessel he had never seen before, even in a photograph.

A familiarly coloured bow came into sight, followed by the words *Port New Plymouth* on the white apron. As she was towed past the *Port Nelson*, Jack was truly astounded by what he saw once the fore end of the vessel had passed. Maritime craft, like human beings, are all built slightly differently from each other, and what might be admired by one observer may not suit the taste of another. However, to his eyes the ugliness of everything abaft the bridge of that vessel was astonishing by any standard, let alone those of the design principles for which Port Line was renowned. The superstructure

Port New Plymouth (Courtesy D. Western)

was utilitarian, with a ridiculously small and out-of-proportion funnel, followed at the stern by a poop deck whose prominence destroyed the hull line. For the purpose of earning revenue through her cargo-carrying capacity, her design was, no doubt, from the owner's point of view, a success. But what Jack was witnessing was, he felt, a travesty of modern ship design.

The *Port New Plymouth*, the first Port Line vessel to carry the name, was a twin-screw vessel of 13,000 tons, with her Sulzer engines capable of producing a cruising speed of 18 knots. Built by Swan, Hunter & Wigham Richardson Ltd at their Wallsend yard, she was launched and handed over to her owners in 1960. From a mariner's point of view she looked very heavy on deck, with 20 derricks and no straight run of working decks: not unusual in some of the larger post-war Port Line vessels. The other side of the working coin was that she had mechanically operated steel McGregor hatch covers with some other labour-saving devices. Jack saw the *Port New Plymouth* berth ahead of the *Port Nelson*, and would have loved to have had a conversation with another rating relating to the beauty or otherwise of the then largest vessel in the Port Line fleet. But as he was a deep-sea mariner, the shore gang did not speak to him except for essential work-related matters, and similarly Jack made no attempt to converse with them socially. Probably for the first time in his employment with the company, he felt quite isolated.

Within hours, Jack was told to report to the dock office. There he was told to move to the *Port New Plymouth* so that over the next few weeks he could familiarise himself with her, as her deck setup was identical to that of his new ship, *Port Nicholson*. He was greatly relieved to be seeing the last of the shore gang and the charge hand.

Jack digested this information with dread. Was his new vessel as ugly as *Port New Plymouth*? The pleasure of being asked to join the new vessel by Captain Young and joining a new vessel for the first time was dampened by the likely design of his new appointment. When he found himself a berth – a very comfortable cabin aboard the *Port New Plymouth* – he met several of the deep-sea crew still aboard to do the home trade voyage with her. Jack asked them their opinion of their vessel. None of those who had sailed in her had many complaints, and all liked the superb accommodation. When Jack casually mentioned the design of their vessel, the only response he received was 'a big awkward sod'.

Jack's other slight concern at that time was the lack of ratings outside the dock office. In the past when a new Port boat was approaching her maiden voyage a queue of ratings would form for a berth on the 'new 'un', but he had seen no such queue for *Nicholson*. In his time with Port Line, Jack had witnessed the jostling long-term planning of various run jobs, in order to be ready when the 'new 'un' was delivered and requiring a crew. Had the men already been selected, like himself? If they had, then surely during this time in London or on his home trade runs he would have met some of them. Despite his misgivings, he made the best of his time aboard the *Port New Plymouth*, not least because the galley supplied him with three meals a day: no more visits to the North Woolwich Greasy Spoon, thank goodness.

Ten days after the *Port New Plymouth* docked at King George V, the rest of her home trade crew were assembled, ready to sign on. This was the signal for Jack to leave his comfy cabin and make his way to the dock office for a post to occupy him until he was sent to Belfast to join *Port Nicholson*.

TSMV *Port Vindex*

'Pick up *Port Vindex* at Hull, take her to the Continent, and bring her back here in time to get to Belfast. A day or two either way won't make any difference. If the vessel's return is delayed, you'll catch the ferry back to Hull.' With these words the man from the dock office sent Jack north to join the *Port Vindex*.

The ship had a most interesting past; she had started life in 1941 in the yard of Swan, Hunter & Wigham Richardson at Wallsend, on the Tyne, as a twin-screw vessel of 10,500 tons, to be named *Port Sydney*. Those were the very darkest days at sea, particularly in the North Atlantic, with the wholesale destruction of Allied shipping by enemy submarines. One of the more effective methods of defeating the menace of the German submarines was aeroplanes. At that time the land-based planes' range was very limited, so carrier-based aircraft policed the convoys. But the aircraft carriers were, at the slow speed of the convoys, vulnerable to submarine attack, so to counter this risk, smaller, cheaper aircraft carriers were needed. While some of them, known

TSMV *Port Vindex*

as 'Woolworth' carriers, were built in America, in Britain it was not unusual for the Admiralty to purchase merchant ships under construction with hulls and engines completed; the hulls were adapted to Admiralty requirements and the vessels were completed as escort carriers, to defend merchant ship convoys. *Port Sydney* was one of the two Port Line hulls purchased by the Admiralty for that purpose.

As HMS *Vindex* she carried out sterling work for the Admiralty before being purchased back by Port Line in 1947 and then rebuilt as originally designed: a refrigerated cargo ship. To honour the important role she had performed during the war, when she entered service for Port Line in 1949 it retained her name– unique amongst its vessels. All its other vessels bore names of places in New Zealand, Australia and Canada, a practice started by the company of William Milburn, one of the major shareholders in the formation of the Commonwealth and Dominion Line in 1914. Her completed design was in the same vein as *Port Victor*, *Port Napier*, *Port Pirie*, *Port Phillip*, *Port Wellington* and the *Port Jackson*, the originator of the design.

Once aboard and signed on, Jack was allocated to a watch, and the *Port Vindex* sailed from Hull, bound for Hamburg. At the mouth of the River Elbe, Jack was surprised to see several masts protruding from the sea off Cuxhaven. As he steered the vessel, still under the North Sea pilot, he decided that this was a dangerous place to navigate. He mentioned to the officer of the watch the surprising number of submerged vessels in such a small area. The response was that the vessels were probably victims of the wartime minefield, as yet uncleared. The officer kept a straight face, and Jack was not too sure whether he was playing him for a fool – not a difficult task – or if there really was a minefield there. So he decided that he would check the chart of the area. In the event, there were just too many officers around he abandoned his excursion into the chartroom, and never established the truth. And then the frantic activity in Hamburg took the matter from Jack's busy mind.

As the *Port Vindex* passed up the river amid a winter snowstorm, a recording of the British national anthem was relayed over the water. It would appear that such an appropriate honour was customary to a vessel of any nationality en route to Hamburg. The moment the gangway was lowered onto the quay wall, the dockworkers streamed aboard, the hatches opened and work began at a pace that put the British dockworkers to shame. All-day and all-night work soon had the cargo discharged, and it seemed that in no time the *Port Vindex* was under way again, en route to Bremen. Jack was on watch again as she went quite a way into the North Sea before taking a widely curving course off Cuxhaven, and he overheard the pilot telling the master, 'Better safe than sorry; you never know what might still be there. Anyhow, this is the course I recommend.'

Were they talking about shallows, or were they talking about a minefield? Yet again, Jack's curiosity was never to be satisfied. *Port Vindex* then entered the Weser, passing Bremerhaven, and steamed upriver to Bremen.

On Jack's final voyage aboard the *Port Hobart*, he had painted the windlass in a smart red, white and green colour scheme. He had never forgotten the mate's comments: 'You can paint over that. If you think I'm going to have a windlass looking like an Italian ice cream, you can think again – *get rid of it*.' Much to his artistic dismay, Jack had obeyed, and changed it to a very boring white.

Now, ashore with some colleagues in an almost deserted Bremen on a Sunday afternoon, Jack, exploring alone for a while, was interrupted by one of his companions reporting that they had found a place selling ice-creams. Jack went in and ordered one. His companions were already tucking into theirs so he joined them and marvelled at the intricate colours at the top of his cone. When he paid for his ice cream, the man behind the counter thanked him in English with a distinctly Mediterranean accent – and Jack's mind flashed back to the fo'c'sle head of the *Port Hobart* and the mate's comment about an Italian ice cream. Never until now having seen one, or even known what was so special about it, the colours and the accent all made sense to him; his ice cream was Italian and truly delicious, making the trip to Bremen a treasured memory.

On the return to London, a clerk from the dock office was waiting with a note for Jack from Mr Lofthouse and a first-class rail warrant for him to join the *Port Nicholson* in Belfast. However, first class did not extend to the ferry across the Irish Sea. Jack decided that an error had been made somewhere, but if the gods smiled upon him, who was he to argue the point? The salmon fillet in the dining carriage had tasted very good, and he mentally thanked dear old Lofthouse yet again.

10

TSMV *Port Nicholson*

Alpha: from the builders' yard

Arriving in Belfast, on his first visit to Ireland – the home of some of his ancestors – Jack was met by the Port Line agent for Belfast and taken to his digs. This turned out to be a spotlessly clean house run by a very pious lady, who dictated where in her house Jack could and could not go; the latter area included a room containing a grand piano with a photograph of a young man in the graduation gown of an eminent university. At breakfast the following morning, the lady said grace before Jack and a couple of other men about to join the *Port Nicholson* could tuck into their bacon and eggs. The men were taken by the agent to the Queen's yard, and the fitting-out basin of Harland & Wolff where in the incessant drizzle they sighted their new vessel.

Jack was used to working aboard vessels undergoing repair or their tri-annual surveys amid the soul-destroying mayhem of dirt and never-ending dockyard equipment. But the sight which welcomed him did not exactly stir the blood. As he viewed his new vessel before ascending its brow he noted, with considerable pleasure, that the *Port Nicholson* had a funnel in proportion to her size, unlike the *Port New Plymouth*'s upended flowerpot. Whilst his new vessel would never be attractive in his eyes, the more appropriately sized funnel made an ugly superstructure slightly more acceptable to him. Aboard the vessel Jack was approached by the bosun, a younger man than most of his rank with a decidedly east London accent, who gave him the keys to his cabin; much like the cabin aboard the *Port New Plymouth*, it was quite luxurious. Taking a trip around the accommodation, dodging the myriad dockyard workers, Jack found not only the expected recreation room, but also a hobbies room – a previously unheard-of addition to the superior accommodation enjoyed in the more modern Port Line vessels. In a further inspection of his cabin, Jack found that the accommodation was fully air-conditioned. Who would ever have believed that men living under the foc'sle head aboard the early Port Line vessels still in service, such as the *Port Alma* and *Port Fairy*, built back in 1928, could easily join a vessel with superior single-berth

TSMV *Port Nicholson* (Courtesy Fotoflite)

cabins amidships and air-conditioned luxury? When, after a few more days in digs, Jack learned that the accommodation and galleys on the vessel were completed he moved his belongings aboard the first new vessel that he had ever experienced.

Within a few days, still under grey and drizzling clouds, the *Port Nicholson* was ready for handing over to her owner, Port Line Ltd. The 14,942-ton, 18.5–21 knot vessel was due to sail on the evening tide. But Jack was astounded to witness a gang of dockyard workers painting the rain-soaked top of the metal McGregor hatches; one man was using a squeegee to remove some of the excess water, with two others, following him, rolling the paint onto the wet surface. It was a surreal sight for a sailor to see such a wanton waste of paint. It was this type of behaviour, along with countless other examples of really shoddy workmanship by those in the shipbuilding industry, that eventually led, along with the ever-increasing demands of the trade unions and diminishing productivity of the workforce, to the almost total demise of the previously world-renowned British shipbuilding industry.

When the deck crew was assembled, Jack finally discovered why the 'new 'un' had not had the usual queues of hopefuls at the Port Line dock office. The deck crew of the vessel comprised the quartermasters with the usual boy seamen and junior seamen – but a very mixed bunch of other sailors. Amongst these men were deck hands unqualified – DHU. Jack had not previously come across such a rank. These men were older than boy or junior seamen, and in this instance they were riggers recruited from the Harland & Wolff yard. They had little or no knowledge of seamanship and they had to be day workers, because unqualified as they were, they could not be watchkeepers. Port Line, probably for the first time in its history, was reduced to employing labourers to man its vessels. Not quite the auspicious start to a maiden voyage that Jack had expected.

Port Nicholson dressed overall

In the evening the *Port Nicholson* sailed out from her birthplace into a gathering storm in the Irish Sea. Jack went on watch on the midnight to 4 a.m. stint. The first hour found him on a very small metal wheel in an unfamiliar and unique open-plan combined wheelhouse / chartroom. During the course of his trick at the wheel he noticed that on the wheelhouse windows there seemed to be a shadow on the glass – not a shadow of uniform shape, simply an unidentified shadow.

On this particular vessel the lookout was from the crow's nest on the stump mast. En route from the accommodation to the door in the mast, Jack was assaulted by rain and sea water whipped up by the gale force wind. When, at the end of his watch, he returned to the accommodation and removed his oilskins, he found them marked with a grey substance, but eager to get to his warm and welcoming bunk, he just hung them up in the drying room and turned in.

At 8 a.m. Jack, conscious of the rolling of the vessel, rose from his bunk for breakfast. In the November murk at that time little could be seen, but as he approached the mess room he could hear raised voices. It transpired that at what passes for dawn in a gale-whipped sea, the shadow that he had noticed on the wheelhouse windows had turned out to be a film of half-dried grey paint; the wind had lifted the paint applied to a hatch lid the previous day and deposited it all over the forepart of the bridge and accommodation. Only the bosun appeared to be taking the matter calmly. Everyone else – those who had no direct responsibility for rectifying the difficulty – were making a lot of noise (except the Harland & Wolff recruits, who remained silent, as they would have to clean up the mess), berating the men at the shipyard. The sight of the awful mess aboard a brand-new vessel was hard to believe.

Nothing could be done until the vessel turned into the English Channel, with the wind and sea astern. Then the work began: hosing down the superstructure to remove the worst of the mess, and trying to wash it over the side. *Port Nicholson* was equipped with teak decking, and although the working alleyways had been scrubbed at some point in Belfast, by the time the vessel

Port Nicholson wheelhouse

had left the quay wall the decks were very soiled. As the gale had precluded much positive work on the white-painted surfaces, the bosun decided that every effort should now be made to get the vessel's teak decks into pristine order for the arrival, amid pomp and ceremony, in London.

When Jack took over the wheel for the last trick of the watch he found Captain Young on the bridge with his first officer. Although he had been conscious of the first mate when the vessel was leaving Belfast, he could not have described him other than him being the man in the gloom on the fo'c'sle, with an air of authority. Both the officer and Captain Young were in deep conversation, and neither appeared to be too happy. Jack could well understand why.

The only man in the wheelhouse who seemed to be without a care in the world was the Channel pilot. Jack hoped that his quiet whistling was a sign of contentment rather than any nervous disposition manifesting itself through pursed lips. But then, at the time for Jack to be relieved, the officer of the watch whispered to him that the sailor for the 4:00 to 8:00 watch had been detained on deck, and the 4:00 to 8:00 quartermaster was still trying to wash down the gangway. In short Jack's hour-long trick at the wheel would be extended, and by how long he was not too sure. The next officer of the watch, the second mate and navigator, arrived, and after discussions in the chartroom area moved across to the wheelhouse. The *Port Nicholson* was the first merchant vessel to be equipped with the new True Motion radar as standard. Whereas a traditional radar scanner has the transmitting vessel fixed in the centre of the screen, with True Motion the position of the transmitting vessel moves relative to its surroundings. The vessel carried a radar engineer for part of the outward voyage, and the manufacturer took every opportunity to feature a photograph of this officer, albeit in his shirtsleeves, at their console in publications relating to the electronic marine environment.

By 16:15, *Port Nicholson* had yet another surprise for Jack. While the master and his deputy were still in the wheelhouse, in walked an officer wearing a uniform jacket carrying the broad gold band of a commodore. Jack looked once, then again – and yes it *was* a broad gold band. This officer joined the master and first mate in a discussion whose nature Jack could not decipher because of the howling wind. By 16:30 he was relieved at the wheel, and after reporting the course to the second mate he went to Captain Young and reported the course to him. The captain turned and acknowledged the course, realised it was Jack and welcomed him aboard *Port Nicholson*. He then turned to his first mate and told him that he had brought Jack from *Port Hobart*.

Jack had a good look at the first officer, a very tall man. This officer then impressed him by telling him he would look forward to working with him. That was yet another first for Jack: no first officer had ever said that to him. From those few kindly words, Jack decided – quite rightly as it turned out – that this particular officer was truly a gentleman. The commodore took no part in the exchanges between Jack and his superiors, and as Jack turned to leave the wheelhouse he noticed that this commodore had his broad gold band on a bed of blue, the insignia of an engineer. Jack had not realised that there was such a person as a commodore chief engineer in the Port Line. The phrase 'never too old to learn' went through his mind as he walked along the boat deck.

As *Port Nicholson* turned into the Thames estuary she anchored, waiting for a tide, enabling the deck crew to tidy the vessel. ready to enter the Royal Docks. There was much washing down of the white paintwork to remove any semblance of grey paint and salt spray, the working alleyway decks were scrubbed again, by a rotary scrubbing machine, whilst the quartermasters washed down the gangway again, and fitted its canvas side screen carrying the legend '*Port Nicholson*'. While the quartermasters were preparing the gangway for the great and good of the maritime world to come aboard, Jack and his colleagues were readying the bunting to hoist from the prow to the head of the jumbo derrick, then to the radar mast and from there on two wires to the after Samson posts at No 4 hatch. Eventually as much as could be done in advance for the triumphant arrival of Port Line's latest and largest vessel was completed, and she was ready for the grand event.

Above: *Port Nicholson* in Gatun Lock
Right: Maiden voyage at Caracas Bay, Curaçao

True to plan, when the *Port Nicholson* had been secured to the pontoon at No 8 shed, King George V Dock, the great and good and their guests swarmed aboard the £3,000,000 vessel. No matter where Jack wanted to go, there were groups of visitors – mostly men, and a few women – obstructing him in his efforts to get there. He went onto the boat deck for sanctuary, but found himself trapped again, this time by a person in civilian clothes telling a group of avid listeners that *Port Nicholson* was designed to have a permanent swimming pool, a crew hobbies room with suitable equipment, air-conditioning, septic tanks to prevent the fouling of enclosed and coastal waters, 'hydraulic between-decks hatch insulated plugs', True Motion radar and a new ship stability model. Jack had no idea who the speaker was, but there was no explanation of just what the 'hydraulic between-decks hatch insulating plugs' were, or what part they played in the 'revolutionary' *Port Nicholson*.

This discourse did lighten Jack's frame of mind after the stress of mooring the vessel, with the constant demands from jumped-up nobodies for this, that or the other to be done 'now, immediately, this minute'. In the recent brief but hectic hours, Jack had, though, noticed that the first mate had prefixed each request or order with 'Could you', or 'If you would be so kind'. Unsurprisingly, then, the nobodies had their orders carried out when it suited him, whereas the approach of this particular Mr Mate got matters attended to immediately.

The *Port Nicholson* did not load much cargo for her maiden voyage. What little she carried included the royal limousines to be used by the Queen when she arrived in New Zealand for her 1962 visit there. Before any cargo work could begin most of the bunting had to be taken down, to allow the dockside cranes to operate freely. When eventually the No 4 hatch had to be used, down came the last of the bunting, changing the *Port Nicholson* from a rather plain princess to a working ugly duckling.

The maiden voyage

There appeared to be a very large group of people on the pontoon to wave goodbye to the *Port Nicholson* as she set out on her maiden voyage. Then within a couple of days the vessel and her men had settled down to sea watches, and all was set fair for a splendid voyage to Curaçao, Panama and Auckland. Jack found that it was a delight to be working on a brand-new vessel as, apart from the normal overhaul of the running gear, there was little to do other than wash down the paintwork. The paint was new, the decks had been cleaned for all the dignitaries in London, and it was only the metal hatch covers which needed a coat of paint to replace the one which had ended up all over the vessel en route to London.

The arrival of the vessel at Curaçao for bunkering did not cause any noticeable excitement. It was a rumour amongst the occupants of the sailors' mess room that every knot achieved above 17 would double the consumption of fuel. The veracity of the statement should have been, but never was, challenged by Jack. However, it did appear that the vessel took on a considerable amount of fuel. As the vessel had gunport doors in her side, the fuel lines were connected through them instead of the usual place for a pipe terminal, in the working alleyways – very annoying, as the oily decks had to be cleaned after bunkers was completed.

The *Port Nicholson* then made her way to the Panama Canal and the first of her many transits through its locks and lakes. Out of the canal and into the wide Pacific Ocean, where the sea kindly lived up to its name, the *Port Nicholson* ploughed on with ease as she fulfilled her owner's hopes with a constant log reading of 18.5 knots. Apart from the all-inclusive deck golf, Captain Young decided that he would have 'horse' racing in the dining saloon. The horses were the four apprentices, the book-keeper being the purser. The master invited all the off-watch crew, officers, engineers and sailors to join the passengers in this weekly evening of entertainment. But there were a surprising number of men in the deck crew who said they would not attend the racing, and this was because it was in the saloon, with the passengers and officers in attendance. Apparently it was not in their culture to mix socially with such people – reverse snobbery, in effect. Much the same type of social separateness had come to the fore when Jack found that many of his erstwhile colleagues would not sign on for a vessel with single-berth cabins. They claimed that the fo'c'sle head communal cabins were conducive to harmony amongst the deck crew, whereas single-berth cabins amidships turned the sailors into individuals with no sense of comradeship and loyalty to their colleagues. This could well be considered a valid point by some, but certainly not by Jack: an individualist by most standards and, according to many, 'an anti-social git' as well.

Everyone who attended the racing appeared to enjoy it, and while the ratings were normally allowed only two cans of beer per day, the master allowed the men to buy spirits in the saloon providing they did not abuse the privilege. The only people who were not too keen on allowing the 'common herd' into the saloon were the saloon stewards. It was extremely irritating and demeaning of their status, they felt, to have some 'hairy-arsed' AB flicking his fingers for attention and ordering a G&T on account. In order to be sure that the said gin and tonic was not adulterated en route to the table, the sailors took it in turn to watch the stewards carefully as they served the drinks.

When Jack had told his colleagues about the master's idea of crew management prior to leaving Belfast, none had believed that any master would be so charitable to his crew. But after three weeks with Captain Edward Young, they began to believe Jack rather than suspect that he was a plant for the master and senior officers. In the interests of diplomacy, Jack resisted reciting the phrase 'told you so' to his colleagues when they were singing the praises of their treatment by the Old Man: it was a struggle to remain silent nonetheless.

Although the thought had crossed his mind before, when taking the *Port Nicholson* into the gale from her builder's yard, Jack now began to wonder just how 'tender' – lacking in perceived stability – the vessel was. Mindful of the fact that when en route to London she had been empty, and with little fuel, he had not been unduly concerned when she rolled, particularly around the Isles of Scilly and into the English Channel. But now she had a part cargo and she also had the stability given by half of her fuel oil aboard. Approaching Wellington in

Party For A "First"

TO MARK the first visit of the Port Nicholson to her name port, the local director of the Port Line Limited, Mr. J. H. Cook, and the vessel's commander, Captain E. W. R. Young, entertained a large number of guests on board last evening. Here Captain Young (centre) is shown with representatives of most exporting concerns. From left they are Mr. P. T. Norman (Borthwicks), Mr. E. Roberts (Swifts, N.Z. Ltd.), Mr. P. N. Morrell (Co-op, Wholesale Society), and Mr. J. S. Coleman (W. & R. Fletcher Ltd.).

Captain Young at reception

a fierce Southerly buster, she appeared very tender to Jack on the wheel. In similar sea conditions the *Port Auckland* or for that matter the *Port Hobart* would have been reasonably stable despite the appalling seas. When he mentioned his concern to the officer of the watch, he was told that the behaviour of the vessel was because 'the Old Man's not reducing speed; we're behind time for arrival in Wellington.'

Later that day, in his cabin reading the *New Zealand Weekly News*, he was thrown off balance as the vessel appeared to come to a dead halt for a moment. Within seconds the deck crew was called out to an incident described by the watch keeper as 'She took one 'ell of an 'eader and the fo'c'sle is an 'ell of a mess. 'E's drivin' 'er too fast. 'E'll bugger summat up before long.'

As the men made their way along the working alleyway against a considerable roll, the *Port Nicholson* was turned broadside onto the enormous swell in an attempt to prevent her from taking another header into the sea. Looking towards the fo'c'sle, all Jack could see at first was a myriad mooring ropes and composite wires, along with the wooden boxes they were kept in – to keep the fo'c'sle deck clean and the lines tidy – hanging down the bulkhead onto No 2 hatch or intertwined with the railings on the after end of No 1 hatch.

The bosun and the carpenter were the first onto the fo'c'sle, with Jack and his colleagues following. Shortly afterwards the first mate joined them as Chippy opened up the forepeak booby hatch. The first discovery was that there was no electricity in the forepeak. As usual, Chippy, fully equipped for any eventuality, used his torch to look down the hatch. It might well have looked like a comic strip had the occasion not been so concerning, as the officer, the bosun and carpenter all bent over the booby hatch coaming to peer down into the forepeak. One after the other they descended into the darkness, apparently to find that the ladder and the stanchion posts supporting the deck above had all broken off from the 'tween deck they were welded to. It appeared that when the vessel had taken that plunge into the sea, the pressure on the foredeck had pushed it down, bending the forepeak ladder and stanchions, and when the vessel had lifted to meet the next sea, the deck had – like the top of a tin can – bounced back

Ship Carries Painting Of Her Name Port

Pride of place on the Port Nicholson, now in Wellington on its maiden voyage, will be given to an oil painting of Port Nicholson by Don Neilson.

The painting was presented to the ship this week by the Wellington Harbour Board at an official luncheon on board the ship.

It will hang on a bulkhead facing the passenger's combined lounge, smoke room and library.

The painting will have plenty of company, as this new vessel is lavishly decorated with prints of famous paintings. The prints, the general colour scheme and decor were chosen by two directors of the Port Line, instead of having the selection made by the woman who launches the ship, as is usually done.

Modern furniture and colours have been used throughout the 12-passenger accommodation and in the officer and crew quarters, giving more of an impression of a luxury hotel than a ship.

Following the vogue for light and easy to clean companionways, plastic has been used, combined with veneer panelling.

Captain E. W. R. Young has a suite comprising lounge, office and bedroom, panelled in African maple with dark green carpets and a green-backed chintz for curtains and furnishings.

The Chief Engineer and commodore engineer of the line, Mr. James Robertson, has similar accommodation, an electric fire with mock coals and a collection of model ships to complete his home away from home.

One, a model of a Viking longship was specially made for Mr. Robertson as he comes from the Orkney Islands, once invaded by Vikings.

The longship has a history, having been started by a captain of the Port Brisbane and then handed over to a refrigeration engineer for completion and presentation to Mr. Robertson.

A small, but modern galley staffed by six men under the chief chef, Mr. F. Clark, cooks for the 84 crew members and 12 passengers.

A large pressure cooker in three compartments, which can be used to cook three different types of food at once, a butchery and compact bakery are features of the galley.

Passenger cabins have chests and dressing tables in African walnut with chairs in powder blue upholstery and sofa-beds in coral. Double cabins have built in ward-robes, large size beds, rather than bunks, and each cabin has its own toilet facilities. All cabins are on 'A' deck with fares ranging from £210 single from New Zealand to Britain.

For those who want a sea voyage, but don't want to spend too much time afloat the Port Nicholson's time was 25 days from the wharf at Royal Albert Docks, London, to Aotea Quay, Wellington.

The Port Nicholson, with the biggest ship's cubic capacity for refrigeration in the world today, also has a swimming pool in blue mosaic for the passengers and crew. A combination chart room and navigation bridge with a new prototype radar are other facilities making the ship one of the most modern afloat.

Press cutting about the painting of *Port Nicholson*

into position, breaking the ladder and stanchions. Within the hour the mooring lines and composite wires had been returned to their respective boxes, which were then secured to the nearest ringbolts or other permanent deck-based structures. The vessel's electrician restored the electricity, and the lid to the booby hatch was sealed. When the vessel was brought back on her original course it was noticeable that her speed had been reduced. The *Port Nicholson* was now coping with the swell rather well, with only the occasional 'green 'un' covering the fo'c'sle.

When the vessel rounded Cape Palliser she was met by a ferocious gale in the Cook Strait. She weathered it well, considering that it appeared her speed had increased. Although Jack did not know the details at the time, he noted that the vessel did not slow down to embark a pilot. As soon as she passed Wanganella Reef, the off-watch sailors were called on deck, to be told that there would be a reception for the great and good aboard the vessel when she had berthed, and everything on the port side was to have the salt water washed off before the vessel was secured alongside the quay.

The men were busy cleaning the saloon and other windows and using fresh water to wash the bulkheads, railings and even the deckhead above the top of the gangway: the quartermasters and two apprentices were helping out, as well as washing off the gangway. From one of the apprentices, Jack heard that the weather at the Heads had been too rough for a pilot to come out to the vessel, so Captain Young, with 40 years of experience of entering her namesake body of water, Port Nicholson, Wellington Harbour, was taking her in himself. By now it was dark, so at least there was no need to hoist bunting, for which Jack was thankful.

The men were called to their harbour stations. When they were in sight of their destination, Aotea Quay, a pilot boarded the vessel for the last few yards. Apparently this was to comply with pilotage regulations, insofar as the ship was technically required to be under the direction of a pilot when in the waters of Port Nicholson.

Within half an hour of the final mooring line being secured, the first of the guests were streaming aboard and causing some mirth on their arrival at the head of the gangway. In Jack's previous vessels at official receptions it was only the master who received the guests at the top of the gangway. But at Wellington the guests were received by not only Captain Young but also Commodore Chief Engineer Robertson. Because of his broad gold band, several visitors thought of him as the senior, and profuse apologies ensued as he introduced Captain Young to the guests rather than the captain introducing the him – but of course as Captain Young was a most genial person, he would have been the last person to take umbrage over an understandable mistake by those not versed in the diplomacy of maritime rank and command.

At Wellington the royal cars were unloaded a couple of days before HM Yacht *Britannia* arrived, to berth ahead of the *Port Nicholson*. *Port Nicholson* did not let the British Merchant Navy down, and was dressed for the occasion with much dipping

Arresting Features:

MAIDEN TRIP OF PORT LINE VESSEL

The ship was behaving excellently and on her first trip from London to Wellington did not experience any engine trouble at all, which was truly remarkable for a new vessel of any kind, the captain of the £3,000,000 Port Nicholson, Captain E. W. R. Young, told the "Star" yesterday when the ship berthed at Port Chalmers.

The Port Nicholson is the longest, widest and largest of the Port Line ships and is the largest refrigerated vessel on Lloyds Register.

She has a gross tonnage of 13,847 tons, a length of 573.6ft, breadth of 75.9ft and draws 30.09ft of water. She has a loaded displacement of 25,099 tons.

Her refrigerated space is more than 600,000 cu. ft. and she has a further 2,225,021 cu. ft. of uninsulated space.

Of the most modern design, the Port Nicholson cruises easily at 20 knots. She reached 21 knots on trials, Captain Young said, and her service speed was set at 18½ knots.

The ship was a little more than an hour late in arriving at Port Chalmers from Wellington yesterday when she encountered heavy fog off Timaru.

The fog was extremely dense and he cut down speed in spite of having the most up-to-date radar system available, passing out of it in three hours, Captain Young said.

A genial master, Captain Young, whose hobbies are reading and an occasional hand of bridge, has been at sea all his life. He has spent 41 years with the Port Line.

He showed the "Star" over the luxury living quarters of the ship. A new feature in design was having his working office (large and with every facility) next door to the wheelhouse and chartroom, which were also combined units in his ship.

The vessel has the latest fire control system where an outbreak in any part of the ship can be detected and dealt with immediately.

The ship is loading cheese and lamb and discharging general cargo. She leaves tomorow for Timaru.

A luncheon to mark her first visit to the port was held in the Port Nicholson today, when invited guests from shipping and transport organisations attended.

Press cutting about *Port Nicholson*'s maiden voyage

of her ensign when required. During the vessel's stay at Aotea Quay a regular launch service appeared to be maintained between *Britannia* and the various wharfs nearer the centre of Wellington. The formality of the launch crews, whilst in the best tradition of the Royal Navy, was pretentious to say the least – particularly to professional mariners of the Merchant Navy, or (to quote some of Jack's colleagues), 'Real seamen who go to sea all the time.' Jack could only nod, but silently agreed with his colleagues, mindful of what his naval officer uncle had told him when he had said he wanted to join the Royal Navy.

At some point Captain Young, and presumably other masters from vessels of British and Commonwealth countries, were invited to dine aboard the royal yacht. Jack was not too certain whether or not Captain Young was a passenger aboard a royal launch as the craft passed down the starboard side of the *Port Nicholson*, but at that precise time the starboard side of the boat deck was being washed down and scrubbed. Almost inevitably, the hose was directed over the side of the vessel just as the launch was abeam. Jack was below the boat deck in the alleyway as the shot of salt water went towards the launch. Jack, closer to the launch than anyone else, was positive that the water did not hit the launch – but it was a very near miss. At the inquiry into the incident, it was claimed that the direction of the hose was totally unintentional, and apologies were expressed by all concerned. However, mess-room lore would have it that, 'The 'ole bloody pantomime were drenched. Pity the Old Man were aboard' – 'E's all right.'

The round of various ports continued with the bunting being hoisted for arrival at Port Chalmers, Timaru, Lyttelton, New Plymouth and Auckland for another meeting with the royal yacht – this time berthed well away from the *Port Nicholson*.

At Timaru Jack entertained his hosts from his previous visits aboard his ship, and was then invited to their home – but in a piece of bad timing he called when his former sweetheart was there, with her fiancée. To make matters worse for Jack they announced the date of their marriage. If ever there was a time to withdraw with as much dignity as possible, this surely was that time. He did, with a heavy heart, and with awakened feelings that he had hoped were long past.

In New Plymouth, one of Jack's favourite ports, the *Port Nicholson* arrived at the weekend with beautiful sunny weather to greet her. As the vessel was opened to the public the sunbathers and swimmers from the distinctive black-sand beach swarmed aboard. There was so much bare female flesh on display, particularly around the permanent swimming pool, that Jack and his colleagues did not know where to look: there were delightful and stimulating scenes wherever their eyes rested. Testosterone was in full flow in New Plymouth on that not-to-be-forgotten day.

The men of the *Port Nicholson* were challenged to a cricket match at the truly wonderful Pukekura Park. The team did a little better than the team from the *Port Hobart* that had played at Wyndham, but the Kiwi team still ground the vessel's team into abject submission. But the celebrations afterwards made up for any disappointment at the result.

During the stay at New Plymouth, Jack went to evensong at the church of Saint Mary, an almost perfect copy of the churches he was used to in Somerset, except that it was festooned with reminders of the Maori wars and the unique history of that beautiful area. On the bare stone walls were plaques to the regiments that had been stationed in Taranaki during the early days of the colony. From the top of the walls hung some old, tattered and discoloured flags which represented those very sad times for both the Maoris and the new settlers; the Maoris had felt rightly aggrieved that their land was being taken by the settlers, whilst the settlers had seen it as their right to develop the land to make a living often denied to them in the country of their birth.

The quiet and serenity of several Anglican churches in both Australia and New Zealand gave Jack a little relief from the hurly-burly of life aboard whatever vessel he was serving in. However, St Mary's Church provided Jack with that indefinable aura of belonging which to him was necessary at that particular time of his life. Although his messmates knew of his visits to various churches, in all the vessels he served in, they never poked fun at him no matter what their faith or lack of it, their upbringing or their social standing. It was easy for some commentators to dismiss men of the merchant marine as the 'scum of the Earth', as Nancy Astor MP had allegedly done. But it was these 'scum' who had saved the nation during two world wars, and in so doing had lost more men and women, pro-rata, than any of the British Navy, Army or Air Force. Without the Merchant Navy no aircraft would have flown, no ships would have been built and no soldiers would have been equipped, and the British population would have starved. Jack had perhaps been lucky to have sailed with, for the most part, people of reasonably good character. The other side of the coin was that in some instances the title 'scum' could, just as in other strands of society, be deserved by the conduct of some British seamen.

As Jack had previously discovered, some vessels – in particular the *Dominion Monarch*, owned by the Shaw Savill & Albion Company, and the *Captain Hobson*, managed by 'Paddy' Henderson of Glasgow for the MOT – had a justified reputation for employing some sailors and stewards deemed unsuitable for employment in reputable companies. Unsuitability generally arose from receiving a dishonourable discharge from a merchant vessel (equated with earning a Decline to Report on their ability and general conduct) which was then entered in their discharge books. If there was trouble involving British seamen in any port in New Zealand, particularly in Auckland, Wellington and Lyttelton, it could be usually laid at the door of seamen from those two ships. On this, the maiden voyage of the *Port Nicholson*, the first manifestation of trouble for the British merchant fleet came from crews of these two, along with some crew from Blue Star Line cargo vessels. In particular, from amongst the catering staff came the insidious rumblings of a trade union-inspired plan to disrupt the status quo

TSMV *Port Nicholson* at Avonmouth (Courtesy PBA - BM & AG C. Momber)

of the Merchant Navy. If any sailors or others should by chance be ashore and meet with seamen from these particular vessels, mostly immigrant-carrying liners, then almost revolutionary ideas could be propagated to demand a living wage and radical changes to the terms of the discipline code of the Articles of Agreement between ship owners and their employees. In Jack's case these matters were of little consequence as, in general terms, he was quite satisfied with his lot – other than his dismal study efforts for his second mate's ticket. This particular learning difficulty was nothing but his own fault: his being a mathematical dunce had nothing to do with his employer. However, since joining his first vessel he had objected to being forced to join a trade union by the ship owner and the MOT before he could go to sea.

After New Plymouth, the vessel eventually arrived at Auckland where Jack met up with a most attractive girl, a sister of a previous shipmate. Great fun was had until the film *D-Day the 6th of June* was showing at the Civic cinema. This girl then lectured Jack as to the suffering of the Soviet people, which 'you Capitalists' (meaning Jack and his ilk) 'totally ignore'. Jack discovered that his attractive girlfriend was a political activist, so for the rest of the vessel's stay at Auckland Jack, 'the capitalist', spent most of the time aboard or at his uncle's home in the suburbs. He was still in shock from his involvement with a politically motivated female and his meeting with his former girlfriend. He made a resolution, sailor or not, that he would eschew any further opportunity for involvement with the fairer sex.

In London, courtesy of Captain Young

Loaded down to her marks, the *Port Nicholson* sailed for London, the homeward trip almost a mirror image of the outward-bound maiden voyage. The vessel performed well, with no incidents to liven up the otherwise predictable return to London. On arrival Jack was asked to return to the vessel for the next voyage, which would see her revisiting New Zealand.

Putting his resolution to abstain from any further association with eligible ladies to one side, Jack invited Jennifer, his lady acquaintance from the far-off days at Butlin's, to go with him home to Wraxall for a holiday. Result: presumed limited romantic equilibrium restored.

Second voyage

Following his very pleasant leave, Jack returned to London and rejoined the *Port Nicholson* in the Royal Victoria Dock, where she was loading cased motor cars for New Zealand. As the weekend approached, he arranged for Jennifer, who lived not far from London, to join him and see what his shipboard life was all about. After a detailed visit Jack and Jennifer decided to finish off a good day by going 'up West' for a walk along the embankment followed by a meal at their usual Italian restaurant in Soho. As they went down the gangway, Jack noticed that Captain Young was on the quay wall with a lady, presumably his wife, and as they stepped onto the quay Captain Young bade them good day, and introduced his wife. Jack in turn introduced Jennifer, and the captain, having established that they were going to central London, invited them to join him and his wife in a taxi. After a very convivial journey, they arrived at the Strand. Jack was not too sure of the protocol of paying his share of the taxi, but as he made a move for his inside pocket Captain Young told him that the matter was already dealt with. After profuse thanks from Jack, and good wishes from the master and his lady, Jack and Jennifer headed for their walk and dinner.

When he returned to his cabin, Jack thought back on the day and wondered which of all the masters that he had served with during his time at sea would have given a rating a lift in a taxi. Other than possibly Captain Craig, probably at the behest of Mrs Craig, none but Edward Young would, he felt, be so generous.

Other than the lack of bunting and the lack of royal motorcars, *Port Nicholson*'s second voyage was almost a repeat performance of her maiden voyage. This time, however, much of the cargo comprised steel and machinery for the Marsden Point petrochemical works being developed in the North Island. After crossing the Pacific, the first port of call in New Zealand was Opua in the Bay of Islands; then, after passing the many islands in the vicinity, including the Hen and Chicken Islands and the Poor Knight's Island, on to deliver the steel and machinery. Marsden Point is a promontory at the entrance to Whangarei Heads and the beautiful bay leading up to the town of Whangarei in Northland. To Jack it seemed a shame that such an attractive area should have such a monstrous industrial plant blighting not only the area of construction but also the otherwise scenic views extending for miles around the plant. However, even in New Zealand the presence of industrial complexes is an economic necessity, and in a country with more natural beauty than anywhere else in the world, some part of that beauty has to be sacrificed to attain the goal of self-sufficiency – in this case the production of refined petroleum.

From Marsden Point it was a very short run into the Hauraki Gulf and Auckland. The incident Jack experienced involved a nocturnal (and forbidden) visit to the nurses' home. He discovered that the window could be pushed up to allow access by a reasonably fit, and in his case flexible, sailor after his lady friend had turned off the lights. In theory, he should have made a soft landing. But unbeknown to him, immediately under the window was a glass-topped dressing table covered in bottles. The sound of Jack hitting the dressing table and the bottles flying everywhere was only a few decibels above his shout of anguish as he shot into the room, his shoulders and head hitting the window sill as his feet decided that the ceiling was their destination. As his body hit the floor, followed by a wall-shaking thump as he met the doorpost, the thought crossed his mind that it might not be quite his evening for breathless romance.

'Quick, quick, get the hell outa here. Oh, Christ, they're coming!' screeched his lady friend. Not bothering to ask who was coming, despite his painful anatomy, Jack smartly departed again, but rather slower than on his would-be grand entrance. As he legged it across the lawn the darkness was dissipated by a myriad lights from the home. On reaching the road, he walked as nonchalantly as possible, recovering his breath and trying not to limp as every step brought out yet another pain. Not for the first time Jack resolved to ignore his hormonal urges and stay aboard with a good book.

From Auckland the *Port Nicholson* paid her usual visits to Napier, Wellington, New Plymouth, Lyttelton, Timaru and Port Chalmers, finishing the discharge of cargo, then loading with butter, lamb, tallow, casein, cheese, fruit and wool, in some cases returning to a port a few weeks after leaving it. When the vessel was in Wellington, Port Line – or perhaps the city – paid for a coach trip inland to Palmerston North and the surrounding area. It was a splendid day out; for those of the crew who had not seen the inland parts of North Island it appeared to be quite an eye-opener, particularly in the hills.

On return to Auckland, notwithstanding the difficulties Jack had with his lady friends of that city, it was still his favourite place to be in New Zealand, and on this visit he did not lock himself away from the delights of Queen Street and neighbouring areas. However, having not patronised the Mission to Seamen's premises for a while, he decided that rather than lead a hermit's life aboard his vessel, he would again frequent its dances. Although Padre Brown still gave him a rather straight glare when he leaned a little too close to his dance partner, Jack – by now a mature specimen – still managed to enjoy the female company the Mission so kindly provided without upsetting Padre Brown. Jack had assumed that 'what the eye does not see ...', but he soon realised that Padre Brown was not in the least bit fooled by anyone's antics. However, what occurred outside his Mission's doors he chose, in some cases, not to see.

From Auckland the *Port Nicholson* made her lonely way across the Pacific Ocean, loaded down to her marks with her New Zealand produce, towards London and, for Jack, a welcome spell of leave before, at the invitation of the first mate, returning to the vessel for her next voyage to New Zealand. For Jack it was interesting to witness the vessel being discharged of her cargo in the United Kingdom; because he was always the deep-sea crew he would not normally experience that. The last time he had seen a cargo discharge at Avonmouth was aboard his beloved *Port Auckland*, and the *Port Brisbane* many years before. Little had changed since those times; dockworkers were still dockworkers, and as bloody-minded as before – but far less bolshie than their colleagues at Liverpool or, for that matter, London.

During the course of his leave, the *Port Nicholson* docked at Avonmouth, and Jack took a party of his friends and acquaintances aboard to show her off and explain her functions and equipment.

Third voyage

After a long and enjoyable, but busy, period of leave the rail warrant arrived at Wraxall to take Jack to Liverpool. This was the first time that his vessel had

The superb handiwork of Boatswain Frank Butler

signed on Ship's Articles anywhere but Belfast and London. On his arrival, Jack found a few of his former colleagues aboard ready to re-sign Articles, but also many new shipmates, including two new men – DHUs – formerly of the Royal Navy. Although one of them had served in submarines for nine years, the furthest he had travelled with the Navy was Belgium.

Starting with the employment of the riggers recruited from the shipyard in Belfast, the *Port Nicholson* was being slowly starved of reliable 'time servers' from the company. This was around the time when National Service was abolished. Many merchant seamen had joined just before their 18th birthday to avoid being pressed into the Army, and once they had achieved their 27th birthday they could leave the Merchant Navy without any threat of National Service. Although these men were branded 'army dodgers' they made, with few exceptions, very good and efficient seamen. In contrast, men such as Jack, who had joined as boys, were considered to be career seamen, the backbone of the various British shipping companies. There was little doubt, certainly in Port Line, that the need to recruit 'anyone off the dole queue with two arms and two legs' as a seaman was a direct result of the end of National Service. So Jack sailed on his third voyage aboard *Port Nicholson* with mixed feelings about his career path with Port Line. He was not too comfortable with the calibre of his new and untrained colleagues, and this, coupled with his difficulties in the mathematical part of his studies for his Second Mate's Certificate of Competency, produced in him a very disquieted spirit as the *Port Nicholson* entered the waters of the Mersey on her third voyage.

Apart from some junior officers, the vessel's officers were similar to those before, and the outward voyage followed much the same pattern as the previous ones, but this time it included a visit to Fiji, docking at Suva. There the officers and crew of the *Port Nicholson* were invited to a grand ball with the commander and officers of HMS *Crane*. The evening went well, and yet again Jack fell head over heels in love: this time with a beautiful Eurasian girl. They danced the night away, but unfortunately for Jack, as midnight struck so did the girl's father, a large New Zealander; his arrival to take his daughter home denied Jack the opportunity of a romantic waltz under the tropical moon – yet another frustration for him to cope with.

On arrival at Auckland the first thing Jack noted was *Megantic*, the new Shaw Savill & Albion Company vessel, on the opposite berth. Shaw Savill had not been known for any particularly distinctive ship design since the advent of the pre-war Empire Food Ships era. So Jack was fascinated by the modern lines of the *Megantic*, so different to her fleet predecessors, and with her name from the lexicon of the White Star Line rather than the traditional Maori names of the pre-war fleet. The New Zealand Shipping Company with Federal Line vessels had a distinctive but traditional silhouette, which continued until the 1970s. Blue Star Line, another competitor shipping company trading in Australasia, did not follow Port Line with curved superstructures, but chose instead

Megantic

a mixture of traditional superstructures, their modern vessels having very distinctive and attractive lines shaping the hull.

As in his more recent visits to Auckland, Jack resisted the parties – mostly with the nursing fraternity – for fear of becoming involved in nefarious activities with the delightful females of Auckland. His record of achievement with the ladies of Auckland in recent years had been dismal by any standards. He had no intention of becoming involved again … but inevitably he did. She was a Maori girl, named Edith and she was another nurse – but unlike the other nurses Jack had associated with, she took a very pragmatic view of matters, particularly relating to British sailors. Jack spent many happy hours in her company, especially as she demonstrated much tact and understanding relevant to keeping young Jack in his place. One evening she invited him to a Maori Farewell. The occasion was to say goodbye to a newly married couple who were migrating to Australia: not quite the destination Jack would have chosen had he been a Maori. At the door of the house, in central Auckland, he was welcomed by an elderly Maori, the father or perhaps grandfather of the emigrating girl. The first impression Jack had was of a most dignified man as he welcomed the sailor to his home. Inside many people were gathered, with the young couple sitting on the far side of the room. With the others he sat on the floor and the ceremony began, Edith translating in whispers. The whole experience was very moving, and most of the people in the room were crying as they sang the Maori Farewell; Jack had to really control himself to prevent the tears from rolling down his cheeks. When the migrating couple left the house, amid even more demonstrations of love and loss, Edith led him towards the door, there to be met once again by the now very distraught, father/grandfather.

Despite his loss and despair, the man most graciously thanked Jack for attending the ceremony and wished him well.

Of all his experiences over many years in New Zealand, that Maori Farewell stood out as an example of the love, the sense of loss and the emotion associated with the departure – long-term departure – of a Maori to another country. Jack was spellbound by the occasion, and Edith explained succinctly the considerable difference between her culture and that of the Europeans.

When the time came for the *Port Nicholson* to continue her visits to the other ports of the country, Jack was in for yet another disappointment. Although there had been a noticeable lack of lust in their brief relationship, it came as quite a shock when on their last evening together in an Auckland restaurant, Edith announced that she would not be in Auckland when the vessel returned. She did not explain why or say where she would be going. Her only explanation was, 'I have loved being with you, but now is the time to part; it will be the best for both of us.' Jack could elicit no further explanation, and after a final kiss they went their separate ways.

On this particular voyage the *Port Nicholson* took Jack to a port in New Zealand that he had not previously visited. The port was at Bluff, sometimes known as The Bluff, the southernmost port on the South Island, with only Stewart Island and several small mid-ocean islands between Bluff and Antarctica. It was the seaport of the city of Invercargill. Because of Bluff's latitude – in the Roaring Forties – it was subject to very strong winds, which meant the use of a very large mooring line, known as the insurance wire, for the vessel. This was the first time that Jack had to use this large and unwieldy piece of equipment, and its deployment from the vessel to the bollard ashore tested the seamanship of the deck crew to the limit. The thought of de-mooring was not welcome to the sailors, either.

Bluff and its environs were, in most respects, very similar to those found beyond the Great Glen in Scotland. For the sailor there was very little to do in Bluff itself, and Jack spent his time searching the sandy beaches for beautifully coloured paua shells, unique to New Zealand; they are home to an oyster-like mollusc, a type of abalone much favoured as a delicacy by the Maori. The beach at Bluff was littered with these shells, but most of them were damaged or in pieces. However, the search for them passed the time until departure and the cursed insurance wire.

The return voyage took in the usual New Zealand ports until the vessel was fully laden, even to bales of wool stored atop the after hatches. As was the custom when leaving the final loading port homeward bound, Jack and his colleagues would, unless otherwise occupied, lean over the rail by the gangway watching the arrival of the passengers and deciding which ones would survive the voyage to see the 'old country' and those who, despite the doctor's very best efforts, might not. As ever, the only female under 40, and certainly the most attractive, was the doctor's wife. There were a few exceptions to this unofficial rule, and one of these came into

Jack's view as she mounted the foot of the gangway, soon to alight on board *Port Nicholson*.

There was an audible intake of breath as the rest of the spectators caught sight of a very attractive woman with a figure most women would die for – and many a sailor would happily do the same in her embrace. By general consent, from the viewing sailors, her age would be in the early twenties. However, taking her face and figure into consideration, who would worry if she was 50? Later in the mess room there was little talk of any shipboard matters, but plenty relating to the passenger, and what, in very crude terms, the orators would like to do with her: it certainly wasn't to enjoy a game of deck golf.

Eric was a bedroom steward and, as was often the case with Port Line bedroom stewards, somewhat effeminate, but he was a jolly nice chap who – unlike many of those of his sexual persuasion – would cheerfully talk to the sailors without any ulterior motive. Purely by chance – or that is what was claimed – one of the ABs found himself in Eric's presence, and casually asked who the young woman was, how old she was and what her name was. Eric – as always, discreet in the extreme – told his inquisitor that he did not know, and could dally no longer as he had to help the woman's husband with his luggage. The mood in the mess room took a turn for the worse as that information sank into the collective mind of its occupants. Jack thought about the dire mood that had arisen in the mess simply because an attractive passenger had her husband aboard with her. In most cases, the sailors' sexual desires would have just been sated during the vessel's leisurely voyage around the New Zealand coast, so their testosterone-fuelled desires would not normally arise again until the men had had a dose of the 'Channels' and returned to 'the little woman by the fire'.

After a few days at sea, Eric imparted the information that the husband was a professional photographer. The first time Jack came into contact with the couple was at the first lifeboat drill after putting to sea – a drill better known as 'Board of Trade sports'. Some passengers, including the couple, were assigned to No 2 lifeboat, the first boat on the port-hand side. The boat crew, which included Jack, helped them don their lifejackets, and they were instructed to line up against the bulkhead adjacent to the boat. As the boat was swung out the husband moved forward to photograph the boat as it swung out from the davit. Captain Young appeared on the bridge wing, and seeing the man and camera by the boat winch indicated to the officer to put the man back in his place. The officer did so. When the boat was bowsed to the fishplate, the sailor in charge of the plug boarded it with the apprentice, who shipped the rudder. A full audit of the personnel and equipment took place, and the boat was hoisted back into the davits. As the boat was about to land on the chocks the photographer again broke ranks, to crouch by the winch and take what appeared to be a skyward photo of the bottom of the boat. Instead of telling him to get out of the way, the officer ignored him as two sailors messed up his shot by leaning over the camera – to ensure, of course, that the boat was firmly back in its davits. Captain Young reappeared on the bridge wing and witnessed the scene. In the four years that Jack had sailed with him this was the first occasion when he saw him plainly annoyed; he spoke strongly to both the officer in charge of the boat and the photographer, much to the delight of the assembled sailors.

It was a beautiful Pacific afternoon, and some of the sailors were working near the door to the passenger accommodation when they heard the sound of a crash – glass or china – and metal. With natural nosiness the sailors went towards the door, but before they got there the door slammed open against the bulkhead and Eric appeared, very red in the face.

'The bitch, the bloody bitch, she did it deliberately: bitch, bitch, bitch!' He stamped his feet as the words shot from his lips. Drawing a swift breath, he continued, 'I'm not going in there again.' A long pause followed, no doubt for effect, then, '*Ever!*' In those few seconds, Jack stepped into the accommodation to see a mixture of crockery, tabnabs, the remains of a teapot and a silver tray on the deck outside the couple's cabin door. He returned to the working alleyway, where he found Eric holding on to the rails and staring out to the broad horizon, visibly shaking. Jack started to approach him, but was stopped by another sailor who said, 'Best leave 'im alone, mate, just make sure 'e don't jump over the bleedin' side.' After what seemed an age, Eric turned away from the rail and walked into the passenger accommodation, quietly closing the door behind him.

When Jack enquired from his colleagues what the fuss was all about, he was told that Eric had gone to the couple's cabin with afternoon tea as requested. He had knocked on the door and heard the woman telling him to come in. On that vessel the bed turned into a couch when not in use, and as Eric had entered the cabin, lying on the couch was the photographer's wife in a pair of minuscule knickers, otherwise – except for a necklace – naked. While most of the crew, and certainly the entire deck crew, would have fully appreciated the situation, Eric took the bare breasts and the almost exposed crotch as a mockery of, and insult to, his presumed sexual orientation.

Whenever Eric spoke to Jack for the rest of the voyage he never mentioned his altercation with the passenger, and Jack, diplomatically, never asked – but he knew that Eric had removed himself from dealing with that particular couple. The incidents with firstly the lifeboat drill and secondly the unfortunate Eric certainly spiced up what would otherwise have been a routine voyage home. When the sailors of the deck department had ogled the young woman passenger boarding their vessel with, no doubt slightly more than a passing interest in her sexual allure, little did they think of the entertainment that she and her husband would give them on the voyage home.

The *Port Nicholson* was fast approaching her third birthday, and her paintwork was beginning to need attention. The first mate decided that the deckhead of the starboard alleyway was in need of a lick of white paint. The pristine teak deck was covered with a canvas sheet, then with trestles and stages set up, the sailors used sugi wads to wash the salt off the deckhead. Once the sugi-mugi water had dried, the sailors set to work

The working alleyway of *Port Nicholson* prior to painting

painting. They achieved quite a lot of coverage before they went to their tea and tabnabs, leaving their equipment in place, their paint kettles suspended from piping, and the brushes steeped in paint. Port Line was on one of its usual bi-annual clampdowns on overtime payments, so Jack was off watch when, despite the doors being closed because of the air-conditioning, he heard a cry of anguish from outside the accommodation. He decided that it could be well worth his time to investigate.

It was apparent from the raised voices in the starboard alleyway that something was amiss there. He saw several sailors swearing loudly, along with the bosun and the mate. Jack swiftly decided that it might be best if he slipped away, particularly as Mr Mate, a very mild-tempered man, looked downright angry.

Within 30 minutes, Jack heard a brief knock on his door; his watchmate came in and, with excitement emanating from his eyes told him of the happenings in the starboard alleyway while the men were at smoke-ho. The story had begun with, of all people, the photographer and his wife. Because all the men had disappeared, the chap had decided that was the perfect opportunity to use the deserted alleyway as the backdrop for some photographs of his wife in a very brief red bikini. Jack thought about the yarn so far and decided that if the colour red was mentioned the story was going to be in very fine detail and of course spiced up by the colour.

The plan for the photo shoot had apparently involved the woman walking along the alleyway towards the camera. In order to get the shots that he wanted the photographer crouched down and remained so while walking backwards until his feet touched the canvas deck protector, when he suddenly stood upright – underneath a suspended paint kettle, resulting in best quality International Paints Topside Gloss White covering him, his camera and the canvas protector. The chap then hot-footed it, leaving a trail of white footprints on the hallowed teak deck leading into the passenger accommodation and his cabin door.

As his informant drew a welcome and very necessary breath, Jack enquired how he knew such facts, to be told, 'I was behind 'im – I saw it all and buggered off to tell the Bose about it. ... If you don't believe me come and 'ave a look.'

Jack was well aware that what he had seen matched the description he had just been given, giving it a ring of truth, though understandably slightly exaggerated for effect. But it would be worth a look if nothing else, so he followed the excited sailor to the starboard alleyway. As he walked up the companionway he was just in time to see the canvas sheet being pitched over the side – and sure enough, there were the white-paint footprints leading to the passenger accommodation door. Going into the door was the lamp-trimmer carrying a can and an armful of cotton waste. Yet again, Jack thought it sensible to retire gracefully from the scene of such obvious disgrace, his ears ringing with demands that 'the bastard should be made to clean up 'is bleedin' footprints and scrub the bleedin' deck, the *bastard*.'

Jack later discovered that the passenger had indeed been requested to clean up the mess he had made on the deck, but other events foiled that plan. Jack saw the lamp-trimmer going into the passenger accommodation with a can and cotton waste. When the passenger had made his way back to his cabin covered in paint, he had taken off his paint-sodden clothes, dropped them on the deck, and gone into the shower in an attempt to wash the paint from his head, feet and hands. As could be imagined, the paint – best waterproof oil paint – was adhering to every surface in the shower cubicle. The stewards – less Eric – had attended, and seeing the mess, called in their superiors. They in turn summoned the lamp-trimmer with his white spirit, which the stewards used to clean both the cabin and, apparently, the passenger.

Because of the time factor, it was left to the sailors to clean the footprints rather than wait for the passenger to do it. For Jack, the unanswered question about this incident was just what happened to the now white-painted and presumably expensive camera. Within days scuttlebutt from the catering department had it that the photographer's shapely wife, in an effort to help her husband, had ended up with her minuscule bikini covered in paint as well as bits of her well-exposed skin. She too did not take lightly to white spirit on her flesh. To make matters worse, she had to wait the stewards to clean the shower and then, because her husband was in so much distress from the effects of the spirit, she had to wait while he showered before she could use it. Again, allegedly, the kindly-meant offer by one of the heterosexual stewards to wipe her off was surprisingly – and most certainly, from the steward's point of view, firmly – refused. For the remaining homeward voyage, neither the photographer nor his wife were seen on deck very much. The deck department were delighted at the absence of the photographer, but less than delighted to miss the pleasure of viewing his wife in her multi-coloured apparel variations at the swimming pool.

While on the New Zealand coast Jack had begun to suffer with stomach pains. Both the doctors in New Zealand and the doctor aboard the vessel were not too certain what was wrong with him, but kept issuing bottles of antacids which to an extent relieved the pain. To add to that, the homeward voyage was not too happy an experience for him, in that there were two seamen who had brought a record player aboard and, except when they were on watch, would play Cliff Richard and the Shadows at high volume. The pair claimed to be nephew and uncle, but there was an undercurrent of something not quite right about the relationship – and certainly there was nothing right about the non-stop din from the record player.

So for Jack, berthing in London and paying off could not come quickly enough. As before, the first officer offered Jack a berth for the next voyage, which he accepted, subject to his health.

Omega: fourth voyage

On his return to the *Port Nicholson*, Jack found that the vessel was bound for New Zealand again, but this time via Australia. Again, the deck sailors comprised a motley crew of skilled and unskilled men working under the same bosun, but with a new first mate, who Jack had sailed with aboard the *Port Auckland.*, Jack had enjoyed a good relationship with the previous first mate, who was now going to command his own vessel, and he was sorry to be sailing with him no longer.

Jack was leaning over the starboard bridge wing, idly watching the comings and goings of the Port Line shore gang and their self-important bosun, when he became conscious of the Irish quartermaster alongside him. In his charming lilting voice he told Jack, as they watched the shoreside scene, 'Everything you now see and experience with this company will soon disappear. Now that they employ anything in trousers and the trade unions get more militant with the scum of the Liverpool waterfront leading them, the Merchant Navy's finished, and Port Line with it. If you stay long enough, you'll see I'm right. Think me a fool if you like – but remember what I've said.' With that the quartermaster vanished as quietly as he had arrived.

When a vessel is ready for sea it is customary, particularly if the engines have been under any form of maintenance, for them to be tested whilst the vessel is alongside. The test involves doubling up the mooring lines, obtaining permission from the dockmaster and warning nearby vessels about the trials and the consequent wash.

That day the engine trials for the vessel were set to begin at 13:00 hrs, when the dockworkers went ashore for their lunch. Over the previous hour the deck crew had been doubling up the forward and stern mooring lines, and the same on the forward and after back springs. By noon all was ready for the trials, and an officer went ashore to the vessels ahead and astern of the *Port Nicholson* to warn them, and to give the vessel astern time to rig extra mooring lines if necessary. Just before the appointed time the sailors went to their harbour stations.

Jack went up onto the poop deck and took in the view of the Royal Victoria Dock. As he approached his station he saw what appeared to be a mast astern of the *Port Nicholson*. Closer inspection revealed a fully-rigged Thames sailing barge loaded with bulk grain or animal provender, newly moored between his vessel and the ship astern.

To see a barge in its traditional rig was a matter of considerable interest and, to him, unique in the Royal Docks. The one man who appeared to be working the barge was rigging a tarpaulin over the cargo.

As 13:00 hrs approached, the officer in charge of *Port Nicholson*'s after docking party took his place on the docking bridge. He looked around him and appeared to take little interest in what he saw. Jack and the lamp-trimmer, in unison, pointed out to their officer the presence of the barge right under the stern of the *Port Nicholson* – now a very precarious place to be. Whether the officer took any note of what his two men had told him was open to question, as he made no effort to warn the barge-master of the impending turbulence, or even to ring the bridge and tell them of the obstruction. Realising that nothing was being done, Lampy called out to the barge-master to warn him of the imminent engine trials.

'I ain't movin' till I got the sheets on, so you can wait for me,' the bargee shouted back.

With that the officer appeared to wake up to the situation and reached for the telephone – just as the screws were slowly turned. As the *Port Nicholson* strained against her mooring lines the barge broke her single, elderly, mooring line and swiftly shot out between the two vessels into the centre of Royal Victoria Dock. The scene as the barge-master screamed at the men and waved his arms was worthy of a Giles cartoon. Suddenly, above the fo'c'sle bulwarks of the vessel astern there appeared several turbaned heads and two wearing naval caps, as the crew of that vessel, on standby for the engine trials of the *Port Nicholson*, looked out to see what the shouting was about. Although there was amongst the after crowd of *Port Nicholson* some sympathy for the barge-master's predicament, it was soon dissipated by the vitriol shouted towards them by the irate figure disappearing with his barge down the mighty Royal Victoria Dock.

The *Port Nicholson*'s voyage began with the usual tasks of taking the mooring lines below deck, clearing the detritus from the docks and from the coasting voyage, and beginning to overhaul the cargo-handling gear – and the obligatory lifeboat drill, this time without any interfering photographer. Strangely, but probably coincidentally, the No 2 lifeboat was allotted to Jack, just as on the preceding three voyages.

The Atlantic, Biscay and the Mediterranean were kind to the ship, and the work on deck was well ahead of schedule by the time she reached the Suez Canal, where she took on fresh water. As usual on this vessel, the first officer remained on the bridge for harbour stations, other officers taking charge of the forward and after gangs of seamen.

Jack was part of the after mooring party. The Egyptian buoy jumper had perched on the buoy, ready to lift the eye of the line when it was slackened off, so that it could be taken into the vessel before the twin screws revolved. Then the after mooring party heard a double fart from the funnel: Slow Ahead. Normally, the officer in charge of the after party should by that time have received an order to let go of the singled-up stern line – but there had been no order, so the line was still fast to the buoy.

As the vessel moved slowly ahead the buoy began to tilt alarmingly towards the departing stern of the vessel; but there was still no order to let go the line. By now the officer was on the telephone to the bridge, presumably asking for the – plainly forgotten – permission to let go. The request was made through the phone-operating apprentice on the bridge, who asked the first mate about giving the permission, the mate in turn asking Captain Young for his permission. This took time. So before any response could be received from the bridge, the wire was taking the weight of 14,000 tons of vessel at Slow Ahead. Everyone on deck kept clear, expecting the line to part. When the lamp-trimmer, taking the initiative, rather than parting the line – still a major offence in the Port Line – began taking the turns off the mooring bitts, the remaining two turns of wire gave in to the weight on it and speedily released itself from the bitts. At the sudden release of tension, the buoy shot back to its moored position before continuing beyond it to the opposite extent of its anchor cable, and in so doing deposited the buoy jumper, like a circus acrobat doing cartwheels, into the waters of Suez. Seconds prior to the unfortunate Egyptian being unceremoniously deposited in the water, the officer turned from the phone, to announce belatedly, 'Let go aft.' The engines stopped, and as the buoy returned to the upright position the swimming buoy jumper, with commendable devotion to duty, returned to the buoy and lifted the eye of the now slack mooring line, seemingly quite unconcerned by his involuntary bath.

Travelling down the Red Sea, Jack was on the wheel on the 12:00–16:00 hrs watch. Under normal deep-sea circumstances the steering would have been by the Iron Mike, but Captain Young, probably because of the traffic on this stretch of water, decided to have human hands on the helm. With a favourable sea and the engines, thanks to efficient engineers, running at identical revolutions, Jack found that only the very lightest touch of the wheel was necessary to keep the gyro repeater from its normally incessant ticking as the degrees passed the lubber line of the course set.

Towards the end of Jack's trick at the wheel, Captain Young came from the chart complex into the wheelhouse, went out onto the bridge wing and looked astern. He then returned to the wheelhouse, said something to the duty apprentice and took him out to the bridge wing; both of them looked astern. On their return to the wheelhouse the master told Jack that the apprentice would take over the wheel. With the formalities for the changeover completed, Captain Young took Jack and the third mate to the bridge wing, and as they looked astern Captain Young pointed to the perfectly straight wake, spoilt only by the swerve as the apprentice had taken over the wheel. As if speaking to himself, without addressing either the officer or Jack, the master stated while looking at the wake, 'That's perfect steering – no Iron Mike could compete with that.' Then, turning to Jack, he said, 'You can go back to the wheel now. Well done.'

While Jack dwelt on the master's words, his pride was tempered by the thought that perhaps the Old Man was subtly reminding him of his often less than remarkable ability to steer a straight line. After the years with Captain Young, Jack knew that a backhanded compliment was sometimes his way of making a point. They returned to the wheelhouse and Jack took over the wheel again. For the final ten minutes of his trick, he worked harder than ever to avoid a kink in the wake and was mightily pleased when relieved by the quartermaster. Over the years he had taken little pleasure, if any at all, from steering the various vessels he had served aboard. The master's unexpected praise was, he felt, a double-edged sword, in that his achievement in steering a straight line was unusual.

The *Port Nicholson* entered the Gulf of Aden and berthed at Aden for fuel oil. As the first mate of the vessel was the Naval Reserve officer from the *Port Auckland*, with his understandable demands for everything to be in order and every person to be in their place, leaving little room for any deviation from his naval-orientated beliefs, the visit to Aden was the perfect opportunity for good discipline to manifest itself. As Jack had been trained by naval officers and instructors, he took the mate's attitude in his stride: his response was to stand up smartly, say 'Yes Sir', and carry on doing whatever in his own sweet way. The officer would have known that it was all humbug, and Jack certainly knew it was. But the officer had exerted his authority over an inferior, and all was well with his world.

However, the idea of a naval officer, even a reserve one, lording it over them did not go down too well with many merchant seamen, real and very independent-minded sailors to their fingertips. It had to be said, though, that in keeping all but an apparently carefully chosen couple of bumboat men off the decks of the *Port Nicholson*, the first mate gained some kudos with his deck department. Although the men still resented what they saw as his affected naval aura, they sometimes grudgingly admired his professionalism – a professionalism which from Jack's point of view was never in doubt from their days together aboard the *Port Auckland*.

For the first time, despite visiting Aden for many years, Jack went ashore and had a look around what had been a British Protectorate since the days when coal-fired steamships used Aden as a coaling port en route to India and the Far East. The town centre was slightly cleaner and less troubled by beggars than Djibouti. There was a certain hostility from the locals, but order appeared to be maintained by British soldiers from the garrison there. In past voyages some of the crew had gone ashore in the evenings to visit the infamous area known as the Crater, a favourite destination of naval men, to seek some carnal relief after their 'long' time at sea. On Jack's last voyage aboard the *Port Hobart*, an unqualified deck hand – formerly of the Royal Navy – had gone to the Crater, and had experienced what he described as 'an extremely doubtful sense satisfaction'. In the total darkness of a tent he was never sure quite what he had coupled with. As he had already paid his money and even in his drunken state had noted the daggers – which were not of a ceremonial nature – on his 'guide' he decided to leave without complaint and made a mental note to see the quack in the morning. Such were the perils of the Crater. When the sailor had seen the quack he felt a little better, but he had to attend the clinic several times because, the vessel being homeward bound, any diseases transmitted to its crew from human or other flesh had to be cured before the crew member's return to his spouse at the rose-covered cottage door. Some time later, when aboard the *Port Nicholson*, Jack met up with the sailor, by now a qualified deck hand, who following the Crater incident had forgone any extramarital sex ever since – or so he claimed. The memory that tale was on Jack's mind as he returned to the *Port Nicholson* and looked up at the Crater area, bathed in the extreme brightness of the unforgiving Arabian sun.

With her fuel tanks full, the vessel slipped away from Aden in the comparative cool of the evening. Jack, on the wheel, noticed that the officer of the watch and the previous officer of the watch were in deep conversation on the starboard side of the wheelhouse. Captain Young was almost in the centre of the wheelhouse, quietly talking with an apprentice. When the two officers finished their conversation, the senior one went to the master and quietly said something to him.

'I wouldn't think so – no, leave her where she is,' was the master's clear reply. The officer collected his colleague and the two went into the chartroom, now curtained off. Within minutes the officers returned to the wheelhouse and at great length studied the radar console. Eventually, the pair of them approached Captain Young, and the senior officer said to him, 'Sir, perhaps you might consider taking her out a little. We're uncomfortably close.' Captain Young opened the port side wheelhouse door, and with both officers and the apprentice, went to the bridge wing. Jack could distinctly hear the wash of the vessel striking the shore, then he realised what the various looks, movements and words of the officers and master were all about; the *Port Nicholson* was very near the rocks, and the sound of the wash proved just how close the vessel was to a dent or three. Thankfully, the vessel was so stable that she almost steered herself, and in view of the sound of the vessel's wash striking the nearby rocks Jack was, like the officers, getting a little concerned, aware that any mistakes on his part would not just be a case of a touching-up paint job.

Captain Young looked his usual urbane self as, with his very concerned-looking entourage, he re-entered the wheelhouse. He spoke to the officers, and everyone in earshot, to inform them of his maritime history with the enquiry, 'Have I told you of the time on the Tyne when I took a plate out of the *Port Brisbane*? The pilot suggested that we might move over a little and I made the judgement that of the possible choice between striking the bank and bouncing into the fairway or striking the approaching vessel a glancing blow, I preferred to take the chance that by maintaining the present course we would just miss her. We did not.'

The alarm on the officers' faces in the dim light of the wheelhouse, illuminated by a full Arabian moon, was a picture indelibly etched in Jack's mind. As the master's arm raised to emphasise his point that his judgement had on that occasion damaged the *Port Brisbane* he continued by addressing the senior of his two officers, 'I understand your concern, although I do not necessarily agree with it – but if it makes you happy, take her out a few degrees.'

No sooner said than done; starboard helm was applied and the *Port Nicholson*, on her new course, began mixing with the ex-Suez vessels from the Red Sea, heading out into the Gulf of Aden and the Indian Ocean. The master left his officers and the front of the wheelhouse, walking towards the light of the chartroom area. As the master came abreast of Jack, a broad and very telling smile crossed his face. Jack wondered if he had told his story about the *Port Brisbane* just to have fun with his doubting officers: knowing Captain Young, quite probably it was.

During the voyage across the Indian Ocean towards Australia nothing out of the ordinary occurred, and it could be considered either boring or quiet and restful. The only matter of note to Jack was when a junior officer was found by Captain Young to be less than competent at calculating his noonday sight. He was given a period of instruction by the navigator. The officer, who held a certificate of competence for the rank of second mate, clearly did not live up to the mathematical standard required of his rank – a matter of annoyance to Jack, as he struggled to reach the standard of mathematical competence required for his own ticket.

The only notable event during the coastal voyage around the south and east coasts of Australia was when the vessel did not go under the Sydney Harbour Bridge and was berthed away from the usual Port Line berth at Pyrmont. Instead, she tied up at a berth at Woolloomooloo, adjacent to the Botanic Park and the Domain, giving the crew a very pleasant walk into town via the parkland: quite a change from the cityscape walk from the Pyrmont berth.

Little of note occurred as the *Port Nicholson* discharged the last of her cargo at Brisbane before heading out into the Pacific Ocean en route to New Zealand via the northern Tasman Sea and Lord Howe Island – where the Shaw Savill & Albion vessel *Runic*, one of the largest pure refrigerated cargo-carrying vessels in the Australasian trade, had sat aground intact for the past 12 months. Under certain conditions the *Runic* offered the illusion of being afloat with many fathoms of water under her keel. In years past Alan, Jack's chum, had sailed aboard her.

As the *Port Nicholson* was crossing the often very unsettled Tasman Sea approaching North Cape, the peninsula at the top of North Island, the weather was not as good as it might have been. She was an empty vessel, with the tendency to 'roll in wet grass' or 'roll in dry dock'. She began rolling when approaching the coast, and on rounding the North Cape ran into a Southerly buster, which caused her to roll severely. The day working deck crew were engaged in washing down the boat deck and the rolling was so bad that they were swinging off the awning spars, preferable to sliding about on deck and striking unforgiving metal objects.

On arrival at Auckland the loading of the homeward cargo began and, for probably the first time in his seagoing career, Jack was looking forward to the end of the coastal voyage and the prompt return home. His health was not as good as it might have been, and the indifferent capabilities of some of his fellow sailors was making him decidedly irritable, bit by bit removing any pleasure he found in both his career with Port Line and his presence in New Zealand. The quartermaster's words in London at the start of the voyage had been playing on his mind during this, his fourth, voyage aboard *Port Nicholson*. As Jack sat in his cabin those prophetic words seemed relevant, as troublemaking seamen from other ships sneaked aboard the *Port Nicholson* to stir up her crew relating to overtime payment, hours of duty, the system of discipline, the appointment of a workers' representative (a trade union appointee) the taking of grievances to the master etc, etc. The stability of the whole British shipping industry was slowly being eroded by the ship owners' often seemingly total lack of interest and by the activities of a few politically motivated people. If such activity was allowed to continue the result would indeed eventually be the loss of not only Port Line but the British Merchant Navy.

When the *Port Nicholson* was alongside in Wellington, a Christmas tree was hoisted aloft to celebrate the occasion. This practice was generally observed by most British shipping companies, and in the ports of New Zealand and Australia, where there was a predominance of British shipping, it was welcomed by the locals as a symbol of British tradition and values. However, the Christmas tree failed to influence the conduct of some British seamen; when alongside for Christmas it was the perfect occasion for them to get as drunk as possible, apparently in order to alleviate the homesickness of being apart from their families at that time of year.

In Jack's case, of course, he much preferred Christmas on voyage. It was an occasion for much lazing about and usually excellent food from the galley, even if with only two cans of beer per person. This year, with the *Port Nicholson* in her namesake port, Jack and his chums were invited by some nurses to spend Christmas Day on the beach. Like the British sailors, they were off duty and away from their families and homes. It was agreed that, subject to the weather on the day, the girls would supply the picnic food and the sailors the beer, plus a large groundsheet.

Christmas Day dawned slightly overcast, and as the men replaced their pants with trunks under their trousers the hot summer sun appeared and they went ashore in high spirits to meet the nurses. The entrance to the beach was through a gap between rocks with an archway onto the sand. As they walked along the beach looking for a suitable site Jack noticed that there were very few people there on such a beautiful day. Before he could make a fool of himself by making his observation public, he realised that it was Christmas Day, so everyone else would be at home celebrating. Eventually the girls decided that they had found the perfect place, and they settled down and looked around. In the distance there were some people in the sea, but otherwise the nurses and sailors were alone.

The girls, getting restless, more or less ordered the Poms into the sea. Then they got up and began stripping off, and Jack and the other sailors began doing the same. 'Christ,' Jack heard as he turned around to see two of his four chums with their trousers around their ankles and a surprised and shocked – even for worldly British seamen –

expression on their faces. He followed their gaze and much to his surprise saw one of the nurses stark naked while her three chums were removing their clothes. On reflection, it was quite a shock to witness the obvious embarrassment of these 'I've seen it all before' sailors as, without a care, the girls swiftly shed their clothes to stand in all their glory, looking very amused at the Poms, only half-undressed, in trunks.

'Jees, can't you lot get out of your strides quicker than that?' enquired one of the girls.

Amid much mirth, another observed, 'They've still got togs on!' and demanded, 'Are you wimps, or what?'

That was a challenge too far for the men. Amid much raucous laughter – because the men without exception turned their backs to the girls while they sheepishly removed their trunks – they were eventually naked. The next difficulty they experienced was the question of whether nature would take its course and rear its head at the over-exposed female flesh. However the circumstances rather curtailed the likelihood of any extra embarrassment, in that it appeared that the men were there simply to give some sort of amusement to the Kiwi nurses. The girls agreed between themselves that the 'Poms' had nothing to boast about and that they saw better every day – a very hurtful opinion to such sensitive souls, surely the cream of British manhood.

With that, the girls ran past the subdued sailors into the sea. That did nothing to dampen the animal urges of the mind and most certainly the body. But for all except one of the men, much to their relief, nature still had not physically caused any change from the normal condition. So with the one sailor still holding on to his genitals, and

MV *Somerset*, from a painting by Robert Blackwell

Canvassed, roped and painted in Somerset by Jack

as a result running with the gait of an ape, they all took to the sea, which, quite cold, inhibited any sign or even thoughts of lust, to join in the briny frolics. In time the sailors became used to the situation and began to enjoy themselves: Jack even forgot that he was naked. After quite some time the group headed ashore, only to find several other groups and pairs of people were now along the beach, most naked, with a few still in swimwear. To Jack it was all a very surreal experience, but after the initial shock it almost seemed normal as they sat eating their picnic before a brief period lying in the sun, after which they joined most of the other people in the perishing sea.

If the sailors were thinking that because of the nurses' liberated conduct they would succumb to their sexual advances, they were mistaken. They soon learned, much to the disappointment of some, that public nudity was not a passport to licentious behaviour. For fear of ridicule, Jack and his chums said nothing in the mess room about their bare-bottomed adventure. There were no further excursions to the beach, but for the rest of the vessel's stay the nurses were regular – and chaste – visitors to the *Port Nicholson*.

In very private conversations relating to the nudity episode, it was generally agreed that it had been a good experience once the initial shock and embarrassment had been overcome. The only disappointing feature of the whole Christmas Day story was that with the one exception, the men could not account for their failure to rise to the occasion. That their masculinity could be questioned at the very peak of its development did cause concern until one of them suggested that the chill of the sea would have been the reason. Even the stud of the party was pleased to accept that explanation rather than there being any doubt about his masculinity.

Apart from his excursion to the beaches of Wellington, the other highlight for Jack was the appearance of the dainty vessel *Somerset*, of the Federal Steam Navigation Company. This smaller, traditionally designed craft had the easily recognisable outline of her parent company's vessels, evident since the Second World War. That she had the name of his home county was all the more significant for Jack, as he passed her in his vessel leaving Wellington en route to Lyttelton. The *Somerset*, and her sister vessel *Piako*, of the New Zealand Shipping Company Federal Line, were the last vessels with the traditional profile of those united shipping lines.

When, after visiting Lyttelton, the *Port Nicholson* arrived at Port Chalmers, the peace of the crew accommodation was shattered by the arrival of a vessel carrying the brother of one of the *Port Nicholson*'s Belfast unqualified deck hands. After a few days of disruption, and a complaint by Jack to both the bosun and the deck hand involved, nothing improved. Plainly the bosun was loath to become involved, and Jack found that the rest of the men were not inclined to voice their protest – but he did, in no uncertain terms.

The upshot was that, with the courage found in beer ashore, the brothers headed for Jack's cabin. There they found him sitting reading a book, and decided to beat him up. Fortunately for Jack he was sitting in the narrowest part of his cabin under the porthole. As they barged in, semi-inebriated, they fell over each other in their rush to get at Jack who, despite the punches thrown when they disentangled themselves, easily fended them off. He managed to land several punches on one of them – in the mêlée he was not sure which one he hit – but when the *Port Nicholson* brother sheepishly appeared at breakfast the next day he had a shiner and an abrasion on his face.

This was the first time during his maritime career that Jack had been subject to a physical attack, and after the incident he was told of the brothers attacking the donkey-man, a senior engine-room rating, because he was a Roman Catholic. It was a silly mistake by these sub-humans, as when the brothers were parted by the departure of the other vessel, the donkey-man – a young tough chap – took terrible revenge on the brother who remained aboard the *Port Nicholson*. While the officers must have been aware of the donkey-man's assault, nothing was said. Quid pro quo.

After the usual round of ports – Napier, New Plymouth, Timaru, Auckland and

Queen Charlotte Sound

Lyttelton – the *Port Nicholson* returned to Auckland, this time for quite a stay. It was here that the first mate demonstrated his initiative, probably influenced by his naval training, by offering anyone who wished to obtain a lifeboat certificate the opportunity to gain it. Almost every day the lifeboat was launched for practical knowledge to be obtained, whilst the chanting of the compass quarter points could be heard as that vital part of the examination was absorbed. Most of the candidates passed the test, examined by an official of the New Zealand equivalent of the British MOT. The New Zealand certificates were written on a vastly superior document to the paper versions that the British issued. Jack, overlooking the officer's sometimes pretentious naval attitude, held him in high regard: the idea and practice of educating his men in practical seamanship were, Jack felt, commendable.

Interestingly, the two first mates who had over the years demonstrated their superlative seamanship skills to Jack were at the opposite ends of the Port Line senior officer range. Whereas the *Port Townsville*'s first mate had a rough tongue, the other, sometime senior officer of the *Port Auckland* and now aboard *Port Nicholson*, was the very embodiment of the public perception of a reserve officer and a Port Line officer.

From Auckland the *Port Nicholson* went south to Wellington and the nurses again, and from there to a port Jack had not visited before: Picton, at the end of the beautiful Queen Charlotte Sound.

During the transit of the sound Jack saw the remains of a substantial sailing vessel on the bank. On arrival at Picton he established that the vessel was the *Edwin Fox*, a former trading ship, passenger ship, convict ship and latterly a freezer hulk, abandoned to her fate. After Picton, the *Port Nicholson* went back to Lyttelton to complete her homeward cargo by loading bales of wool. With her passengers aboard, she was ready for sea, but the sailing time was put back time and time again until sailing that day was cancelled altogether. The reason given was that 14 bales of the wool cargo had not arrived. It could be considered an understatement to say that most of the thinking crew thought it ridiculous that a £3,000,000 vessel with millions of poundsworth of cargo would be delayed for just 14 bales of wool to arrive for shipment – but delayed she was. Jack heard Captain Young explaining to some passengers that the 24-hour delay would not be considered a financial loss when compared with the loss of the goodwill of the shipper if his wool failed to reach the British auctions at the prime time.

When the wool arrived, the *Port Nicholson* put to sea, heading for Panama. At the same time a vessel belonging to a German company, Hamburg Sud, trading between New Zealand and Central and South America, also sailed from Lyttelton heading in the same direction, and for many days Jack saw the twin masts of the German vessel appearing and disappearing as the swell lifted one or the other of the vessels. To Jack, the scene was reminiscent of photographs of sailing vessels in the same sea: so near each other but so far, with only the topmasts visible in the lifting seas of the South Pacific.

Nothing of any note occurred during the long transit of the Pacific Ocean and the Panama Canal, but instead of refuelling in Caracas Bay, Curaçao, the *Port Nicholson* was sent to the island's capital, Willemstad. This port was another first for Jack, and as the vessel went into the harbour it became apparent which nation had colonised the island: the waterfront houses looked as if Amsterdam had been transposed into that warm and sunny island off the coast of Venezuela. By this time the *Port Nicholson* was two years old, and parts of her definitely needed a new coat of paint. Rust had been beginning to appear on the foredeck, and the deck crew were removing it and red-leading the bare steel; this activity coincided with the ship's arrival at Willemstad.

With remarkably bad planning on someone's part – and with, in consequence, much coarse language – the crew had to attempt to moor the vessel without stepping on the wet paint, usually unsuccessfully. For Jack, whenever he subsequently thought of Curaçao, two scenes came to mind: Henry Morgan's fort at Caracas Bay, and the Dutch scene at Willemstad, with red lead everywhere except where it should have been.

From Curaçao, the vessel headed for Galveston, the port for Houston, Texas. Jack was off watch and asleep in his cabin when he was woken by a change in the tempo of the engines. Above his cabin he could hear voices, then the sound of the gangway striking the hull. By this time the engines were beating a very slow rhythm, and Jack decided that something, somewhere, was wrong. In shorts and shirt, he emerged on deck to see the first mate, a group of seamen and a lady passenger at the gangway, looking out on the mirror-like sea under a cloudless sky. Following their gaze, he saw a small boat with people trying their best to row away from the ship. The gangway was lowered until it was just above the sea as the vessel, with her engines at Slow Ahead, circled the craft. Avoiding the glare of the morning sun on the water, Jack made out what appeared to be a woman in the stern sheets of the boat, holding a large effigy of the Madonna, as the men in the boat still appeared to be rowing away from the *Port Nicholson*.

The passenger, clearly a fluent Spanish language speaker, went down the gangway and shouted to the people in the boat to come alongside. Eventually the *Port Nicholson's* engines were reduced to Dead Slow ahead, and Captain Young manoeuvred his very large vessel alongside the very small boat, no mean achievement by any standards. By now Jack had armed himself with his trusty Zeiss Ikon camera, and he photographed the boat and its passengers as the *Port Nicholson* fell gently alongside it. The woman holding the Madonna, then the men, women and three children came up the gangway and onto the deck. With the passenger acting as interpreter, it was established that these people were escaping the communist regime in Cuba and heading for sanctuary in America. The reason that they were originally attempting to get away from the vessel was that Port Line colours – topside grey, topped with a red and black funnel– had led them to believe that the vessel was Russian – an understandable mistake. Soon afterwards another small boat was sighted, and along with the original craft it was lifted aboard by a hastily rigged derrick of No 4 hatch. The two boats were in a parlous state of repair. Both had rotten, very primitive, sails which were far too fragile to have been of any use. The first boat aboard did have an engine – but that too was useless, as it was seized and inoperable.

Once the refugees realised that they were not going to be returned to Cuba, the spokesman for the group produced dozens of huge green Cuban cigars for their rescuers. Jack made no attempt to smoke his, but several colleagues did. They eventually decided that green cigars, Havana or not, were not their choice of a smoke, and the cigars were quietly disposed of in order not to offend the generosity of their guests.

With the maximum engine revolutions, the *Port Nicholson* was soon under way and back on course for Galveston, with a cargo of succulent prime fillet steaks and chilled lamb. The crew became 'quality control officers,' thanks to Harry, the chief cook, and the under-zealous tally-clerks in New Zealand. To overcome any discrepancies, the latter had allowed excess boxes of steak aboard, just to be on the safe side. By nothing

Left: Roberto with his sisters. **Right:** Refugee boat at sea

less than a maritime miracle – or more commonly sleight of hand – several boxes of prime fillet steak found themselves in the galley cold room. The men found the beef of excellent quality, but it was decided that their finding should not be broadcast, in case some over-stuffed official took an unhelpful interest in how beef of such superb quality graced the plates in the sailors' mess room. It was yet another case of what the eye does not see, the heart does not grieve over – the slogan of the deck department in most British merchant vessels of that time.

At Galveston, they handed the refugees to the American Immigration Department and their boats to the harbour authorities. The discharge of cargo was a speedy process, without any boxes of beef fillets going astray. To Jack, bringing beef products to Texas seemed to be a case of coals to Newcastle: of all bovine-orientated places in the world, Texas was the prime example. He later discovered, when enquiring why tons of chilled lamb had been left on the quay wall to thaw in hot sunshine, that while the beef was welcome the lamb was not. It was a case of importing something from New Zealand in order to be able to export American products, mostly aircraft and machinery, to New Zealand – at a greater value to America, of course.

From Galveston the *Port Nicholson* went to Charleston, South Carolina. It was here that, particularly amongst the black workmen, Jack witnessed workers driving superb motor cars, but apparently living in very run-down accommodation, some of it nothing more than tar-paper shacks. He found it a very strange society, but both black and white people were welcoming to him nonetheless.

The next stop for the *Port Nicholson* was Philadelphia. It was fascinating to see all the laid-up Naval Reserve vessels as the ship made her way up the Delaware river. In Philadelphia Jack was told by his colleagues that this city was the best place to buy American KD. Not quite too sure what that meant, Jack tagged along with the group of seamen heading for the KD store. It turned out to be an enormous clothing shop specialising in American khaki drill trousers and shirts. Many dollars were spent fitting out the seamen, and it reminded Jack of American wartime naval films, when all the officers were dressed in their khaki drill No 2s. Eventually he was to find that the high regard KD enjoyed amongst his colleagues was fully justified by the number of years it took him to wear out the clothes he had bought that day. After a look at the Liberty Bell, Jack returned to his vessel and found that his purchases that day had drained his wallet so for the last few days in Philadelphia he remained aboard.

On a previous voyage the bosun of the *Port Nicholson* had decided to stop smoking, and Jack was very impressed by his willpower, not only in stopping smoking but for the rest of that voyage in keeping a packet of State Express cigarettes on his desk in full view every time he entered his cabin. Such willpower was an inspiration to Jack after an incident on leaving Philadelphia when he leaned on the rails at No 3 hatch; his cigarettes, kept in the waistband of his shorts, decided that they preferred a watery grave to being smoked. As he watched the packet cartwheel

The U.S. Coast Guard training ship *Eagle*

in slow motion into the briny, Jack, a man of notably short temper, demonstrated his displeasure to one and all with a vehement fit of temper directed at cigarettes, the sea and his waistband. On past occasions, a deep satisfying draw on a cigarette would restore the required equilibrium for normal life to continue for Jack – even if not for those at the receiving end of his tongue. But now, mindful of the resolve of the bosun relating to smoking, Jack decided there and then that he would stop smoking – and much to his surprise, he did. This course of action was fully supported by his two brothers, the beneficiaries when he took home his allowance of 200 Benson & Hedges.

From Philadelphia the vessel made her way to Hamilton, Bermuda: not a regular destination for peacetime Port Line vessels but a pleasant change from the routine ports. After the tricky entrance to Hamilton, the *Port Nicholson* tied up astern of the U.S. Coast Guard training vessel, *Eagle*, a sailing ship. Soon invitations were flying back and forward between the two vessels, and Jack and his colleagues enjoyed their escorted tour of this beautifully presented vessel.

The weather was just as depicted by the brochures: sunny and balmy, with a few cottonwool clouds. When ashore, Jack found that certainly Hamilton, and probably Bermuda as a whole, was an enclave of wealthy Americans; they were the only people who could afford the cost of living there or even to visit Bermuda. In order to use up what remained of his Bermuda sub, Jack went ashore to the nearest off licence to buy some brandy, quite forgetting the cost of everything in this expensive island. When faced with a price beyond his means, Jack settled for a bottle of Bermuda rum from under the counter. It was a plain black bottle with no label, and with the neck and cork dipped in pitch, as in all good Caribbean pirate films. On his return to the *Port Nicholson* with his liquid purchase, he was much ridiculed for being so stupid as to buy a bottle of unbranded something. However, when the pitch was removed, along with the cork, the contents were in fact rum – rum with a flavour that was appreciated by the many 'experts' who sampled it. Jack promptly changed his tipple from brandy to rum. His only disappointment was that it being an anonymous beverage, he could never buy the same again. But the memory and taste never deserted him, a constant reminder of his one and only visit to colourful Bermuda.

The next destination for the *Port Nicholson* was Liverpool. It was to be the first time in her four-voyage career that the vessel had not paid off in London.

'I understand from the chief officer that you won't be joining us for the next voyage.' As the words left Captain Young's lips, Jack had a flashback to Captain Townshend's words when he had decided to leave the *Port Auckland*, four years previously. The major difference was that in the case of Captain Townshend it was, with one exception, the first time in two years that he had spoken to him. In contrast, over the two and a half years that Jack had sailed with Captain Young there were very many occasions when the master had initiated a conversation – not least when he had given Jack and Jennifer a lift into central London.

Jack, hoping to avoid any offence, told the master that he thought in order to further his maritime career he should leave Port Line. In his reasons for leaving the company that had given him so much pleasure during the past nine years, he carefully omitted the quartermaster's ominous words, which during the ensuing months had begun to manifest themselves.

The master voiced his regret and offered Jack a personal reference. When the reference arrived, it was so good that Jack read it twice. The reference, addressed 'To whomever this may concern,' related to Jack's service whilst under the command of Captain Young. It commented very favourably on his character, appearance, efficiency and dedication, concluding with the somewhat ambiguous words 'moving forward' to describe his future. On Jack's second reading of the document he noted with some relief – just in case a future company might think that the reference was Jack's own work – that it was written on company notepaper, with the ship's stamp under Captain Young's signature.

Jack went down the gangway of *Port Nicholson*, and fought through the jostling dockworkers, lorries and dockside mayhem before joining a colleague in a taxi. 'Exactly what are you looking at?' enquired his travelling companion in his distinctly enunciated words and modulated drawl while Jack stared through the taxi window at his final Port Line vessel.

Jack did not reply immediately, but after a long pause let out a heartfelt sigh and replied with a somewhat dejected voice, 'Full and away,' and after a throat-tightening pause continued, 'Onwards and upwards.' There was a silence as the taxi left the quay wall. As the vehicle approached the dock gate the silence was broken with laconic words from Jack's companion, 'Oh! Buggah orff, you big tit.'

11

Epilogue

By the middle of the 1970s the prophetic words of that wise Irish quartermaster aboard the *Port Nicholson* had come to pass; while the ubiquitous shipping containers and the vessels suitable for their carriage were being built, Port Line and its trading competitors were selling or scrapping their ships as fast as possible. Yet Port Line and its parent, Cunard Line, were still having refrigerated cargo ships built, as well as fast, smaller fruit boats.

After leaving Port Line in 1965, Jack continued his career ashore amongst his ships and as in 1964 he had been at the beginning of the commercial life of the *Port Nicholson*, in 1979 he stood once again on the bridge of that ship before she, at her commercial end – even though in pristine condition – sailed from the Royal Portbury Dock en route to the breakers' yard at Kaohsiung.

In seemingly no time at all Port Line and its competitors, while disposing of vessels, were dabbling in the refrigerated container ships owned by groups of the previously competing companies. But this too soon came to an end. With its parent company, Cunard (now owned by, for want of a better term, an investment company) Port Line Ltd – which, unlike its competitors, had had every one of its ships, wartime vessels excepted, built in Great Britain, and had only employed British officers and crew – reached the end of its existence, and

Port Line Ltd
C/o Cunard House
88 Leadenhall Street
London EC3

became but a wonderful memory of a premier British shipping company.

Wakey, wakey, rise and shine;
All aboard the old Port Line.
Sea boots and oilskins – decks awash:
Ice cream served in the sun lounge.

Farewell